UNEQUAL JUSTICE

UNEQUAL JUSTICE

The Prosecution of Child Sexual Abuse

Based on a comprehensive examination of criminal courts
conducted under the auspices of the NCJW Center for the Child.

ELLEN GRAY

Ellen Gray

THE FREE PRESS
A Division of Macmillan, Inc.
NEW YORK

Maxwell Macmillan Canada
TORONTO

Maxwell Macmillan International
NEW YORK OXFORD SINGAPORE SYDNEY

The Free Press
A Division of Macmillan, Inc.
866 Third Avenue, New York, N.Y. 10022

Maxwell Macmillan Canada, Inc.
1200 Eglinton Avenue East
Suite 200
Don Mills, Ontario M3C 3N1

Macmillan, Inc. is part of the Maxwell Communication
Group of Companies.

Printed in the United States of America

printing number

1 2 3 4 5 6 7 8 9 10

Library of Congress Cataloging-in-Publication Data

Gray, Ellen.
    Unequal justice : the prosecution of child sexual abuse / Ellen
Gray.
        p.   cm.
    Includes bibliographical references and index.
    ISBN 0–02–912663–0
    1. Child molesting—United States.   2. Prosecution—United States.
I. Title.
    KF9323.G7   1993
    345.73′025554—dc20
    [347.30525554]   92–38229
                                                                  CIP

This publication is based on a study funded by Grant No. 90-CA-1273, National Center on Child Abuse and Neglect (NCCAN) Administration for Children, Youth and Families, Office of Human Development Services, U.S. Department of Health and Human Services, awarded to the NCJW Center for the Child, and also by the National Council of JewishWomen. Certain analyses were also supported by a subcontract of NCCAN Grant N. 90-CA-1402, awarded to the American Bar Association. The views expressed herein are not necessarily those of NCCAN, the Administration for Children and Families, the U.S. Department of Health and Human Services, or the American Bar Association.

For my daughter, Emily

CONTENTS

Note to the Reader

Established in 1893, the National Council of Jewish Women (NCJW) is the oldest Jewish women's volunteer organization in the United States. Its 100,000 members are represented in 500 communities throughout the country. NCJW programs affect the lives of people of all races, religions, and economic backgrounds. The organization focuses on family issues, with a special emphasis on women and children.

In addition to community service, advocacy, and education, NCJW has had a long-standing commitment to research that benefits children. Founded in 1968, the NCJW Research Institute for Innovation in Education (RIFIE) at The Hebrew University of Jerusalem develops, implements, and evaluates projects concerned with the education of Israel's at-risk children, youth, and families.

In 1983, NCJW established the Center for the Child, a research institute in the United States. Its mission is to conduct research to promote the well-being of all children and families by increasing public awareness of children's issues, improving programs and services for children, and influencing public and private policy affecting the welfare of children and families. Research on Head Start, the Home Instruction Program for Preschool Youngsters (HIPPY), the experiences of employed, childbearing women, and family day care typify the Center's concern with the social problems affecting children.

NCJW volunteers play a vital role in putting the Center's research into action at local and national levels. The Center also calls upon NCJW volunteers across the country to conduct field research in their own communities, with training and support from its professional research staff. In so doing, the Center is continuing the NCJW tradition of volunteer research. NCJW volunteers conducted the first definitive nationwide survey of day care facilities and services and published their findings in *Windows on Daycare* in 1972. The 1987 *Mothers in the Workplace* study was a nationwide volunteer survey, conducted by the Center for the Child, of the challenges and difficulties faced by new mothers in combining employment and family responsibilities.

NCJW volunteers have a long history of concern for the plight of children entangled in the social welfare and justice systems of this country. In the mid-1970s, they conducted a nationwide survey of the juvenile justice system and published their findings in *Children without Justice* in 1975. In 1979, NCJW helped initiate an experimental program to develop Court Appointed Special Advocate (CASA) projects. Volunteers were trained to assume the role of guardians *ad litem* in juvenile and family courts for child victims of neglect and abuse. In 1982, NCJW published *Children at Risk,* a manual to guide local needs assessment and development of CASA projets. NCJW Sections and volunteers around the country continue to be involved in the national CASA program. In these various studies, the contribution of volunteerism to the research enterprise has been effectively demonstrated.

Unequal Justice, based on research conducted by the NCJW Center for the Child, continues in this traditon of volunteer research. This pioneering study describes the history of child sexual abuse cases from the time they enter the criminal justice system. In eight jurisdictions throughout the United States, trained NCJW volunteers tracked 619 cases of sexual abuse for a period of one year. The task cannot be underestimated: they conducted interviews, reviewed records, and observed courtroom procedures dealing with material that was often disturbing. Their assignment was especially daunting . . . being privy to instances of abuse affects even the most experienced child welfare professionals.

This study highlights the problem of child sexual abuse and helps remind us that children are easily victimized. While the instances of child sexual abuse described in this study have come to the attention of the criminal justice system, it is important to remember that child sexual abuse is largely a hidden phenomenon. By documenting how the criminal justice system handles child sexual abuse cases, we hope this study will help protect the rights and welfare of children.

Joan Bronk
President
National Council of Jewish Women
1993

INTRODUCTION

We have reached a curious and problematic juncture in our history as it relates to childhood. We have begun to acknowledge the possibility that adults—even parents—use children sexually to feed their own compulsions and quiet their own demons. This information has been available to us for a very long time. (Historian Linda Gordon, chronicling family violence from 1880 to 1960, concludes that "incest patterns changed less than any other form of family violence over the last century." [1988, p.210]) However, as the iconoclastic psychoanalyst Alice Miller and other have shown us, there are serious psychic costs to admitting the existence of this behavior. Indeed, the medical/psychiatric field, wittingly or unwittingly, has participated in a "coverup" of the extent, nature, and consequences of the sexual abuse of children that is still influencing our perceptions of the victims of this crime.[1] We have just now begun to allow into our minds the possibility that sexual abuse of children—not always violent, not necessarily classifiable within current mental health typologies, and not only at the hands of strangers—happens extensively.

Although we know that the child-welfare/juvenile-court system is not mandated to provide services in cases of non-caretaker abuse, we have also recognized that this social service system is inadequate to its designated task of rehabilitating cases of intra-family abuse. Our knowledge about child sexual abuse *has* progressed to the point that we

1

recognize its difference from physical abuse and child neglect. The therapeutic viewpoint from which we in the field of child welfare regard those who strike out at their children in frustration or neglect them out of poverty—poverty of material necessities or poverty of a nurturant upbringing of their own—is neither sophisticated enough nor coercive enough to protect the sexual abuser from his compulsions or protect future victims of the sexual abuser.

Accordingly, we have entrusted the criminal justice system with redressing what we now see as crimes. But this system, which has served us so well for two hundred years, sometimes falls short in its task because child sexual abuse cases are so peculiar. These are crimes often with no evidence of the sort we are accustomed to taking seriously. These are crimes often with no witness, except the victim, and that victim is often of an age that we usually regard as not credible.

If we are worried for these children, we are also worried for our husbands and brothers and neighbors. There is the possibility that the word of a little child—a child who might be pretending, who might be lying, who might have been coached—could ruin the life of a respectable member of the community. We are worried for our justice system. We wonder about the apparent willingness of some to abrogate the constitutional rights of the defendant to confront his accuser, or for the court to suspend hearsay and leading-question prohibitions for these young witnesses when these prohibitions must apply for everyone else.

We play out all of our ambivalence about children, sex, and civil liberties in the criminal court cases of child sexual abuse. However, because we are still under the influence of the unspoken commandment, "Thou shalt not be aware,"[2] our motives remain largely unconscious. These unconscious motives contributed to the "hysteria" surrounding the McMartin day-care case. They are responsible for the accusations that the child abuse professional community is engaged in a "witch hunt." They have created the "battle and the backlash."[3]

Out of a conviction that facts offer a way out of the emotion-bound intermediate state of affairs that we are in, the National Council of Jewish Women (NCJW) Center for the Child sought to investigate what was really going on in these cases across the country. The research center was awarded a grant from the National Center on Child Abuse and Neglect, and this author was hired to design and direct the study. We first conducted a preliminary survey of fifteen jurisdictions across the country through questionnaires and interviews administered by local NCJW volunteers. We then mounted a yearlong intensive collection of data on virtually all filed cases of child sexual abuse in eight of these jurisdictions, (and, for one very large jurisdiction, on the referred cases that were not filed, as well). These data also were collected by NCJW volunteers—this time, by reading prosecutors' case records and observing courtroom proceedings. The eight jurisdictions that are represented in the study by no means give the picture of the entire nation. But they were not selected for being atypical, either. We believe they offer us a place to start in understanding the current state of criminal prosecution of child sexual abuse.

The findings were eye-opening. Over 90% of the cases presented to prosecutors do not go to trial. Over half the cases prosecutors see are not charged or are dropped after charging. A large percentage of cases in some jurisdictions are diverted to "treatment," a loosely defined mandate for some form of counseling. Plea-bargaining is used extensively in these cases, and may leave a convicted defendant with a record not easily identified as child molestation.[4]

These figures, when they began to emerge, shaped the remainder of the study and framed much of this book. If the *preponderance* of child sexual abuse cases that are referred to the criminal justice system never arrive in the courtroom, then—we reasoned—the handling of these invisible cases in the system must be exposed to public scrutiny if we are truly to be informed about the criminal prosecution of child sexual abuse.

The study also revealed serious inequities in the system for both victims and defendants. For instance: if you are black, you are more likely to be accused of child sexual abuse (even though studies show you are not more likely to *commit* child sexual abuse); you are more likely to enter the criminal justice system; you are likely to be charged with a more serious offense; and, once in the system, you are less likely to have your case diverted to treatment and away from prosecution. If you are a female victim of sexual abuse, your case is more likely to be admitted into the criminal system than if you are a male victim (even taking into account the different rates of victimization). If you live in certain locations and are accused of sexually abusing your daughter, your case may be diverted to psychological treatment and away from prosecution; in other locations, that option does not exist. But diversion to treatment is less often an option to you if you are a black man, or if you abused someone else's daughter rather than your own—even in locations that practice such diversion. If you are a very young child victim, chances are your case will be plea-bargained or dropped. If you are five or six years old, chances are greater that the case will go to trial. If you are a teenager, however, chances are very slim that a trial will be held. If you are a resident of one particular county, your case is likely to last just over a month; in another, it is likely to drag on for almost a year.

Work associated with this study showed that for those cases that do get into court, there are biases that are likely to operate there as well. For instance, whether the child witness is poised or befuddled has a different effect on the jurors' perception of her credibility depending on the type of expert testimony that is offered in the case.

While many of these findings are disturbing, this study should be seen as an overview of the current state of affairs, not as an exposé of the system.[5] Many of the practices and biases found here are not peculiar to sexual abuse cases (although some surely are); it is just that they have not been revealed in this context and are not known by this audience. The nonprofessional citizens who serve as advocates for abused children in the courts are unlikely to know in any detail how these courts operate in general, let alone with specific regard to sexual abuse. It is hoped that the combination of a social scientist (rather than a lawyer) as the principal investigator of this study, and local lay people as data collectors increased the chance that what the general public might want to know about the system was uncovered. To a large extent, we went into the criminal justice system with the questions and misconceptions of the average person, rather than the "matter-of-fact" knowledge of the socialized insider.

This is not, in the first instance, a legal text, although there is much here that may be of use and interest to lawyers. There exist elsewhere several very good compilations of statutory authority for prosecutorial innovations for dealing with child sexual abuse cases (e.g., American Prosecutors Research Institute, 1992, 1992a), and other materials that prescribe prosecution strategy in detail (e.g., Toth & Whalen, 1987). Therefore, there are few legal citations and lengthy discussions of case law in this book. Instead, this is an investigation of current implementation practices.[6]

Another note about the method of this research: it is eclectic. Even in this multidisciplinary field of child abuse, combining the methods of several disciplines in one study sometimes stirs up in readers representative of each discipline a certain anxiety. Nonetheless, the choice to include survey research (sociology), laboratory study (psychology), courtroom observation (anthropology), and the act of venturing into the criminal justice system at all (law) seems warranted here, given the questions involved, and is squarely within the tradition of my own field of training, social work, which borrows from each of the social sciences selectively.

One very important purpose of this research is to inform action. There is much interest across the country now in reforming the criminal system as it deals with child sexual abuse. Some of the reforms of the recent past, however, are turning out to be less than useful. It is my hope that the information presented here will be used as grist for the mill for more exploration and more appropriately targeted activity. We collected this data on many aspects of the defendants, the victims, and the process in the belief that we cannot know where we should go until we know where we are. The chapters that follow begin to tell us where we are.

1

Child Sexual Abuse: Isn't It a Crime?

Child abuse in the United States is widespread and well-recognized. There are somewhere between one and three million cases a year, by various estimates. By 1982, according to a Harris poll conducted in that year, 90% of the American public perceived child abuse to be a serious problem (N. Peterson, National Committee for Prevention of Child Abuse, personal communication, 1992). The percentage may be even higher today. Even more distressing to the public, however, is the newly "discovered" extent of child sexual abuse in this country. Exact incidence figures do not exist, but there were 155,900 countable cases of child sexual abuse in 1986, according to the National Incidence Study (NCCAN, 1988), and more than 200,000 new cases per year by 1984 estimates that took underreporting into account (Finkelhor, 1984). Thanks to blanketing public-awareness and education efforts, the general public now recognizes (albeit reluctantly) and has some understanding of the neglect or physical abuse of children resulting from the breakdown of their parent's ability to cope with the vicissitudes of life. Until recently, however, most people seemed incapable of *ac-*

knowledging the phenomenon of child sexual abuse. The perpetrators of these acts were not impaired in any obvious way, save their sexual interest in children. There was no safe way for us to identify with these abusers, and no comfortable way to empathize with their victims. It was simply easier to deny that the phenomenon existed. But the situation has changed: now, unless we refuse to read newspapers and magazines, watch television, listen to the radio, or talk to others, we Americans must concede child sexual abuse as a fact of life.

In truth, rather than being a strictly linear process of discovery, society's recognition of and legal response to child sexual abuse through history has been somewhat intermittent and contradictory. References to the sexual maltreatment of children and youth alternately surface and disappear throughout the literature on children and childhood.[1]

America's religious and cultural heritage provides the backdrop for this hide-and-seek approach to the protection of children from sexual assault. In antiquity, children were not thought of as full human beings. Infanticide by exposure or other means was common and accepted as a way to regulate population, destroy females when males were desired, or be rid of deformed births. DeMause refers to a typical gynecological writing of the times entitled, "How to Recognize the Child That Is Worth Rearing," and tells that children who didn't meet the criteria it presented generally were killed. Those who were spared extinction lived "in an atmosphere of sexual abuse" (deMause, 1974). Legal redress for this abuse was inconsistent. The ancient Code of Hammurabi, the Babylonian king, for instance, held that a man who raped a young virgin was to be killed. If this child were his own daughter, however, his punishment was merely banishment from the city.

Hebrew law dealt with the defilement of children in a context of economic justice. Because a young girl was considered property, the Talmud decreed that recompense had to be made for raping and deflowering her; her father had to be paid a sum of money, and the girl became the wife of the defiler (as she was now unworthy of anyone else). The Greeks and Romans protected some children from sexual abuse by adults (it has been speculated that the "pedagogues" provided as companions to "free-born" upper-class young males in Athens in the classical period may have served this function [Sommerville, 1990]), but used other children for precisely this purpose, with impunity. Christian law was obsessed with "affinity," and sexual relations with a relative were outlawed. If the relative was under seven years of age, however, the act was not punished, as it was not recognized as "valid" (Rush, 1980). The concept of children considered worthy or unworthy of protection from sexual abuse with regard to their "quality" as well as their age persisted throughout this time. Evidence of this attitude is that girls abandoned to exposure were sometimes rescued only to be raised as prostitutes.

In the Middle Ages, infanticide faded out slowly, but the sale of children, and abandonment—both literal and emotional—prevailed. With the advent of civil law in England (through the Statutes of Westminster, the first of which was enacted in 1275), statutory rape was defined—although specified as sex with a child under twelve, rather than sixteen or eighteen, as it is in most states today—and prohibited, but it was designated as a misdemeanor crime.

DeMause describes the Renaissance attitude toward children as ambivalent. Children were still physically harmed to a great degree, but they were part of their parent's emotional life. They were regarded with hostility and fear in addition to being seen as the responsibility of their parents. Nursing was seen as an enormous inconvenience, and children were shamed in the belief that shame would make them honorable. This was the era during which the idea of child molding that has been with us to some degree ever since, began. To illustrate the tenor of these times, deMause notes the proliferation of child-instruction manuals. Thus, while children of this period were beginning to be seen as vulnerable to sexual abuse and worthy of protection, they were also beginning to be regarded as responsible for this protection themselves. They were told they must keep adults from molesting them (Rush, 1980), presumably by not being "provocative" in their "look" or behavior. This was in keeping with the general legal attitude toward rape during this period.

Even though the Second Statute of Westminster had amended the classification of rape to a felony by this time, according to Susan Brownmiller little had changed: "The later giants of jurisprudence, Hale, Blackstone, Wigmore and the rest, continued to point a suspicious finger at the female victim and worry about her motivations and 'good fame'" (Brownmiller, 1975, p. 22).

The English Poor Law of 1601 marks perhaps the first time there was a systematic and legislated attempt to deal with orphaned, neglected, destitute, or otherwise needy children outside their own homes. Through this set of statutes, children were "bound out" as apprentices or servants to willing individuals who would teach them a useful trade. This arrangement effectively removed the children from homes and parents deemed unsuitable by the standards of the day, but the motives were far from current child welfare tenets. Historians are quick to point out that the major reasons for these child placement practices were economics and social control, not protection from physical and sexual abuse by their caretakers. Binding-out relieved the community of the financial cost of supporting these children and the social cost of coping with what the Virginia Statutes at Large of 1646 termed "sloth and idleness wherewith such young children are easily corrupted . . ." (Bremner, 1970, vol. 1, p. 65). Furthermore, placing these children in servitude to nonrelated overlords itself created new opportunities for sexual abuse.

In the 1630s, New England's Puritan laws criminalized incest, defining the act broadly to include sexual relations and marriage between near relatives. However, Elizabeth Pleck tells us that at that time, "criminal laws against family violence were intended mainly to serve symbolic purposes—to define the boundary between saint and sinner, to demonstrate to God and community a vigilance against sin, and to shore up the proper authority in the household and society" (Ohlin & Tonry, 1989).

After this period of symbolic attention, there followed two centuries of no legal acknowledgment of the sexual abuse of children. However, Samuel Radbill points out that some pressure regarding child sexual abuse was brought to bear on the public by periodic literary works highlighting the problem. He cites Richardson's *Pamela* in the eighteenth century, Scott's *The Heart of Midlothian* in the nineteenth century, and Victor Hugo's *Les Miserables*—as well as many of Dickens' works—as examples (Radbill, 1987).

Destitute children continued to be indentured throughout the eighteenth century, but in the nineteenth century they were commonly placed in workhouses to be taught a trade, or in almshouses, simply to put them out of sight and mind. The Industrial Revolution in England is well-known for its physical abuse of children, but less so for the rampant sexual abuse. C. John Sommerville, in his book, *The Rise and Fall of Childhood* (1990), quotes an exposé by Friedrich Engels to show that the period's reliance on child labor allowed factory owners to indulge themselves in this type of abuse: "In ninety-nine cases out of a hundred, the threat of dismissal is sufficient to break the resistance of girls who at the best of times have no strong inducement to chastity" (Engels, 1968, orig. 1865). The early history of child welfare activity in the United States after the era of binding-out and almshouse care was dominated by religious institutions. The establishment of these institutions for dependent and neglected children marks the beginning of the varied approach to child care that we have today (Lundberg, 1947).

Concern about the sexual abuse of children peaked again during the late nineteenth century, spurred by the feminist movement. This was the beginning of a connection that has persisted though most of the history of concern with family violence.

> For most of the 110 years of this history, it was the women's rights movement that was most influential in confronting, publicizing, and demanding action against family violence. Concern with family violence usually grew when feminism was strong and ebbed when feminism was weak. Women's movements have consistently been concerned with violence not only against women but also against children. (Gordon, 1988, p. 4)

Beginning in the late 1800s, Societies for the Prevention of Cruelty to Children proliferated, numbering 300 by the cen-

tury's end, representing the conviction that protecting children
(even from their parents) is the responsibility of the state (Pleck,
1989). There were complicating attitudes embedded even in this
seemingly child-centered approach, however. Historian Linda
Gordon speaks about the prudish, anti-immigrant, anti-Catholic,
classist ideology that now allowed recognition rather than denial of
incest (at least in some quarters), but eventually led to the victims of
this crime being "reconstituted" as tainted sex delinquents, and
their mother labeled as neglectful. Finally, this reconceptualization
focused on the stranger as child molester and away from fathers as
perpetrators (Gordon, 1988, p. 215).

During the Progressive Era, child abuse—at least those instances that took place within the family unit—was again oper-
ationally if not legally decriminalized, this time in favor of a
therapeutic approach. No particular distinction was made between physical and sexual abuse in this regard. All family
problems were thought amenable to benevolent intervention,
and, it was reasoned, resorting to the criminal courts could only
stigmatize emotionally ill parents, break up families, and cause
economic hardship. A parallel court system was developed in
1899—the juvenile, or family, court—that concerned itself with
the protection and welfare of the child in these intra-family cases,
rather than the punishment of the offending parent.[2] While a
"finding" of child abuse or neglect could be made by such a
court, the extreme outcome of this finding would be removal of
the child from the custody of the parents. Court "supervision,"
carried out by a social worker was a much more likely outcome.
It is through this less formal judicial system, not the criminal
system, that most physical abuse cases, virtually all neglect cases,
and the extremely few emotional maltreatment cases that are
brought to any kind of justice system are taken, even to this day.

While hailed as a major child welfare milestone by many (Platt,
1969), the development of this alternative "justice" system can
be said to have done a grievous disservice to children's rights
(Platt, 1969; Dziech and Schudson, 1989). In this forum, confidentiality of the proceedings worked to the benefit of the
parental defendants and, arguably, against the child victims.
The relaxation of the standard of proof in this court from

"beyond a reasonable doubt," required in criminal proceedings, to "preponderance of the evidence" or "clear and convincing evidence" in Juvenile Court may have inadvertently minimized the offense. Charles B. Schudson, a Wisconsin Court of Appeals judge and his co-author sum up the unintended consequences of this reform:

> Thus, without intending to do so, the juvenile courts prevented child sexual abuse from coming to public view. Although they provided the first formal intervention in cases of abuse or neglect, they did so by conceding that most of these were family problems, not crimes. The irony was that these courts designed to protect children also protected those who abused them. (Dziech and Schudson, 1991, p. 26)

There was a brief return around 1940 to the criminal model that, interestingly enough, coincided with the rise in popularity and legitimacy of psychiatry, leading to a curious liaison between this "science" of mental health and the law. Exemplifying this trend, California enacted in 1939 one of the first sexual-psychopath laws in response to a spate of child sex-murders several years earlier and the subsequent public outcry, making the law specifically applicable to child molestation. People convicted under this statute were committed to psychiatric treatment facilities for the long term, or at least until they were deemed no longer dangerous to society. Around 1950, spurred by the psychiatric community, which had been less than successful in treating these "sexual psychopaths" through in-patient therapy and who now eschewed the label as imprecise and dynamically insignificant, the laws were changed to refer to perpetrators as—in Illinois—"sexually dangerous person," or—in California—persons who are "predisposed to the commission of sexual offenses to such a degree that [they are] dangerous to the health and safety of others" (Weisberg, 1984).

At about this same time, physical child abuse was newly seen as within the domain of medicine. This recognition was largely due to the development of the x-ray as a diagnostic device that first revealed that fractures of the long bones of infants and bleeding under the outer membrane of the brain often occurred together, and eventually permitted the debunking of parents' fallacious explanations of their children's injuries, documenting a history of previous similar injuries in many cases. Physician C. Henry Kempe and his colleagues studied these cases and elaborated the "syndrome" in the early 1960s, publishing "The Battered Child Syndrome" in the *Journal of the American Medical Association* in 1962, and the book, *The Battered Child,* in 1968. Because there was no corresponding technology for measuring sexual abuse, however, it often went unrecognized.

Advocacy for child-protection activity began in earnest after that. The U.S. Children's Bureau drafted model protective legislation for the states. The American Humane Association followed suit with their own model legislation. Child-abuse reporting laws were enacted in all fifty states between 1963 and 1967. Aimed first only at physicians, these statutes were rapidly broadened and eventually empowered all citizens, and mandated child care professionals—such as teachers, doctors, social workers, nurses, and day-care workers—to report child abuse by parents or caretakers to an officially designated, public, child welfare agency charged with investigating the allegation. Reporters were (and are) free of liability even if the report is unfounded as long as they made the referral "in good faith," and in about half the states, mandated reporters were (and are) subject to liability for *not* reporting child abuse they became aware of in their professional capacity. It is likely that these laws were as liberal as they were because of the general climate of optimism in the 1960s regarding our ability to solve social problems in a noncoercive manner. The therapeutic stance was so empathic toward the parents in these cases, that "referring" them to the child welfare system was seen (at least by those in the system), as providing a service rather than making an accusation.

It was largely through the work of Vincent DeFrancis, a lawyer and a social worker, that the understanding of child abuse only as battered babies was broadened to include neglect, psychological abuse, and sexual abuse of children. DeFrancis enabled the inclusion of this last category of maltreatment, first by conducting research in New York in 1965–1968 that illuminated the incidence and nature of child sexual abuse, and then by testifying before a Senate committee considering national child abuse legislation and urging that this broadened definition be adopted in the legislation.

When child sexual abuse did come to the attention of these newly constituted child welfare authorities, it was treated in much the same way as the physical battering and child neglect cases of the day. It was understood to be the behavioral product of a generational cycle of maltreatment in which mistreated children grow up without the self-control and nurturing skills to adequately care for and avoid hurting their own children, who in turn grow up without these skills, and so on. The response that grows out of this understanding is one in which the family structure is preserved, the "sick" member is treated, and some additional measure of social control is imposed on the situation (juvenile court supervision, and/or new "rules," such as the father and his daughter will not be left alone together).

In 1974, the National Child Abuse Prevention and Treatment Act was passed, thereby establishing the National Center on Child Abuse and Neglect of the federal government. This agency's mission is to compile information; operate a clearinghouse for programs showing promise of success in prevention, identification, and treatment of child abuse; publish training materials; provide technical assistance to public and nonprofit agencies, fund research into the causes and other aspects of abuse; operate resource centers, demonstration projects and state grant programs and study changes in incidence. Child sexual abuse has remained a major focus of these activities.

Meanwhile, the legal system was working hand in hand with the therapeutic community on child molestation cases. In 1975, the California legislature passed a law ensuring the funding and dissemination of a prototypic treatment program for incestuous fathers and their families that was started in Santa Clara, called the Child Sexual Abuse Treatment Program (CSATP). It was this legislation that first relabeled (intrafamily) child molestation as child sexual abuse in the legal literature (Weisberg, 1984). However, excepting this program developed by Henry Giaretto and his associates, in which an essential component is criminal-court-mandated participation, the noncriminal approach to child sexual abuse—particularly that abuse occurring within families—has continued until very recently. As evidence, between 1976 and 1981, the number of treatment programs for child sexual abusers and their families grew from 20 to 300, according to Josephine Bulkley (1985).[3]

At the same time, however, there were changes being introduced into the legal system with regard to adult rape cases that foreshadowed the reforms that would be called for in child sexual abuse cases when the pendulum swung back to a more punitive approach. Again, it was the feminists who spearheaded these changes. Women's rights groups called attention to the revictimization of raped women caused by the assumptions and practices of the courtroom. In the 1970s and 1980s, feminists pushed for counseling and preparation of victims for trial, the provision of victim advocates throughout the prosecution of the case, closed courtroom proceedings, and the banning of the victim's prior sexual history as legal evidence of her complicity in the crime. And in 1980, California enacted legislation to outlaw requiring evidence of victim resistance in order to validate rape charges and return a guilty verdict, a requirement that had been held over from seventeenth-century law (Dziech & Schudson, 1991).

In the last ten years, there have been many calls to approach child sexual abuse cases differently from battering and neglect cases. That is, there has been a concerted push toward criminal prosecution of these cases, although not without controversy. Some experts, such as Massachusetts Attorney General, Scott Harshbarger, and the staff of the National Center for the Prosecution of Child Abuse of the American Prosecutors Research Institute (APRI) in Alexandria, Virginia, take the unconditional position that child sexual abuse is a crime, and no less so because the perpetrator is the victim's father or other relative (Harshbarger, 1987). While these individuals do not hold that every one of these individual cases should be prosecuted, they are not prepared to exempt any particular categories of child sexual abuse (cf. Peters, Dinsmore, & Toth, 1989).

Other authorities in the field advocate selective prosecution. For example, David Sandberg, the director of the Program on

Law and Child Maltreatment at the Boston University School of Law, lays out certain factors to be considered in the decision of whether to prosecute or not: 1) victim desire and/or consent for prosecution (he advocates acceding to the wishes of an adolescent but employing a "best interest of the child" criterion to cases with younger victims); 2) whether an intra-family or stranger assault is involved (here, the important issue is whether the child has access to at least one supportive parent or parent substitute); 3) the child's developmental status ("is the child developmentally age appropriate?", "how will criminal prosecution affect this child?"); 4) the presence and effectiveness of existing district-court action (court supervision, orders of protection, transfer of child custody); and 5) whether the criminal prosecutor is equipped to prosecute the case in a child-centered manner (providing victim advocates, monitoring the child for signs of unwillingness to go through with prosecution, having various services available to orient the child to the courtroom process) (Sandberg, 1987). As Patricia Toth, director of the National Center for Prosecution of Child Abuse of APRI points out, Sandberg leaves out any consideration of the danger the offender presents to other children—"Almost always a concern for the responsible prosecutor who knows anything about child molesters" (Toth, personal communication, July 9, 1992).

There is still a voice for the therapeutic approach to child sexual abuse cases, or at least against prosecution in these situations. The desire to prevent further trauma to the child has led some to suggest that prosecution of child sexual abuse should be avoided, as legal efforts to protect children and punish offenders may exacerbate the trauma experienced by sexually abused children (cf. Conte & Berliner, 1981; Newberger, 1987). Concomitant to this is a movement in the direction of pretrial diversion of accused individuals to treatment professionals and facilities.

Criminal prosecution of sexual abuse does have, on balance, a significant emotional cost for some child witnesses (Berliner, 1985). The literature is replete with opinion and case documentation by clinicians, prosecutors, and child-abuse experts to the effect that children are caused additional psychological harm by insensitive legal procedures (DeFrancis, 1969; Burgess and Holstrom, 1978; MacFarlane, 1978; Bulkley, 1981; Weiss and Berg, 1982; Sgroi, 1982). Repeated questioning and cross-examination by a series of strange adults can frighten children and leave them with the impression that it is they who are guilty (Tufts–New England Medical Center Study, 1984).[4] Our defendant-oriented, adversarial court system, in which the Constitution's Sixth Amendment has guaranteed the right of the accused to physically face his accuser, places an additional emotional burden on the child. (Although, *Maryland v. Craig*, a recent U.S. Supreme Court ruling [June 27, 1990] held that in certain, narrow circumstances, this confrontation need not be face to face.) Unlike defendants, witnesses do not have any constitutional rights to protection during either the investigation of their allegations or the trial, even if they are children. Consequently, the prevention of additional trauma to child victim witnesses has recently emerged as a concern among medical, legal, mental health, and social service professionals (Conte, 1984).

Some, however, have argued that the seemingly contradictory goals of protecting children from secondary trauma, on the one hand, and of more persistently and effectively prosecuting the perpetrators of child sexual abuse, on the other, might both be served by the same systemic reforms (Gothard, 1987). It is said that various efforts by child protective-service agencies, law-enforcement agencies, and the courts to lessen stress on the child—reducing the number of occasions on which statements are taken, consolidating or coordinating investigations by the several agencies involved, relying upon specialists (by training or experience) to conduct investigations, and customizing the courtroom procedure to the age of the child—may also increase the efficacy of prosecution, primarily by improving the accuracy and credibility of testimony.

Still, there is much to learn with respect to children as witnesses, particularly as witnesses to their own victimization. For many years, in accordance with principles of English Common Law, young children were considered incompetent to testify and had no place in court at all. In 1895, this situation changed dramatically when the U.S. Supreme Court in *Wheeler v. United States (159 U.S. 523, 524–26 [1895])* ruled that a five-year-old boy could testify at a trial concerning his father's murder by a stranger. In recent years, when determining competency, courts have placed primary emphasis on the child's ability to distinguish truth from falsehood and his or her expressed understanding of the obligation to tell the truth (Melton, 1981). Now that children's testimony is generally admissible as evidence in criminal court proceedings, there remains the question of how best to elicit testimony from children that is both accurate and credible, providing a solid basis for prosecution and conviction.

With respect to the uses of victim testimony in child sexual abuse cases, disagreement abounds. On the one hand, as the National Legal Resource Center for Child Advocacy and Protection of the American Bar Association (now the ABA Center on Children and the Law) has pointed out, the child victim's testimony in sexual abuse cases is often critical, since other admissible evidence rarely exists in these cases. The child, then, becomes the prosecutor's most valuable resource. On the other hand, the prosecutors in many jurisdictions are not getting the experience with child witnesses that they need in order to learn how to use their testimony effectively, because they bring so few of these difficult cases to trial.[5] Both the President's Task Force on Victims of Crime (1982), and the Attorney General's Task Force on Family Violence (1984) recognized this problem and criticized prosecutors who are hesitant to charge or anxious to plea-bargain because these cases are often difficult to try. Then again, others have criticized on opposite grounds: that ambitious assistant district attorneys sometimes go to trial needlessly with child sexual abuse cases in order to bolster their own careers with sensational publicity; and they point out that plea bargaining is a legitimate, appropriate, and often superior route to prosecution of child sexual abuse.

Public opinion is strong that, if child sexual abuse cases go to court, special measures should be taken to adapt the process to the emotional and cognitive level of the child witness. A great hue and cry has been heard for making certain physical accommodations to the child in the courtroom, such as providing a smaller witness chair, allowing children to testify via videotape or closed-circuit television or otherwise shielding the child from the gaze of the defendant during testimony, allowing the children to demonstrate their allegations by manipulating anatomically complete dolls rather than being required to present the story verbally, and allowing questions that are somewhat more leading than would be permitted in questioning an adult witness, among other accommodations. However, for each of these reforms there is a counter opinion that the rights of the accused are being mitigated in direct proportion to the latitude given the victim witness.

It is clear that an increasing number of child sexual abuse cases are coming to the attention of the criminal courts. It is also clear that there is public disagreement about the advisability or fairness of criminally prosecuting child sexual abuse cases, particularly when the case rests solely on the child's testimony. At one end of the continuum, the argument against prosecution stresses the shortcomings of the criminal-justice system and the dangers inherent in overlooking the structural and philosophical causes of abuse. At the other extreme, the reasoning of anti-prosecution advocates is illustrated vividly in a quotation from a *New York Times* article excerpted in *By Silence Betrayed* by John Crewdson. The speaker is Ralph Underwager, a psychologist from Northfield, Minnesota, who testified as an expert witness in one of the more famous child sexual abuse cases of recent years, the so-called Jordan Minnesota Case. Crewdson quotes Underwager as saying that it is "more desirable that a thousand children in abuse situations are not discovered than for one innocent person to be convicted wrongly" (Crewdson, 1988). Apparently, there is a great deal of fear that this latter occurrence is just what will happen. In a 1988 random population survey of over 1000 people, 41% agreed (and 2% strongly agreed) with the statement: "In the current social climate, it is virtually impossible for a person accused of child sexual abuse to get an impartial trial" (Minnesota Center for Survey Research, 1988).

Needless to say, the issues inherent in this dispute are many and complex, and not adequately evoked by these polar characterizations. However, the data on which this debate for and against criminal prosecution of child sexual abuse cases is based is sketchy and mostly anecdotal. We do not have a comprehensive current picture of the criminal justice cases, nor do we know what is really going on inside the "black box" of the criminal justice system.[6] Who are these perpetrators sent to criminal prosecution for sexually abusing children? Which abused children are the ones whose cases are referred to the criminal system for prosecution? What happens to the cases once they are there: do they plead guilty; are they dismissed or tried? Are the defendants allowed to undergo psychotherapy and to avoid acquiring a criminal record? Do they plea bargain, admit to all the charges against them, argue their case before a jury, go to jail? If they go to jail, how long do they stay? Are the answers to these questions different if the child is very young, if the child is a teenager, if the defendant is black?

This lack of information leads to the adversarial character of the discussion. Opponents become entrenched and attack each other's integrity and professionalism rather than marshalling the particulars to make their arguments. The interested public is forced to declare loyalty rather than make an informed judgment.

Actual practice in child sexual abuse prosecution, as with any criminal prosecution, is infinitely complicated. Contrary to what the general public may think, there is not a clear set of criteria, easily administered, that determine whether a case of child sexual abuse is to take the civil or criminal route, or both, to resolution. And if the case embarks on the criminal path, there is no checklist of factual elements that, if present, determine which way to turn at each decision point from intake to final disposition. Discretion operates at every node on the "decision tree," and we need aggregate information to see the patterns in these discretionary choices. The vast majority of the cases are decided at one of the junctures before jury trial. The real story may be in these earlier stages.

It remains the case, however, that the furor is over the cases *in court,* rather than those that do not face a judge and jury. Even here, though, there is a dearth of accurate information about what actually transpires. Many questions remain. It is not generally known if the technological advances that have been touted and criticized in the newspapers—videotaped testimony, closed circuit TV from the judge's chambers to the jury—are revolutionizing the prosecution of child sexual abuse cases. Are these reforms currently in widespread use and, if so, does the trying of child sexual abuse cases in the criminal court threaten to weaken the constitutional rights of the accused—a fundamental tenet of American jurisprudence?

On what basis are the jurors making their decisions in these cases? Are they swayed by experts who give information about abused children and their typical behaviors? Do they believe the children who are facing them and telling terrible stories about unspeakable acts? What is the state of the medical evidence?

What would the average citizen see if she observed child sexual abuse trials in criminal court? Are the proceedings overly technical and difficult to follow? Are they dramatic and heartrending? Does the defense attorney further traumatize the child by questioning her credibility? Are the jurors attentive? Does the judge seem impartial?

Consider the following:

A thirty-two-year-old male who had been convicted on several prior charges of drug possession allegedly fondled his eleven-year-old neighbor as she was playing in the front yard of a friend. The case went to court. There were two eyewitnesses who testified, and the victim also testified. The defendant was charged with indecency with a child, but was not convicted.

A four-year-old girl complained that her "bottom hurt" one night when her mother was putting her to bed. She was taken to the doctor and diagnosed with gonorrhea of the vagina and mouth. When questioned, she acknowledged that someone had "poked me with his thing," but would not tell who. The police questioned several male relatives of the child with ambiguous results and sent the case to the District Attorney's office. After interviewing the child once, the prosecutor sent the case to the child-welfare office, closing the criminal file.

A father was accused of attempted intercourse and anal penetration of his seven-year-old daughter. The abuse was said to have occurred over a period of a few months. The defendant had prior convictions on two counts of murder and drug possession. The case went to trial and the child took the stand. There was definite medical evidence of sexual abuse that was used in court. The examining physician and the police investigator provided corroborating testimony. The defendant was convicted and given a life sentence.

A four-year-old boy was repeatedly subjected to rubbing of his penis and anus by his father. This was reported to the department of social services by the boy's mother and investigated by a social worker and the police. During questioning, the child could not recall times and places of the incidents, although he reported that they had taken place, and he was visibly shaken by them. The father, from whom the mother was now separated, denied the abuse. The police and social services closed their cases for lack of evidence, without referring to the district attorney.

A fifty-five-year-old man with previous sex-related charges and one conviction on a non-sex-related charge, was accused of fondling and digital penetration of a ten-year-old, and her nine-year-old cousin. The nine-year-old was visiting her aunt and cousin who were boarders in the defendant's house. There was medical evidence of abuse for one child. Both children recanted, but the younger child ultimately testified about the abuse. The ten-year-old stuck to her recantation, and did not testify. The defendant was acquitted.

A forty-year-old defendant was accused of having intercourse with his eleven-year-old daughter. Medical evidence included slides showing a three-centimeter hymen (enlarged). He was convicted and sentenced to 4–10 years in prison. The defendant had previously pled guilty to incest charges with his older daughter and had been sent to treatment instead of prosecution by the same judge who sat on this case.

A six-year-old girl was questioned by the police after her mother called the authorities saying that a man lured her behind a nearby house by asking if she would help him find his lost model airplane. According to the report, the man told the child to close her eyes if she wanted a lollipop, and the girl said that she "peeked" and saw him unzip his pants. As soon as she could, she ran away and told her mother that he stuck something in her mouth. Although the police had a suspect—a seventeen-year-old youth—he would not admit anything. They dropped the case.

A forty-three-year-old man had allegedly abused his eight-year-old stepdaughter over a period of about a year by fondling her and penetrating her vagina with his fingers. The abuse stopped when the stepfather moved out of the house. The child did not disclose the abuse until almost three years later. Her mother kept getting notes from school saying that she was doing poorly, and finally the child "confessed" to her mother. There was no medical evidence of abuse. The child did testify, although there were no other corroborating witnesses. The defendant was convicted and sentenced to 15 years in prison.

A state Supreme Court overturned a man's sodomy conviction because he was barred from attending a hearing to determine whether two sisters, one seven years old and the other eight, were old enough to testify accurately about the allegations. The state court said the pretrial hearing was essential to the prosecution, and that the defendant had a right to confront his accusers in this forum.[7] The man had allegedly abused the girls and a five-year-old boy after their mothers left them with him while they shopped for a birthday cake for him.

A twenty-eight-year-old man with a prior conviction of aggravated sexual assault was indicted for "taking the victim's penis into his mouth." The victim was the four-and-a-half-year-old son of his live-in girlfriend's foster sister, for whom he occasionally babysat. During the trial the child also described the defendant putting his penis into the child's mouth and ejaculating. Apparently, the abuse had occurred several times but charges were filed on just one incident. The child ultimately took the stand, although the mother was difficult to persuade to allow this. While testifying, the detective on the case referred to the defendant's prior record. Consequently, a mistrial was declared.

These vignettes, representing actual cases that were presented to prosecutor's offices in the eight states of this study, suggest the complex relationship between the allegations of abuse and the final outcome of the criminal case. The association between the apparent seriousness of the acts that were alleged and the disposition of a case is not necessarily a direct one. Instead, there is an intricate configuration of contextual and legal factors that contribute to each decision. Nevertheless, there may be a pattern to these decisions, and if there is a pattern, it has not heretofore been discernible, because the statistics have not been available up to this point.

It is telling that figures regarding the number of cases coming to the attention of the prosecutor's office, the number of indictments given, the extent of plea bargaining, the number of cases going to trial, the number of convictions won, and the various sentences handed down are unavailable in most jurisdictions. It appears that prosecutors and their staff are so occupied preparing and trying these cases that they do not have time left over to compile statistics on their activity. The preliminary survey to this study uncovered that virtually no jurisdictions in this sample or the few other areas surveyed had the figures for these decision points broken down by age of the child victim, and there were many missing data in the aggregate statistics as well. Furthermore, the figures that were retrievable did not necessarily add up to the totals provided. With such inadequate information at the jurisdiction and state level, getting a national overview is impossible. Lois Herrington, former Assistant Attorney General, decried the situation that exists at the federal level in a keynote speech at the Fourth National Conference on the Sexual Victimization of Children in 1986, a portion of which is reprinted in David Hechler's book, *The Battle and the Backlash: The Child Sexual Abuse War* (1988). She admitted that the federal bureaucracy has not done a very good job of keeping statistics on child sexual abuse. Discussing the two national data bases on crime, she pointed out that the FBI's Uniform Crime Report has no information on child sex abuse and very little on family violence. Futher the National Crime Survey of the Bureau of Justice Statistics doesn't ask questions of subjects under twelve and often conducts interviews of child victims in the presence of the entire family, seriously compromising the completeness of the data.

It is appalling that as individuals, as communities, and as a nation we do not know what is happening to the child sexual abuse cases we refer to our justice system, let alone what is happening to the lives of the people who make up these cases. The purpose of this study was to take the first of these steps: to track the child sexual abuse cases that were presented to the prosecutor's offices in eight geographically and procedurally diverse jurisdictions across the country for the period of one year—September 1987 through August 1988—capturing the decisions made on each case, and to explore the case and system factors that predict these decisions.

2

Methods and Sample Used in This Research

All field data were gathered by National Council of Jewish Women (NCJW) volunteers.[1] NCJW is made up of volunteer members who are involved in community service, advocacy, and education in communities across the country. These volunteers also participate in field research of such timely topics affecting children and families as work and family, day care, and juvenile justice. Volunteers from forty NCJW Sections (chapters) were given the opportunity to complete a preliminary survey of the criminal jurisdiction serving their geographic area by interviewing local officials. These jurisdictions were chosen for a variety of reasons, having to do both with their statutory status (that is, what combination of laws related to child sexual abuse cases existed on the books in that state) and their demographic makeup. Sampling was designed to represent legislative variation and demographic diversity. Fifteen jurisdictions completed the preliminary survey interviews with the prosecutor's office, the child welfare agency mandated to receive reports of child abuse, and the police. Eleven of these NCJW local Sections agreed to participate in the full study, but two were unable to do so, for different reasons. One very small jurisdiction was dropped from the study for lack of cases. In the end, there were eight jurisdictions in the full study. Those jurisdictions, and the NCJW Sections that collected data from them are as follows:

Study Jurisdictions and Participating NCJW Sections

Baltimore County, MD	Baltimore Section
Clay, Duval, and Nassau counties, FL	Jacksonville Section
Dallas County, TX	Greater Dallas Section
Jefferson County, KY	Louisville Section
Johnson County, KS	Greater Kansas City Section
Orleans Parish, LA	Greater New Orleans Section
St. Louis, MO	St. Louis Section
San Francisco, CA	San Francisco Section

Site coordinators were selected from among the volunteers in each participating NCJW Section. These Site Coordinators (two to a site) were brought together in New York and trained to collect the data for the project in a two-day intensive session. The first day, local and national experts presented to the group thorough information regarding child sexual abuse and the typical progress of a case through the criminal justice system. The second day was devoted to explaining to the volunteer site coordinators the sampling requirements of the study and use of the data collection forms. Training and technical assistance continued by telephone, mail, and occasional meetings as the volunteers encountered the intricacies of their local justice systems.

Data regarding the referral source, alleged crime, circumstances of disclosure, characteristics of victim and offender, and case disposition were gleaned from the prosecutors' case records, to which the volunteers negotiated access with the author's help (see "Defendant Case History" and "Child Case History" in the Appendix). While this information is technically public record, the genuine willingness of the district attorneys to cooperate with lay people going through their files and taking up scarce office space to laboriously record the details of each case was an unexpected bonus. These members of the prosecutors' offices were found to be very dedicated and hardworking individuals who, rather than being defensive about their shortcomings in handing these very difficult cases, were enthusiastic to learn the results of our investigation and put them into practice.

Data regarding trials were collected in a different manner. Volunteers observed the proceedings in the courtroom. Their observations were guided by and recorded on checklists and closed-ended questionnaires pertaining to the procedural techniques employed in the case (e.g., closed-circuit televised testimony, anatomically correct dolls), the process of determining competency of the child witness, the conduct of the child witness and her questioners, and the testimony of other courtroom witnesses (see "Child Competency Examination Checklist," "Child Witness for Prosecution" instrument, "Daily Observation Sheet," and "Prosecution Techniques" checklist in the Appendix). In addition, there were two questionnaires for jurors. The first was an attitude survey, designed to be completed before the deliberations, and the second, a form on which to record the elements of the case that were pivotal in the juror's decision regarding conviction or acquittal (see "Attitude Survey" and "Juror Questionnaire" in the Appendix).

All instruments were developed by the author for the purposes of this study. They were pretested by the author and several consultants in local New Jersey prosecutors' offices and courtrooms. That is, prosecutors' records were read and the data transferred to the "Defendant Case History" and "Child Case History" forms, to see if the desired items were actually retrievable. Courtroom proceedings were observed and recorded on the several observation forms to determine whether the tasks being asked of observers were realistic and achievable.

It is important to note that all the data collected for this study were "once removed" from the defendants, victims, and witnesses in question. That is, no first-hand accounts were collected from any of these individuals. This was deliberate. Although the richness and empathy that often results from hearing people's stories in their own words cannot be denied, records and statistics provide a dispassionate, aerial view of the situation that cannot be seen "from the ground." It is easier to detect patterns, trends, and bias from that height. Not interviewing victims, witnesses, and family members also avoids the unintentional, but very real, intrusion and exploitation of these already beleaguered people that can result from one-on-one data collection.

The fact that this study used community volunteers as data collectors had definite methodological benefits for this portion of the study. As ensconced citizens of the locales served by these jurisdictions, these volunteers are reasonable representatives of other citizens of their areas; and—presumably—when they enter the courtroom, their perceptions of what goes on there are also representative. They were then well placed to follow up the study findings and their own experiences as data collectors with community-level advocacy and programming efforts.

In addition to this standardized information, volunteer data collectors were encouraged to keep a diary of notes regarding the cases they observed. While the gathering of this information is decidedly unscientific, it provided the study with two things: additional data regarding cases that may not have been fully captured on the existing forms, and the perspective of the volunteer, who, although she was trained for her task in this project and became increasingly experienced as the data collection year proceeded, was nevertheless a reasonable stand-in for the average citizen. This perspective is important because the discrepancy between what actually happens to child sexual abuse cases in criminal court and what the "person on the street" thinks happens is rather wide and constitutes one of the underlying themes of this study.

In keeping with the emphasis on the accessibility and utility of this study, technical information will be kept to a minimum in the presentation that follows. However, it is necessary to report the basic design of the study, strategy for selection of sample cases, and the techniques for data analysis in order for others to assess the validity of the findings. Therefore, the following section may contain a few words or ideas that are foreign to the lay reader. When practicable, these will be translated into everyday words.

DATA ANALYSIS

This is an exploratory study. Data were analyzed using descriptive and inferential statistics (statistics that summarize, and statistics that draw conclusions about the entire population on the basis of a sample drawn from it, respectively). Certain of the analyses were hampered by the fact that many of the variables in this study are nominal-level, or categorical data. What this means is that rather than being measured in amounts, such as blood-alcohol level or classroom size, they are measured in terms of membership in a category, such as ethnicity or case outcome (conviction versus acquittal). This makes using such typical, multivariate statistical methods as hierarchical regression—which allows one to determine simultaneously the relative effects of several factors on a particular outcome—nearly impossible. Mathematical procedures that accomplish this require that all the information used be able to be converted into meaningful numbers (such that four units of the variable is actually twice the amount of two units). This numerical conversion cannot be performed on qualitative data. Because of this fact, in the field portion of this study there is a heavy reliance on bivariate methods (two variables at a time) such as cross-tabulation, necessitating a focus on simplified questions in a sequential fashion. The laboratory portion of the study makes use of the more sophisticated multivariate analysis tools such as hierarchical regression (explained above); analysis of variance, in which the influence of one or more independent variables on a dependent variable is determined; multivariate analysis of variance, in which the analysis is extended to two or more dependent variables, and these dependent variables are then transformed into their underlying constructs (called canonical variates); and factor analysis, which also determines the underlying structure of constructs.

Another impediment to multivariate predictive modeling in this study is one of "slippery" definitions. The key outcome variables in this study—criminal charges filed and prison sentences assigned—are not uniformly measured by jurisdictions. The roster of criminal charges available in each jurisdiction is different, both in terms of the names given to the different offenses, and the actual elements of the crime that are aggregated to receive that label. For instance, the charge of fondling a child (under fourteen) in Florida is called "lewd, lascivious or indecent assault" and it is considered a second-degree felony, punishable by 15 years in prison. In Kentucky, the charge for fondling a child under fourteen is "sexual abuse," which is a second-degree misdemeanor and carries a punishment of up to 1 year in prison. (Sexual abuse of a child under twelve in Kentucky carries a sentence of 1–5 years). The charges and sentences for anal, oral, or vaginal penetration of a child under twelve are similar in Kentucky and Florida. In Florida, the charge for such offenses is "sexual battery," which is a first-degree felony, punishable by up to 30 years in prison. In Kentucky, the charge for vaginal penetration of a child under twelve is "rape," which is a first-degree felony punishable by 20 years to life imprisonment. Oral or anal penetration crimes are called "sodomy," but carry the same sentence. However, the sentence for these same crimes committed against a child older than twelve is far more lenient in Kentucky than in Florida. In Kentucky, rape or sodomy of a child under fourteen carries a 5–10 year sentence, and rape or sodomy of a child under sixteen carries a 1–5 year sentence. In Florida, sexual battery of a child over twelve is punishable by up to 15 years in prison.

If it were possible to convert the sentences in each of the eight jurisdictions to a common metric, punishment could be used as the outcome variable, and the influence of contextual and legal factors on that punishment could have been assessed. The conversion proved to be too complex to be reliable, and was further complicated by the fact that sentence rendered and sentence served often constitute very different amounts of time in these jurisdictions, and the relationship between them varies enormously, as well. (One prosecutor reported that in his jurisdiction, defendants can expect to serve approximately a third of their sentence, whereas another prosecutor said time served in his state is entirely dependent upon prisoner comportment and level of crowding in the jails.)

The case types that were used in analyzing prosecution routes and sentencing outcomes were developed with factor analysis, using the varimax rotation option to arrive at independent types. Factor analysis "is a statistical technique used to identify a relatively small number of factors that can be used to represent relationships among sets of many interrelated variables" (Norusis, 1990, p. 313). Varimax, and other rotation schemes, are mathematical transformations that simplify the structure of the factor matrix, allowing the factors to be differentiated from each other. This technique was used not so much to get at any underlying constructs—which is the purpose to which factor analysis is most often put—as it was used to determine if certain abusive behaviors tended to cluster together in the absence of others in predictable ways. A four-factor solution was obtained that seemed conceptually sound, and these factors accounted for over 55% of the variance in cases. The four case types were: 1) cases consisting primarily of anal penetration or oral-genital contact; 2) cases consisting primarily of fondling; 3) cases primarily involving sexual offenses that do not include touching the child (for example, exhibitionism, defendant masturbation, taking erotic photographs); and 4) cases consisting primarily of penile/vaginal intercourse or attempted intercourse. These four categories were then used whenever the influence of the abusive behaviors on some legal outcome were being studied.

SAMPLE

There are 619 separate criminal cases represented in this study. Because some cases included more than one child victim, there are data on 670 children. Some incidents involved more than one defendant. Defendants were tried separately, however, so the data represented here are organized around the defendant's case. The sampling of cases for this study is complex for practical rather than theoretical reasons. Ideally, all cases presented to prosecutors' offices in all sites for the entire year would be included. However, there were numerous impediments to this inclusive sampling. One such obstacle has to do with the structure of the various criminal jurisdictions: the screening process is very different in different locations. All referred child sexual abuse cases may not end up in the same organizational unit, even if there is a specialized unit for cases of this type. For instance, in New Orleans, records on cases where no charges were filed were not kept in the prosecutor's office, but in the Office of the Magistrate. Also in New Orleans, the sex crimes unit (which consists of only two attorneys) does not handle all child sexual abuse cases, but only the most legally problematic of these cases. The other child sexual abuse cases are dispersed among the other attorneys in the system. In Dallas County, the records of those who were not formally charged reside with the police.

Another constraint was that in two jurisdictions, San Francisco County and New Orleans Parish, the volunteers were prevented from examining cases in which no formal charges were filed on grounds that it would be a violation of the rights of those who had been accused but not charged. In one jurisdiction, the volunteers were told that the prosecutors did not want to expose to scrutiny their decision-making process regarding whether to file charges or not (although they had no difficulty with their other decisions being analyzed).

One further accommodation that was made to the available sample concerns cases in which the victim is a teenager. Originally, trial data were to be collected only for cases where the child victim was under eleven years old at the time of the last offense, to avoid the added issue of the plaintiff's perceived complicity with the act. When it became clear (very early on) that there were very few trials at all, and that, in particular, cases of adolescents rarely went to trial, the upper age limit was relaxed. While this delay may have resulted in a lost case or two, virtually all the cases that went on trial in these jurisdictions were recorded.

Finally, the fact that data collectors in this study were volunteers had a certain impact on the sample as well as the method. The cost of the project would have been prohibitive if paid research assistants had been engaged for the time-intensive data collection required. Using volunteers allowed the collection of a sizable data set. The disadvantage of using volunteers has to do with their other commitments and their control over their own schedules. While the individuals who participated in this project were particularly dedicated, volunteers cannot and should not be required to perform research tasks on demand, as they are not being compensated. A few random cases were lost due to competing demands on the volunteer's time.

SAMPLE BIAS

Adjustments had to be made to all of the antecedent conditions. These adjustments resulted in an ever-shifting sample in the analysis phase of this study, depending on the particular question being asked. For any given question, all cases that could legitimately be included on the basis that they contain all the requisite categories of data, were included.[2] Many of the cross-jurisdiction analyses, then, have skewed samples, owing to the small number of jurisdictions and the large discrepancy between the numbers of cases in each, introducing bias in favor of the larger jurisdictions (see Table 2.1). (The jurisdiction covering Clay, Duval, and Nassau counties in Florida, for instance, handled 276 child sexual abuse cases during the data collection year. The next largest number of cases was 61 during a four-month period from San Francisco County.) Even if all child sexual abuse cases in each criminal jurisdiction could have been studied for this research, the jurisdictional totals would have been vastly different from one another. In the 1986 preliminary survey to this study, these jurisdictions reported from 43 to 532 individuals charged with sexual abuse of a child in their respective sites, and the number of cases each handled bore no apparent relationship to the size of the jurisdiction.

In addition to bias within the sample, there is the possibility that the sample itself is nonrepresentative of the country at large. Whereas eight jurisdictions cannot represent the full complexity of the many criminal justice systems in the country, there is no reason to believe that there are many features of criminal justice systems or the jurisdictions they serve that were systematically omitted or included. It should be mentioned, though, that the most highly progressive counties in the country with regard to handling of child sexual abuse cases are not included in the group studied.

TABLE 2.1
Study Sample by Case Categories

				Category			
Jurisdiction	Not Charged	Dropped After Charging	Incompe- tent to Stand Trial	Diverted	Pled Guilty/ Original Charges	Plea Bargained	Tried	Total
San Francisco	–*	12	–	2	20	22	5	61
Clay, Nassau, Duval, FL	106	9	4	52	45	50	10	276
Louisville	–	8	–	1	17	20	3	49
Orleans, LA	–	2	–	2	12	15	5	36
Baltimore	–	–	–	2	5	23	3	33
Johnson County, KS	–	5	–	8	9	14	8	44
St. Louis	–	–	–	–	11	4	2	17
Dallas	–	–	–	–	2	–	20	22
Total	106	31	4	67	121	148	56	538

*A dash in this table represents that this category of case was not included in the data collection for the jurisdiction (see reasons in accompanying text), not that there were no cases fitting the description in the jurisdictions.

Apart from size, the jurisdictions represented in the study were very different demographically (See Table 2.2). Their 1986 population figures ranged from 318,300 in suburban Johnson County, Kansas, to 1,833,100 in Dallas County. Affluent Johnson County, Kansas, had a 1985 per-capita income of $16,190, 88.8% of the residents with an education of 12 years or more, only 3.6% of the population living below the poverty line in 1979, and an 1986 unemployment rate of 2.8%. Nearly 97% of those who lived in Johnson County in 1984 are white. In contrast, Orleans Parish had a 1985 per-capita income of only $8,975, just over 59% of the people with 12 years or more of education, 26.4% of its residents living below the poverty line in 1979, and an unemployment rate in 1986 of 11.2%. In Orleans Parish in 1984, almost 61% of the people were nonwhite. The study sample is slightly skewed toward large urban jurisdictions (San Francisco, Dallas, New Orleans, St. Louis, and the counties surrounding Jacksonville), although Johnson and Baltimore

TABLE 2.2
Jurisdiction Demographics*

County	1986 Population†	County Size Ranking	1984 Racial Composition		% Educational Attainment (1980)		1985 Per Capita Money Income	1979 Median Household Income	1979 % Living below the Poverty Line		1986 Unemployment Rate	1985 # Crimes Known to the Police	
			White	Black other	% 12 yrs. or more	% 16 yrs. or more			Persons	Families		Total	Violent
Clay, Nassau, Duval	779,800		84.3	15.6	66.2	13.7	$10,414	$16,764	12.7	10.5	5.6	56,830	8,130
St. Louis	993,200	28	86.3	13.7	73.9	22.9	$14,442	$22,127	4.9	3.5	4.7	36,244	2,586
Baltimore	670,300	60	88.8	11.2	68.3	18.8	$13,982	$21,640	5.3	4.1	4.3	39,861	6,891
Orleans Parish	554,500	83	39.3	60.7	59.2	17.7	$ 8,975	$11,814	26.4	21.8	11.2	48,732	8,222
Dallas	1,833,100	10	79.2	20.8	71.2	21.8	$13,014	$18,571	10.6	7.9	5.7	183,712	17,322
San Francisco	749,000	49	61.6	38.4	74.0	28.2	$13,575	$15,866	13.7	10.3	5.5	60,062	9,667
Johnson	318,300	151	96.9	3.1	88.8	33.3	$16,190	$25,173	3.6	2.6	2.8	11,900	705
Jefferson	680,700	57	82.7	17.3	63.6	15.3	$10,923	$16,644	12.2	9.7	7.4	32,532	2,867

*From U.S. Bureau of Census, County and City Data Book, 1988.
†Figures for each column reflect the most recent U.S. Census data published by county prior to 1987 when this study was conducted. Median household income and percentage of individuals and families living below the poverty line still have not been updated in the *1992 Annual Metro, City and County Data Book.*

counties are suburban in character, and Jefferson County comprises a somewhat smaller metropolitan area.

SOURCE OF REFERRALS TO THE PROSECUTOR'S OFFICE

Another reason for different-size samples by jurisdiction is that the investigation of child sexual abuse cases varies greatly by state, and by jurisdiction within states (See Table 3.1). The participant agencies in the investigation process are the police, child protective services (usually the state or county Department of Child Welfare, Social Services, or Human Services), and the prosecutor's office (state's attorney or district attorney). Each has a defined duty that includes investigation of the child abuse allegation. Every one of the fifty states has a child abuse law that mandates certain categories of individuals to report cases of suspected child abuse. Reports involving family members or caretakers as the suspected perpetrators go to child protective services (CPS), where they are investigated and a service plan is made for the family. The police are charged with investigating and making arrests for the crime of sexual assault. The prosecutor must evaluate and decide whether to prosecute all allegations presented to him or her for which there is probable cause to believe that a crime was committed within the jurisdiction. These responsibilities are standard across jurisdictions. It is how these agencies interpret their roles and work together that is the source of the considerable variation.

In the jurisdictions for which child abuse investigation data were obtained in this study, several different models of cooperation in investigating child sexual abuse complaints can be identified. Among these models, two relationships are common to all of the jurisdictions: the police and child-protective services must report to each other, and the police must report to the prosecutor's office. In every case, these are legislatively mandated reporting requirements, not simply customary notification or professional courtesy. Although, according to the *National Analysis of Official Child Neglect and Abuse Reporting* (American Humane Association, 1979), the police at one time were notoriously remiss in reporting to CPS, that situation seems to be changing, if the few sites studied here are typical.

Most of the jurisdictions surveyed have at least the option of joint response by CPS and the police to child abuse reports, which means that they conduct the initial investigation of the report together (by statute, within 24 hours). Some jurisdictions reported only being able to jointly respond about 50% of the time. In other jurisdictions, CPS can request joint response when warranted by the seriousness of the case. Even though it is not always exercised, the prevalence of the joint response option is different from only a short time ago when Finkelhor, Gomez-Schwartz, and Horowitz found "a tendency for agencies to operate on cases in an isolated way within their own restricted professional network" (Finkelhor, 1984). This finding is probably not a function of this particular sample, however, as there is a nationwide trend toward more coordination between systems charged with responding to child abuse. One obvious advantage of joint response to sexual abuse reports is reduction in the number of times the child victim is interviewed. Also, better communication and coordination between the police and CPS regarding these cases reasonably can be assumed to result.

Three of the sites in the study—Orleans Parish (New Orleans Area), Johnson County (Kansas City, Kansas), and Jefferson County (St. Louis)—follow an investigation model that includes mandated reporting between the police and CPS, joint response to child sexual abuse referrals, and reporting by both the police and CPS to the prosecutor's office. This is a fairly common model, but even as short a time ago as 1986 when the preliminary survey was conducted for the study, the more common model was one that lacked mandated reporting by CPS to the prosecutor's office. Now, only Dallas, San Francisco, and St. Louis, of the jurisdictions in the study, still exempt CPS from the responsibility of reporting their cases to the prosecutor.

Mandatory reporting to the prosecutor's office by child protective services is fairly new as a legislative requirement. The historical function of CPS has been child protection, not prosecution of offenders. The mandated child-protection agency in most states came to see itself as an alternative to the criminal prosecution of child abuse. This was generally regarded to be humane and practical in cases of intra-family physical abuse and neglect that could be ameliorated by concrete and therapeutic services. Sexual abuse cases taxed the effectiveness of this approach, however, and gradually CPS agencies recognized the therapeutic and social need to bring the perpetrators of child sexual abuse to justice, thereby having to develop relationships, both formal and informal, with the district attorneys and state attorneys in their jurisdictions. In 1984, Finkelhor, Gomez-Schwartz, and Horowitz (Finkelhor, 1984) reported that in their sample metropolitan area, the criminal justice agency received only 6% of its sexual abuse referrals from other than criminal justice sources. Legislatively mandated reporting to prosecutors by CPS has raised this portion somewhat. In this study, 15% of the cases were referred by other than the police.

The length of time it took a case to move through the criminal system in each of these jurisdictions at the start of the study (according to the preliminary survey of jurisdictions) appeared to vary without obvious pattern. The shortest length of time it took for cases to progress from arrest to sentencing was reported to be three to six months. Several jurisdictions reported that the typical case could take up to two years to traverse the system, however. This protraction of the investigation/trial period has obvious negative consequences for the child who needs to reach a more immediate resolution of this event in his or her life, as well as making it more difficult to prosecute effectively. If the estimates made by the prosecutors in the preliminary survey to this study were correct, the actual duration figures obtained during the study represent a trend toward moving cases through the process more quickly (see Table 4.5).

In addition to the length of time a case is active in the criminal justice system, another factor that can vary widely is the number of interviews the child is subjected to during the life of the criminal case. Although there may have been several interviews before the prosecutor's office became involved in these cases—particularly when there is not a joint response system in place, or an investigative team drawn from child protective services, the police, and the prosecutor's office—when the study began, most jurisdictions reported that there were three to four interviews with the child from the point of prosecutor involvement to sentencing of the defendant in most of their cases.

PROCEDURAL VARIATION

Once a case gets into the criminal court system, it is still subjected to procedures and practices that are specific to the particular jurisdiction. Existing legislation, mandatory and discretionary procedures, and the frequency with which the procedures were used were reported by members of the district attorney's office in interviews during the 1986 survey preliminary to this study. These profiles are presented in Chapter 3. They give a picture of the perceived state of affairs in these jurisdictions at the time the study was begun. They also provide a baseline from which we can assess movement over time and any discrepancy between procedures that can be documented, and the perception of practice in general.

Although in slightly different combinations, each jurisdiction in the study site already had, at the start of the data-collection year, statutory provisions for most of the innovative prosecutorial techniques (particularly those that affect courtroom practices) that have been advocated across the country in recent years. Of those techniques for which the jurisdictions have statutory authority, however, they reported using only a few.

It is interesting to note that when actual cases are tracked through the system, practices sometime deviate from the descriptions of the process given by prosecutors in interviews (see Chapter 5). There are many possible explanations for this discrepancy other than misrepresentation, some of which will be discussed as these discrepancies are revealed. Both the intention and the reality are important, and the distance between them can provide clues to systemic bias and needed reform.

3

Eight Jurisdictions
A Study in Differences

This chapter presents brief descriptions of the jurisdictions studied in this investigation with respect to demographics, interagency referral, and legal-procedural methods, offered separately in order to allow comparison with one another and other jurisdictions not in the study, and in some cases to preserve the flavor of commentary by professionals who work within each of the systems. The informants were prosecutors currently handling child sexual abuse cases. The material is also arrayed in Table 3.1.

BALTIMORE COUNTY, MARYLAND[1]

In 1980, there were 670,300 people in Baltimore County, which was ranked as the 60th largest county in the United States.[2] Of these people, 88.8% were white, and 11.2% were African-Americans or other people of color, roughly imitating the racial statistics for the country at large. As of 1980, 68.3% of the population had completed 12 years of education, and 18.8% had completed 16 years or more. This places Baltimore near the center of educational attainment among the jurisdictions studied.

TABLE 3.1
Jurisdiction Characteristics

Jurisdiction	Special Sex Abuse Unit	Number of Prosecutors Handling These Cases	Joint Investigation	Police/CPS Notification	Police Report to DA's Office	CPS Report to DA's Office	Innovative Structures for Handling These Cases
Jacksonville	Yes	One	Sometimes	DHRS↔ Police by mandate	Yes, by mandate	Yes, by mandate	Child Protection Team (crisis intervention team)
St Louis	Yes (Adult & child sexual abuse)	6–8 attorneys	Yes, by official policy if interfamilial	DFS must notify police by statute	Yes, not mandated	Not mandated to do so	No
Baltimore	Yes (Adult and child)	Two	No	DSS↔ Police by mandate	Yes, mandated	Yes, mandated	No
New Orleans	Yes - (but only handles most legally problematic cases)	Two	Yes (if interfamilial)	Police↔ DCYFS Yes - if interfamilial DCYFS ↔Police by mandate	Yes	Yes	No
Dallas	Yes - (for sexual abuse of children > 14) set up in 86/87	Six	No	DHS↔ Police by mandate	Yes	No	No police screen
San Francisco	Yes - (for sexual and physical abuse)	Three	Yes	DSS↔ Police by mandate	Yes, official policy	No	CASARC hospital-based multi-disciplinary approach
Johnson Cty	Yes	Four	Yes	Police ↔SRS by mandate	Yes	Yes, by mandate	No
Jefferson Cty	Yes - (for domestic violence)	Three	Yes, (CIT's) mandated	Police ↔CPS mandated	Yes, by mandate	Yes, by mandate	Child Investigative Teams (a unit of specially trained CPS & police work jointly)

DA's Office Screens All Cases of CSA	Typical Number of Interviews	Diversion Program	Grand Jury	Child Must Testify at Grand Jury	Preliminary Hearing Required	Child Must Testify at Preliminary Hearing	Plea Negotiation
Yes	Child not allowed to be interviewed more than 3x's by statute	Yes (Kids in Distress)	No	—	No		Yes
Yes	3x's	No, except for suspended imposition of sentence	Yes	Usually	No		Yes
Yes	Many	No	Optional used often	No, police officer testifies for them.	Yes	No	Yes
Yes, but refers only most problematic to sex crimes unit	3 or 4x's	No	Yes, but only if conviction will result in a life sentence	Not required but usually do	Yes	Only if defense requests child's testimony	No office policy but permitted on occasion
No	6x's before DA's Office	No	Yes	At the discretion of the jurors & prosecutor	Yes	At the discretion of the judge	Yes
Yes	Minimum 4x's	No	Yes, but usually waived		Yes	Not required but usually does	No
Yes	3x's	Yes, only incest cases diverted	No	—	Yes	Approximately half the time	Yes, but never reduce felonies to misdemeanors
Yes	3 or 4x's	No	Yes	No	Yes, but not required	Rarely	Yes

Baltimore County (as distinct from the more economically depressed city of Baltimore) is a place of moderate to high moderate income. Income per-capita in Baltimore County for 1985 was $13,982, with the median 1979 household income at $21,640. However, the percentage of persons living below the poverty level in that year was only 5.3%. The percent of *families* living below the poverty level was only 4.1%. The 1986 unemployment total was 16,331, constituting a rate of 4.3, also not as serious as many jurisdictions in the sample.

There were 39,861 serious crimes known to the police in 1985 in this county; of these, 6,891 involved violence. The Baltimore county district attorney's office handles all criminal cases within the county. The Sex Offense Unit is the special unit within the district attorney's office charged with handling cases of sex offenses against both adults and children. This unit is not mandated by law, however. During the year that data were collected for this study, two lawyers, one law clerk, and two investigators staffed this special unit. Although the overall staffing compares well with other jurisdictions in the study, the number of attorneys is on the low side, especially given the broad scope of the unit.

In Baltimore County, the Youth Services Division of the police handles all cases of sex abuse of children under thirteen. The Division of Social Services (DSS) assigns special caseworkers to these cases. During the data-collection year, Maryland state law mandated that all three agencies—the district attorney's office, the police, and DSS—must notify each other within 24 hours of receiving a complaint of child sexual abuse. However, investigations are almost always conducted independently. Children are typically interviewed once by a DSS caseworker, once by a police officer, and once by an investigator at the DA's office to determine whether charges should be filed. After charges are filed, the child is interviewed at several other points to prepare her for testifying.

All cases of child sexual abuse are screened by the DA's office in Baltimore County. This is common across the country, but not always the case. Usually, the child does not testify at the preliminary hearing, because in Maryland, only hearsay evidence (usually that of the investigating police officer) is required at such hearings. A grand-jury hearing is optional but usually favored by prosecutors, since it is a closed proceeding and the defendant is not present. Children do not testify at these hearings—only police officers.

According to local prosecutors, two of the most significant procedural impediments in prosecuting child sexual abuse cases in Baltimore County are the extreme restrictions placed on the use of hearsay exceptions and on closed-circuit TV, both reforms designed to strengthen and ease the ability of children to testify. The use of either is permitted only if the prosecutor can prove— by putting the child on the stand and demonstrating to the judge the child's emotional distress—that the child is incapable of testifying.

The use of expert witnesses is allowed within limits. Experts can testify about characteristics of abused children, and the behaviors that victims typically exhibit, but they are not allowed to give an opinion as to whether or not they believe this particular child has been abused. In addition, the competency of the individual child witness to testify must be proven.

During the time that data were being collected on child sexual abuse cases in Baltimore County, there were 13 judges trying all civil and criminal cases in the jurisdiction. A representative from the district attorney's office offered the opinion that there was some variation in the degree to which these judges were aware of, and responsive to, the special needs of child victims and witnesses.

While plea-bargaining is permitted in Baltimore County, there is no formal office policy regarding the extent to which charges can be reduced. If deemed necessary, a prosecutor can drop charges from a felony to a misdemeanor, or from a sex abuse–related charge to a nonsex abuse–related charge. Prosecutors defer considerably to the wishes of the parents of the victim in negotiating pleas. Often, parents place pressure on the prosecutor to reduce the charges in order to spare the child from testifying.

Baltimore County had no diversion program during the study year, although there is such a program in place currently.

Determinate sentencing (detailed, progressive penalties stipulated for convictions on particular charges) is used for all offenses. Due to the parole system, however, those convicted typically serve only about a fifth of their prison sentence, whatever the crime.

DALLAS COUNTY, TEXAS

Dallas County is notable because of its extremes. Comprised of 15 independent communities including the city of Dallas, it is the tenth largest county in the nation. Dallas County had a 1986 census of 1,833,100 comprising 79.2% whites and 20.8% people of color. As of 1980, 71.2% of the population had graduated from high school in the public system, and 21.8% had graduated from college.

The Dallas County per-capita income for 1985 was $13,014, with the median 1979 household income a relatively high $18,571 per year. The percentage of persons living below the poverty level in 1979 was 10.6%; families living below the poverty line in that year were 7.9% of the population. The 1986 unemployment total was 63,142, a rate of 5.7%. Although there were three jurisdictions with lower per-capita income than Dallas County, there was only one jurisdiction with a higher unemployment rate in the sample. In addition, Dallas had the highest absolute and proportional number of crimes and violent crimes among the jurisdictions considered. In 1985 in that county, there were 183,712 serious crimes known to the police; of these, 17,322 involved violence.

Perhaps related to these high crime statistics, several informants in Dallas spoke of the Texas attitude toward criminal justice as being different than in other parts of the county. One alluded to the Old West mentality that was in some ways present in the region even now. "We still hang 'em up here," she said, referring to the stern treatment of defendants whose cases go to jury trial.

During the year that data were collected for this study, a child abuse unit was established in the District Attorney's office to handle cases of physical and sexual abuse for children under fourteen years of age. Before this unit was established, child sexual abuse cases had been randomly assigned to a prosecutor in one of the 14 different district courts. Prosecutors frequently rotate to different courts in this jurisdiction, so that victims may have had several different prosecutors working on their case by the time it was brought to trial. The special child abuse unit was set up so that child victims would each have only one prosecutor following their case throughout (so-called vertical prosecution). All cases of child abuse are sent to one of six prosecutors assigned to this unit. While six is a comparatively large number of attorneys for a sexual abuse unit, Dallas is not the most highly staffed among the jurisdictions studied (St. Louis has more prosecuting attorneys). Added to Dallas County's extremely high crime statistics, this makes for a disproportionately high case-load. There are two investigators and an intern who assist the prosecutors. There are 14 judges trying these cases in Dallas County.

Both the Department of Human Services (DHS) and the police have child abuse units staffed by specially trained investigators. Both agencies are statutorily responsible for notifying the other, according to the Texas Family Code. DHS is responsible for notifying the police within 24 hours for serious crimes, and in writing for less serious crimes. Usually, the police and DHS do not conduct joint investigations. Reports from the central hotline number are electronically transferred to DHS, who then conductes the initial investigation. Often, DHS videotapes their interviews with the child in order to minimize the need for further police interviews. However, the police usually find DHS interviews inappropriate for their needs, and conduct their own interviews. Between DHS and the police, a child typically is interviewed up to six times.

In Dallas County, it is the police, rather than the district attorney's office who screen all cases to determine on which to file charges. Only cases being charged are sent to the DA's office, where a grand jury hearing is set in motion. Sometimes, reports from parents go directly to the DA's office special intake section where they are screened for referral to the grand jury; however, this is rare. It is official policy that prosecutors must consult with the parents and child on how they would like the case to be handled. Usually, the prosecutor has enough information on the case from the police, DHS, and medical reports to make an initial investigative interview with the child unnecessary.

In Dallas County, the defense is permitted to request an examining trial (that is, a preliminary hearing) to determine probable cause and the need for a grand jury hearing. However, most cases go straight to grand jury. Children are not required to testify at the grand jury, although the child's testifying is usually recommended to the grand jury if a child is over ten years old.

Texas law limits the use of many important courtroom innovations. The only hearsay exception made in child sexual abuse cases that is not otherwise permitted in criminal proceedings is the "outcry" exception (a "statement relating to a startling event or condition made while under the stress of excitement caused by the event or condition" [Dziech and Schudson, 1989]), and the child must still be available to testify if it is used, which defeats at least some of the purpose of the law. The use of expert witnesses was permitted during the time this study was in progress. The competency of the child is not presumed and must be determined by the judge in a separate hearing. The use of videotaped depositions and statements as testimony is not permitted. The use of closed circuit television for testimony is permitted if the child is unavailable to testify, but this statute has yet to be tested. Other innovations are permitted at the discretion of the judge.

A representative of the Dallas County prosecutor's office commented that the hardest aspect of trying these cases is getting the children to give testimony credible enough to convince jurors, since "it's usually just the word of the child against that of the defendant." She added that once the jury is convinced of the truth of the child's accusation, however, they usually "come down hard on the defendant." She also commented that it is difficult to qualify juries on these cases, because most potential jurors say they could not consider granting probation to someone who had committed child sexual abuse.

Plea-bargaining is permitted in this jurisdiction. There are no formal policies governing plea-bargaining, although the general philosophy is to try not to reduce charges from a felony to a misdemeanor.

Dallas County does not have determinate sentencing, although certain broad ranges of prison time are prescribed for the various offenses (e.g., aggravated sexual assault carries a sentence of five years to life), and stiffer penalties are mandated for repeat offenders. In Dallas County there is no formal diversion program, but it is fairly standard for a judge to order an evaluation and course of treatment for first-time sex offenders as a condition of their probation.

Texas also allows for victim impact statements in criminal proceedings. This is important, as the judge is required to consider the impact of a crime upon the victim at the time of sentencing of the offender. The victim is interviewed and asked to describe the financial, physical, and emotional effects of the crime on her and on her family. This consideration is thought to help promote a just sentence and appropriate restitution.

CLAY, DUVAL, AND NASSAU COUNTIES (JACKSONVILLE AREA), FLORIDA

The jurisdiction serving the three counties of Clay, Duval, and Nassau had a combined 1986 census population of 779,800. This population was made up of 84.4% whites, and 15.6% people of color. The demographics of the area put it toward the more beleaguered end of the spectrum of social problems such as poverty, unemployment, educational level and crime, including child abuse. The per capita income in the three-county area for 1985 was $10,414, with the median 1979 household income at $16,764. A sizable 13% of the population were living below the poverty level in 1979, which amounted to 10.5% of the families in the area. The 1986 unemployment total was 6,769, which was a rate of 5.3%. As of 1980, 66.2% of the population had graduated from high school, and 13.3% had completed four years of post-high school education. This is the smallest percentage of college graduates of any of the study jurisdictions. There were 56,830 serious crimes known to the police in 1985; of these, 8,130 involved violence.

If there is something unique about the area that is relevant to this study, it would be the preponderance of naval bases nearby. This fact was cited over and over by local members of the prosecutor's office as explaining the large number of cases that come into the criminal system in Jacksonville. Although they did not explain the connection thoroughly, respondents referred to the transience of the population, and made reference to runaways being victimized by navy personnel.

Each of the three systems charged with handling child sexual abuse in Jacksonville and the surrounding counties—the Department of Health and Rehabilitative Services (the agency mandated to provide child protective services [CPS]); the sheriff's department; and the state's attorney's office—have specially designed and trained units to deal with sexual abuse cases. The cooperative relationship between the agencies is demonstrated by several arrangements: 1) the fact that the sheriff's officer and CPS social worker sometimes make joint investigations of child-abuse reports, 2) the existence of a multidisciplinary team that staffs child sexual abuse cases and provides crisis intervention services, and 3) the fact that CPS is mandated by law to inform the state's attorney's office of child sexual abuse cases coming to their attention—verbally within one hour, and in writing within three days. When the sheriff's office makes an arrest, they have to notify the state's attorney's office within 72 hours. These are somewhat progressive innovations, shared by many urban jurisdictions at the time of the study, but certain aspects, such as the timeliness of CPS' reporting to the prosecutor's office, are unusually responsive.

In Jacksonville, as in many jurisdictions in the last few years, there is a concerted attempt to limit the number of interviews to which the child-victim is subjected. An administrative order from the chief judge can be invoked to prevent the child from being interviewed more than three times. In this case, the interviews would be the following: DHRS and the Sexual Battery Team would try to do the very first interview together; a prefiling interview would be conducted by the state's attorney, and then, if need be, a pretrial interview would be conducted, also by the state's attorney. In addition, it used to be (during the period covered by this study) that one discovery deposition was permitted to be taken by the defense attorney. Since that time, however, this last interview has been challenged on the grounds that it is excessive and traumatic to the child, and the supreme court of Florida has ruled it unconstitutional.

Like most of the jurisdictions in this sample and most jurisdictions in the country at this time, Jacksonville has a specialized unit of the state's attorney's office to handle child sexual abuse cases. This unit is smaller than most, however, particularly in the number of prosecutors included. During the data-collection period this unit was staffed by a director, one attorney, an investigator, a paralegal, and three secretaries. The other specialized units in the study jurisdictions had two to six attorneys handling these cases, and many of these units had a lower volume of cases.

DHRS has a special intake unit called the Child Protection Unit. They perform the basic investigation. During the data-collection period, there was a special Sexual Abuse Investigative Unit comprised of six specially trained counselors. DHRS has cross-reporting responsibility; by statute, when a case is reported to them, they have to notify the state attorney's office verbally of the report within one hour, and in writing within three days. It is also their responsibility to report to the police or the sheriff's department within one hour. The Florida Child Abuse Registry, to which the cases are also reported, is maintained by DHRS.

The Jacksonville Sheriff's Department has a Sexual Battery Team made up of ten investigators. These investigators are specially trained in interviewing children. They are mandated to report cases they receive to DHRS. The investigators can make an arrest if they have probable cause and they must notify the state's attorney's office within 72 hours of when the offender is in jail. Sometimes, a uniformed patrolman responds first to a report of suspected sexual abuse. He or she will file a report to the Sexual Battery Team and then a plainclothes detective will be assigned to continue the investigation.

Cases, including the results from the initial investigations, are referred to the state attorney's Special Assault Division for screening. In order to help determine whether charges will be filed or not, the child is usually interviewed by an attorney to assess her credibility and how well-substantiated the case is. If it is determined that a case should not be handled in the court system, an attorney may decide to divert it to treatment before charges are filed.

Jacksonville has a special diversion program called Kids In Distress (KID). This program refers defendants, whose cases are diverted, to professionals who are experts in the treatment of child sexual abuse offenders. Professionals in the program report back at least monthly—sometimes weekly—on the progress of offenders and whether or not they are meeting the treatment terms of their probation. If the defendants comply with the terms of their diversion, they will not be prosecuted. Records are not expunged routinely, however, and the offender in most cases will retain a record of arrest for sexual abuse charges. Diversion is perceived as a desirable option to use, when possible, as a way of keeping families intact. In theory, cases are most often diverted when the offender has a history of being a reliable source of financial and emotional support to the family (see Chapter 5).

A representative from the DA's office explained that the underlying philosophy guiding prosecutorial decisions is to maintain the family unit, unless the accused is likely to repeat the offense and to pose a threat to the community. It is thought that the incidence of stranger assault (often committed by repeat offenders) is high because of the heavy concentration of naval bases in the area, which attract transients.

Florida is one of six states that permits a less-than-12-person jury in felony and misdemeanor trials. In this state, six people sit on the jury. This jury must be unanimous in a criminal finding of guilty. There is no grand jury or preliminary hearing system in use in Clay, Nassau, and Duval counties.

The representative from the DA's office stressed that, whenever possible, he tries to prevent children under eleven from testifying in court because he believes that children this young are likely to be traumatized by the experience. Use of a special, statutory, hearsay exception is the most commonly used procedure for protecting children from giving in-court testimony.

Often members of the initial investigatory team (a police officer or DHRS representative) will present the hearsay evidence.

Videotaped testimony is permitted, although rarely used. If the victim is older than eleven, live testimony is preferable so that the jury can see the victim, according to a Jacksonville representative.

The decision to bring a case to trial is made if it is believed that the perpetrator will repeat the offense, and that a trial would be in the best interest of the child. Plea-bargaining is allowed in this jurisdiction. There is no official policy on how far prosecutors can negotiate. This limit is determined on a case-by-case basis.

Clay, Duval, and Nassau counties use a system of "presumptive sentencing," in which judges' sentencing decisions must accord with a set of fairly strict guidelines. These sentencing guidelines are explicit policies and procedures for deciding on individual sentences. Usually, a fairly narrow sentencing range is prescribed for a given offense and then the sentence can be either shortened or lengthened within prescribed limits according to whether there are mitigating or aggravating circumstances. The decision is usually based on the nature of the offense. For example, the prescribed sentence for a particular crime might be probation if the offender has no previous felony convictions, a short term of incarceration if the offender has one prior conviction, and progressively longer prison terms if the offender's criminal history is more extensive.

JOHNSON COUNTY, KANSAS

Johnson County, Kansas, which includes the suburbs of Kansas City, Missouri, and Kansas City, Kansas, is a rarified environment of wealth and relative freedom from urban social problems. The county had a 1986 census of 318,300 and was ranked as the 151st largest county in the United States. As of 1984, the last year for which the figures were available, 97% of the residents of this county were white, and only 3% were African-Americans or other people of color. As of 1980, 89% of the residents of Johnson County population had finished high school and 33% had finished college.

The per-capita income in the county for 1985 was $16,190; the median household income in 1979 was $25,173. The percentage of persons living below the poverty level in 1979 was 3.6%, easily the lowest level of all the areas studied. The percentage of families living below the poverty level was even lower: 2.6%. The 1986 unemployment total was 4,853, which calculates to a rate of 2.8. In 1985, 11,900 serious crimes were known to the police; of these, an astoundingly low 705 involved violence.

The system for handling child sexual abuse cases in Johnson County is fairly progressive. The Child Sexual Abuse Unit is a special unit within the district attorney's office that is set up to handle cases of child sexual abuse. Office personnel include one senior attorney who also acts as the office supervisor, four attorneys who handle cases tried in juvenile court, and three attorneys handling cases tried in the criminal court. There is also a Victim Witness Unit, comprised of three full-time and two part-time employees. They recruit and train volunteers (there were a dozen or so at the time of the study) to act as victim advocates.

The Child Protection Unit (CPU) is the special unit set up by the Social and Rehabilitation Services Department (SRS) to handle these cases. Although the police have no special child sexual abuse unit, almost all of the police departments in the 20 cities within Johnson County have a specially trained detective assigned to work on these cases. The police and the CPU are mandated to notify each other when either receives a report of child sexual abuse. CPU is mandated to refer cases to the district attorney's office as well. The police and CPU conduct joint investigations. The district attorney's office screens cases referred by the CPU, although a prosecutor from the DA's office noted that the CPU and the police do a very good job of referring only well-substantiated cases.

In the Johnson County jurisdiction, there is usually a preliminary hearing, but there is no grand jury system. The respondent from the prosecutor's office said the child testifies at the preliminary hearing in about a third of all cases. Prosecutors try to minimize the number of interviews the child undergoes. In cases that go to trial, a child is typically interviewed about three times: the initial interview with the assistant district attorney (ADA), once before the preliminary hearing, and once before the trial.

Johnson County also has a well-developed and well-utilized, though circumscribed, diversion program. Because only incest cases are diverted and cases can be diverted only before the preliminary hearing, it is always the prosecutor who makes this decision.

Offenders applying for diversion are referred to the Johnson County Mental Health Center where they are evaluated to determine whether they are appropriate candidates for treatment. Only professionals who are specially trained to treat sex-abuse offenders receive referrals from this program. If treatment is completed satisfactorily, the case is dismissed. After formal treatment is concluded, expatients are monitored regularly, a feature that is not standard in these programs. The prosecutor from the DA's office offered the opinion that the diversion program was extremely successful in preventing the recurrence of abuse.

Almost all the currently touted innovative courtroom practices are permitted by statute in Johnson County, although they were used on a discretionary basis during the time of this study. Closed-circuit TV testimony, videotaped statements of children, and out-of-court statements by children to third parties are all allowed when proper foundation testimony has been presented.

The philosophy of the Johnson County Prosecutor's Office is never to reduce felonies to misdemeanors, or sexual abuse charges to nonsexual abuse charges. Prosecutors will rarely agree to probation unless a mental-health professional determines that the offender is treatable. If the offender is not diverted to treatment, he almost always is incarcerated.

Sentencing is imposed at the discretion of the judge, although strong weight is given to the prosecutor's sentencing recommendations. Sentencing is affected by the capacity of the prison system in this jurisdiction, although the informant believes there is a strong effort on the part of those responsible for making parole decisions to leave sex-abuse offenders in prison as long as possible.

According to the prosecutor interviewed, an enlightened attitude on the part of the judges and jurors in Johnson County has been the single most helpful factor in successfully prosecuting these cases, not any particular practice or courtroom innovation. Apparently, the Johnson County jurisdiction has a much higher rate of convictions in these cases than neighboring jurisdictions, which have largely blue-collar populations. Also, Johnson County sends more cases to trial than average. The prosecutor explained this "success" in terms of the fact that at each stage of the prosecutorial process, from initial investigation by the CPU and the police to the trial, professionals exercise a high degree of integrity and good judgment. The police detectives assigned to these cases understand which cases are legitimate and appropriate to refer to the DA's office, and ask questions in a nonleading fashion. Also, the initial joint CPU-police interview is almost always videotaped, which helps prosecutors later if the child recants. Videotapes can be used at trial, if the taped interview is deemed to be nonleading, and if the child is available for cross-examination.

A Johnson County respondent also noted that prosecutors in his office have a much lower burn-out rate than typical, because cases are spread out over three or four attorneys, and the DA's office places its most experienced attorneys on these cases. In turn, prosecutors seem to have a very good rapport with the judges, who respect the integrity of the prosecutor's filing decisions.

Finally, jurors in Johnson County were characterized by a representative of the prosecutor's office there as being more enlightened than average, and "do[ing] a good job of sifting through the evidence." They are also more likely to give the benefit of the doubt to the child, rather than to the offender. However, the prosecutor noted that in general, the "pendulum of public perception is swinging back" towards an increasing concern with protecting the defendant from unfair accusations, and a concomitant attitude of skepticism towards children's testimony.

JEFFERSON COUNTY, KENTUCKY

Jefferson County encompasses the city of Louisville, Kentucky, and the outlying suburbs. In 1986, the county had a census total of 680,700 and was ranked as the 57th largest county in the United States. At that time, the population of Jefferson county included 82.7% whites, and 17.3% blacks and individuals of other races.

Jefferson County is not an affluent area, nor home to a highly educated population. Income per capita in 1985 was $10,923, and the median household income in 1979 was $16,664. The percentage of persons living below the poverty level was 12.2%, and when measured as families, the proportion living below the poverty line was 9.7%. As of 1980, 63.6% of the county residents had completed 12 years or more of public education, and 15.3% had 16 or more years of education. The 1986 unemployment total for Jefferson County was 26,103, making for a rate of 7.4. There were 32,532 serious crimes known to the police in 1985; 2,867 involving violence.

In Jefferson County, the Domestic Violence Unit (DVU)—established by practice rather than legislation—handles all cases of child sexual abuse as well as all other cases of domestic violence against child or spouse. Child sexual abuse cases represent the greatest proportion of cases this unit handles.

The jurisdiction served by the DVU is all of Jefferson County (the 30th judicial circuit court). At the time of the study, unit personnel included three prosecutors, one secretary, and one paralegal. The DVU has a Victim Witness Advocate program staffed by two victim advocates.

The state of Kentucky stipulates that a criminal trial may have a 12-person jury. This 12-person jury must be unanimous in a criminal finding of guilty. Grand-jury indictment is required on all felonies to initiate prosecutions. Not unlike in other places, jury trials are a small percentage of cases filed in this jurisdiction. Most cases that go to trial in the felony court result in convictions.

A special multidisciplinary team called the Crimes Against Children Unit (CACU) investigates reports of child sexual abuse in Jefferson County under three conditions: 1) when there is the possibility of ongoing abuse, 2) when the abuse results in a serious injury, or 3) when there is a question of removal of the child from home. All reports received by either the police or CPS are referred to this unit, where specially trained county and city police detectives and CPS social workers work together in teams, called Child Investigative Teams (CIT teams). The CIT system was developed in Louisville in 1981, although it was not until July 1987 that the CACU was established in order to house the teams in one unit.

Each CIT team consists of a Juvenile Police detective and a CPS worker who function as partners. The partners are supervised by their own agency supervisors. Most referrals are made through CPS. A CPS supervisor evaluates the referrals and makes the assignments. If a case is referred to the police first, then they will notify the Juvenile Police detective at CACU. This joint response is mandated by law. A 1987 juvenile-justice code mandates that all reports of suspected sexual abuse will also be referred to the county attorney and the state commonwealth attorney for review. However, the initial investigation remains the responsibility of the CACU, rather than the state commonwealth attorneys.

Jefferson County has a court system that includes county attorneys who work in juvenile court and county criminal court. These county courts hear less serious, nonfelony cases. If a case is being referred by the police for felony charges, then it goes straight to a higher criminal court called the circuit court. Instead of the county attorneys, state commonwealth attorneys handle these cases. All sexual abuse cases are felonies and thus go to the circuit court. Typically however, these cases are heard in both the circuit and district (civil) courts concurrently. If the case is weak and charges are dropped to misdemeanor or a non–sexual abuse charge, the case remains in district court.

The DVU screens its own cases, although this is not typical of other divisions in the circuit court. Here, the victim typically undergoes two extensive interviews, one conducted by the CACU and one by the DVU prosecutor. The child is usually interviewed a few more times prior to the trial date in order to prepare her. The philosophy of the DVU has been to indict whenever there is reasonable cause to believe a child's story. However, the atmosphere recently has become more conservative, and prosecutors are increasingly willing only to indict in those cases they feel they can prove.

Many of the innovative courtroom practices recommended for child sexual abuse cases were permitted in Jefferson County during the year it was studied. One exception is that the competency of the child witness was not presumed by statute. In addition, the use of expert witnesses was decided on a case-by-case basis, and used only occasionally.

Over the year or two preceding the study in Jefferson County, the courts deemed a number of important, progressive statutes pertaining to child sexual abuse cases to be unconstitutional. A statute permitting hearsay, if determined to be reliable by the judge in a separate hearing, was struck down in January of 1990. Hearsay is now permitted on a very limited basis (excited utterance, and statements made to a doctor during medical exam), and even these exceptions came to be avoided for fear they would be limited as well. In November of 1989, the courts also struck down a statute permitting the introduction of testimony concerning the child sexual abuse accommodation syndrome. This led to many cases being appealed.

A representative from the Jefferson County district attorney's office believes that there is an increasingly conservative attitude toward these cases in Jefferson County that makes them harder to prosecute. Juries, in her opinion, are more "callous" and less sympathetic to the victims than they were a few years ago. Jury members seem to be more aware of the potential harm done to an unjustly accused defendant than of the harm done to a child-victim whose story is not believed. She speculates this may be due to a rash of widely publicized cases that did not result in convictions. She repeats that often her "hands are tied" in prosecuting these cases. During this study, however, the two aforementioned progressive statutes *were* in effect, and it is not clear how much of the conservative trend she referred to was active in affecting case outcomes.

Pleas can be negotiated in this jurisdiction. There are no formal policies governing plea negotiations, although there is a law making sex offenders ineligible for probation. One representative of the prosecutor's office said that this is one of the biggest obstacles to getting a sentence at all. Cases in which there are major offenses but that are unlikely to result in convictions if brought to trial are very difficult to plea-bargain because of this law. In general, prosecutors only drop charges from felony to misdemeanor if evidentiary problems make a felony conviction very unlikely. It is extremely rare for a sexual abuse charge to be dropped to a nonsexual abuse charge.

There are 16 judges in the Jefferson County jurisdiction. The prosecutor representing the district attorney's office felt that the sensitivity with which judges handle these cases varies, but that most seem to dislike handling them at all. Jefferson County has no diversion system. The philosophy in this county is that diversion is not appropriate for sex offenders. Determinate sentencing is used, which limits the judge's discretion in sentencing.

If the charge on which a defendant is convicted is serious (e.g., rape, or sodomy), he must serve at least 50% of the prison sentence before being eligible for parole. For less serious crimes prosecuted in Jefferson County, a convicted person must serve at least 20% of his sentence. These guidelines are much more explicit than in some jurisdictions, where defendants are not likely to serve full sentences, but where it was difficult to find anyone who would venture a guess as to what proportion was apt to be served.

The prosecutor interviewed for this study would like to see more thorough investigations being conducted by the CACU, which is understaffed and suffers from frequent turnover. She also feels public education is extremely important in creating more sympathetic juries and judges.

ORLEANS PARISH (NEW ORLEANS AREA), LOUISIANA

Orleans Parish, although one of the smallest jurisdictions included in this study, had the most dismal socioeconomic statistics of all the counties. The 1986 Census count was 554,500, and the county was ranked 83rd largest in the United States. The population at the time of the study included 39.3% white residents, and 60.7% residents of color (predominantly black). As of 1980, only 59.2% of the population had completed public high school, and 17.7% had completed college or four years of schooling beyond high school.

Income per capita for 1985 was a mere $8,975. The median household income in 1979 was only $11,814. The percent of persons living below the poverty level in 1979 was 26.4%. The percent of families living below the poverty level in that year was 21.8%. The 1986 unemployment total was 27,028; the unemployment rate was 11.2%. In 1985, there were 48,732 serious crimes known to the police; 8,222 of these crimes involved violence. The only county with more crime per capita in this investigation was Dallas, with only a slight edge.

The district attorney's office has jurisdiction over all criminal cases in Orleans Parish (county). The Sex Crimes Unit screens all cases of physical and sexual child abuse. However, attorneys in this unit handle only the most legally problematic of these cases (those in which the child witness is very young, there is a lack of medical evidence or other form of corroborating evidence, or where there is a motive for the child to make a false accusation). The rest are referred to other criminal prosecutors. The Sex Crimes Unit is composed of one investigator and two attorneys.

The Division of Children, Youth, and Family Services (DCYFS) has a special unit called the Child Protection Investigating Unit to handle the investigation of these cases. DCYFS has a mandate to investigate cases of suspected child sexual abuse within 24 hours. When they receive an acute referral, however, the response time is usually one to five hours. Their mandate is to investigate cases of incest or cases where the perpetrator is the caretaker or guardian. The police handle all other types of sexual assaults themselves. The police are not mandated to notify the DCYFS unless the child is in danger. DCYFS *is* mandated to notify the police, and whenever possible (in cases of intra-familial abuse) they initiate a joint investigation from the outset.

The police also have a special investigative unit for child abuse cases, referred to as the Child Abuse Section. District patrol officers may respond to a report of sexual abuse on their patrol, but after their initial involvement they always refer the case to the Child Abuse Section of the police department. The police always refer to DCYFS if they receive a case first.

The police detective and the DCYFS worker take the child to a neutral, private location to interview her for the first interview. Anatomically correct dolls may be used. It is preferred that this be a joint interview—but if not possible, the same procedures are followed by one agency, with quick feedback to the other. They also interview the complainant and nonoffending parent. The police interview the perpetrator, sometimes bringing him into their office, sometimes not. If they feel they have enough evidence, the police swear out a warrant, present it to a judge, and make an arrest. Prior to referring the case to the DA's office, medical evidence is reviewed and interviews with witnesses and other possible victims takes place.

If a case is validated, DCYFS writes a letter to the juvenile court DA's Office. The district attorney's office reviews the letter and if appropriate, they send it to the Orleans Parish Criminal Court. Similarly, once the police make an arrest, they write a report and send this on to the DA. Once the case reaches the district attorney's office, the child is typically interviewed one time to determine whether charges should be filed, and on what offenses. The case then usually continues for one to six months while the disposition of the case is decided. There is a *speedy trial motion* that can be filed on behalf of the defendant, restricting the time from arrest to trial to 120 days.[3] If the case goes to trial, the child is interviewed many more times (usually at least three times) in order to prepare her or him for the courtroom.

Louisiana requires grand-jury indictment to initiate prosecution only in capital crimes. The child is not required to testify at the grand-jury hearing, although she usually does. In noncapital crimes, a preliminary hearing is required and the child must testify if requested by the defense.

For charges that result in a jail sentence (if convicted as charged), Louisiana stipulates that a criminal trial must have a 12-person jury, and 10 out of 12 jurors must agree on a guilty verdict for a conviction. There were 10 judges in this jurisdiction during the data collection period.

With regard to the local laws, standards, and procedures pertaining to child sexual abuse cases, the only hearsay exceptions permitted are the *outcry* exception and the victim's report to the treating physician. While no statutes prohibit use of expert witnesses, they are rarely used because judges often make it difficult to "qualify" them as experts. Children are not presumed competent to testify in this jurisdiction and must be qualified through questioning.

The representative from the district attorney's office mentioned that a law he found helpful in successfully prosecuting these cases was one that gave calendar priority to murder and child sexual abuse cases. He also mentioned the importance of being well prepared for the case, which often means having several interviews with the child.

Specific guidelines prohibit plea bargaining in certain felonies or crimes that involve habitual offenders in Orleans Parish. The formal office policy is not to plea bargain in general, although it is permitted in certain cases. The DA's office representative said it is often ineffective to plea-bargain, because sentencing is very stiff in the parish. There is no mandatory sentencing in this jurisdiction: sentencing is up to the discretion of the judge. There is no formal diversion program in the Orleans Parish criminal jurisdiction.

SAN FRANCISCO COUNTY, CALIFORNIA

One of the largest jurisdictions in the study, San Francisco County includes the city of San Francisco and its outlying suburbs. The jurisdiction had a 1986 census of 749,000 and was ranked the 49th largest county in the United States. At that time, the population of San Francisco County was 61.6% white, and 38.4% black and other. As of 1980, 74% of the population had 12 or more years of public education and 28.2% had 16 or more years of education.

The San Francisco per-capita income for 1985 was $13,575; the median 1979 household income was $15,866. These figures reflect income extremes, with many people at the lowest levels. There were 13.7% of San Francisco County residents living below the poverty level in 1979, representing 10.3% of the families. The 1986 unemployment rate was 5.5%. In 1985, there were 60,062 serious crimes known to the police in the county; of these, 9,667 involved violence.

During the data-collection period, a special unit of three prosecutors was set up to handle cases of child physical and sexual abuse in San Francisco County. All of these cases were handled vertically (by one prosecutor, start to finish). Three other prosecutors handled cases of adult sex crimes. (They have now combined these units so that these six prosecutors handle both types of cases, because handling child abuse cases exclusively was considered too emotionally difficult.)

In early 1987, a new system was developed in San Francisco County whereby various agencies involved with handling child sexual abuse cases (the DSS, the police, the district attorney's office, and San Francisco General Hospital), developed a written agreement specifying how they would handle these cases conjointly. The protocol, as it is known, was strongly endorsed by the mayor, who has taken a special interest in this issue. The protocol works as follows: DSS has a Family and Children's Services Division that handles the Child Protective Service cases. Within this division is the Child Sexual Trauma Intake Unit. This unit has four full-time workers who get involved with any newly reported case of sexual abuse. DSS is responsible only for cases of incest, which they extend to mean any intra-family abuse, even where there is a nonrelated adult who had regular access to the child. When the abuse has been perpetrated by an out-of-home stranger, the police investigate by themselves.

DSS has the primary role of child protection. They can file a dependency petition on behalf of a child in juvenile court. In the event that a perpetrator is criminally charged, there are parallel cases in juvenile court and criminal court. Both the DSS and the police are statutorily mandated to report cases to each other.

The San Francisco Police Department has an active Juvenile Bureau which handles all investigations of child sexual abuse. The detectives in the Juvenile Bureau are specially trained to work with cases of child sexual abuse. DSS and the police conduct joint investigations. Representatives of both agencies wear beepers 24 hours a day, and when a new case is reported, they attempt to conduct the first interview conjointly. In reality, because DSS does not have the humanpower to handle all night and weekend cases, those situations often are handled by the juvenile detectives alone. However, the next day, they coordinate their efforts closely with those of DSS.

A unique feature of the method of investigations in San Francisco is the reliance of the above three agencies on a special program at San Francisco General Hospital called CASARC, which stands for Child and Adolescent Sexual Abuse Resource Center. The services provided by CASARC include: crisis counseling, medical exam and treatment as appropriate, medical evidence collection (they have a colposcope), psychological assessment and short-term therapy groups, advocacy for the victim, court accompaniment and support, referrals to other community agencies, case coordination among involved agencies, and consultation. There is staff available at this hospital-based program 24 hours a day.

Generally, after the DSS Juvenile Detective Team make their initial assessment, they bring the child and family to CASARC for a more in-depth interview and assessment by their highly trained staff. There is flexibility regarding which members of the investigative team sit in on the interview. At the time of this study, CASARC was trying to get a one-way mirror so that this in-depth interview could be observed by relevant members of the team without overwhelming the child with everyone being present. Apparently, they now have the mirror but according to one police officer, it is not used much. What usually happens is that a single police officer and one CASARC worker conduct the initial interview. Typically, one interview is sufficient, although the CASARC worker assigned to the child has ongoing contact and dialogue with the child and her family members. CASARC is part of Forensic Medicine for the San Francisco courts. They also have two pediatric gynecologists on staff, one of whom is bilingual (English/Spanish), which they find very helpful. These two M.D.s do almost all of the medical examinations, so that there is consistent, experienced medical evaluation and diagnosis.

It is the police who assume the responsibility to report cases to the District Attorney's Office. This is not a statutory ruling but rather official agency policy. Based on the preliminary investigation, the police will confer with the DA's office to determine whether there is sufficient evidence to file charges. The police then present their findings, including interviews conducted with the victim and defendant, and medical examination reports. The DA makes the final decision as to whether to file charges on those cases presented by the police. In California, a prosecutor can defer prosecution of a child sexual abuse case for up to six years if it is deemed that the child is not mature enough to be a competent witness.

In San Francisco County, there is a grand-jury system. However, because defendants have a right to a post-indictment hearing and will almost always request one if they are indicted, it is common practice to waive the grand jury and just have a preliminary hearing. The child is not required to testify at the preliminary hearing, but almost always does so, since she is usually the sole witness. Typically, the child is interviewed a minimum of four times by the prosecutor between the time a case reaches the DA's office and when it goes to trial, if that is the eventual outcome.

The representative of the prosecutor's office interviewed for this study stressed the importance of vertical prosecution in these cases. In her opinion, minimizing the number of interviews the child undergoes is not as essential in protecting the child from trauma as is ensuring that the same prosecutor handles the case throughout.

There are no special hearsay exceptions relating to testimony for children in this jurisdiction, although the standard exception for spontaneous declarations is permitted. Testimony from expert witnesses is permitted under certain conditions. The issue to which an expert is testifying must already have been raised in the case. The expert can then present "scientific" information to aid the jury in understanding this particular issue. It is also necessary that the testimony refer to victims of child sexual abuse in general, rather than the individual victim in question. Also, a cautionary instruction must be given by the court to the jury saying that they can regard or disregard the testimony of the expert. The use of closed-circuit TV is only permitted if the child's life has been threatened should she take the stand. Videotaped testimony is not permitted at all. The competency of a child witness is presumed in California.

Some courtroom practices can be adapted to accommodate the child in San Francisco County: 1) child abuse cases can be scheduled ahead of others; 2) leading questions may be used; 3) the child is allowed to demonstrate the abuse with anatomically correct dolls; 4) the judge is permitted to remove his robes, so as to appear less imposing; and 5) testimony can be scheduled around the child's school hours.

There are six or seven judges in Superior Court, in which all felony cases are heard. The prosecutor said that there was some variation in how judges handled these cases. She felt that some judges were more likely to expand evidentiary limits and permit innovative courtroom practices than were others.

There is no diversion in this jurisdiction. However, defendants are always required to complete some type of counseling or treatment program as a condition of their probation. The prosecutor's personal feeling was that these programs were not substantially effective, although she felt they could be effective in certain intra-familial cases when the abuser was not a confirmed pedophile.

Plea-bargaining is not permitted in San Francisco County. Determinate sentencing is used for all types of offenses, but one prosecutor interviewed noted that there was a lot of variation in sentences imposed, according to which judge was doing the sentencing. In general, she was satisfied with the fairness of sentencing outcome. Judges take seriously the sentencing recommendations made by prosecutors. The respondent spoke highly of the state law that requires full consecutive sentencing terms for separate counts or separate victims. She said that typically those convicted of sex abuse crimes in San Francisco County serve about 50–60% of their sentences.

ST. LOUIS COUNTY, MISSOURI

St. Louis County presents itself statistically as a livable, mid-large county. In 1986, it had a census of 993,200 persons and was ranked as the 28th largest county in the United States. Just over 86% of the residents were white, and 13.7% black and other minorities. As of 1980, 73.9% of the population had completed at least 12 years of public education, and 17.7% had attained 16 years or more of education.

The per-capita income for St. Louis County in 1985 was $14,442, the second-highest of the areas studied, with the median in 1979 household income at $22,127. The percentage of individuals living below the poverty level in 1979 was 4.9%; the percentage of families living below the poverty level was 3.5%. In 1986, 25,995 people were unemployed in St. Louis County, a rate of 4.7%. In 1985, there were 36,244 serious crimes known to the police, a rate that rivals affluent suburban Johnson County, Kansas. Of these crimes, 2,586 involved violence.

The district attorney's office in St. Louis County has a special unit called the Sex Crime Team, which handles all cases of adult and child sexual abuse. The Sex Crime Team is staffed by six to eight senior trial attorneys who handle a case from beginning to end. Most reports are made to the Division of Family Services (DFS), which is statutorily responsible for notifying the police. The police and the DFS do not have special units to handle these cases, although many of the larger police departments in the one hundred or so municipalities that make up St. Louis County do have special investigators. In practice, the police notify the DA's office once a report has been substantiated, although neither the police or the DFS are mandated to notify the DA's office. DFS and the police must conduct joint investigations by official policy.

The Sex Crime Team screens all cases to determine if charges should be filed. If there is no confession, the child and the nonoffending parent are brought in for an interview. The child is interviewed once before the grand jury and once before the trial. Usually, the defense attorney interviews the child once to take the deposition.

The procedure followed by the district attorneys is to have the child testify at the grand-jury hearing to observe how well she handles testifying in court, and therefore, how far they can proceed with the prosecution of the case. The prosecutor interviewed said that, generally, the grand-jury hearing is not threatening to the child because the defendant is not present and that the hearing gives the child an opportunity to get used to the courtroom setting.

The prosecutor said that the most beneficial recent innovation in prosecuting these cases was the special, statutory, hearsay exception. Before permitting the introduction of a hearsay statement in court, a hearing must be conducted in the judge's chambers to determine the reliability of the statement, given the circumstances under which it was made.

The use of videotaped testimony is also permitted but rarely requested. Typically, prosecutors would rather use live testimony because the feeling is that the child's live testimony is more powerful and that the quality of the videotape is often poor. The use of expert witnesses is permitted on a limited basis. Doctors may testify about whether injuries are consistent with abuse, but may not testify as to whether abuse actually occurred or give an opinion on the credibility of the child.

It is permissible in this jurisdiction to reduce pleas to lesser charges. It is thought preferable to settle cases out of court to reduce risk of traumatizing the child in court. The philosophy is to plea-bargain whenever possible, in order to get some kind of sentence. In St. Louis, rape and sodomy repeat-offenders get a 30-year sentence with no parole, so that getting any kind of conviction on a first offense, even if on a lesser sex-offense charge, is considered important. The assumption is that the offender may well come back into the system and be sentenced to the 30-year prison term.

In St. Louis County, minimum and maximum ranges are defined for certain classes of offenses. About 80–90% of those convicted receive some period of incarceration. Those convicted must serve at least a third of their sentence. Sentences tend to be short in this jurisdiction, in part because judges and juries are very liberal, and in part because it is difficult to plea bargain.

There is no formal diversion program in St. Louis County, although a judge may order "suspended imposition" of the sentence, meaning that the accused is placed on probation for a certain period, and, in most cases, must receive counseling or treatment during this time. Suspended impositions are most often recommended when a case is weak.

4

The Victims, the Defendants, the Cases

We turn now to a description of the cases in the eight jurisdictions in this study. It is important to remember throughout the presentation of these data that they represent only the portion of all officially known child sexual abuse cases that were referred to the prosecutor's office in the studied geographical areas, and in order to make the jurisdictional subsamples comparable, they also represent only the cases in which charges were filed, unless otherwise stated. (Unfiled cases are compared with filed cases for one sample jurisdiction later in this chapter). As such, the data do not give a cross-section of the universe of child sexual abuse in this country, and may differ from that universe in important ways. Where possible, these differences will be explored as the description unfolds.

THE VICTIMS

GENDER

The alleged child victims in these criminal cases were predominantly female (80.3%, versus 19.7% male, see Figure 4.1). This

FIGURE 4.1
Gender of Child Victims

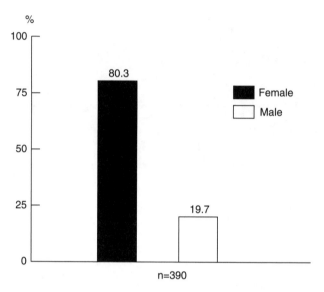

finding is consistent in direction with virtually all prevalence studies of child sexual abuse, but may indicate that the criminal-justice system receives a smaller percentage of referrals of cases with boy victims than the general prevalence rate. Finkelhor (1984), estimates from multiple prevalence studies that two to three girls are victimized for every boy, while the criminal system in these study jurisdictions was, in 1986–87, receiving four cases with girl victims for every case with a boy victim.

This discrepancy is not surprising when it is considered that sexual-abuse prevalence studies and criminal-justice referrals rely on different sources of information. Prevalence often is estimated retrospectively and anonymously from surveys of adults. Referrals to the criminal-justice system require that an act of sexual abuse is known or suspected, and in most cases, requires disclosure by the victim herself. Males have been found in numerous studies to be even more reluctant to report sexual abuse than females (Finkelhor, 1984; Knopp, 1986; Porter 1986; Rogers & Terry, 1984). This has been attributed to the socialization of males to be strong, noncomplaining, self-sufficient, and in

FIGURE 4.2
Age of Child Victim

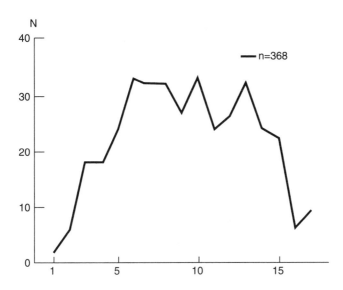

control of their own sexuality, but such theorizing is mostly speculation.

In addition, many of the cases in the criminal system come from the child welfare agency mandated to receive child abuse reports. By statute, all of these cases consist of abuse by parents or caretakers. However, boys have been found to be victimized outside the home by strangers, acquaintances, and professionals a higher percentage of the time than girls (Finkelhor, 1979, 1984; Geiser, 1979; Finkelhor & Russell, 1984; Rogers & Terry, 1984; Groth, 1986; Faller, 1989), thereby lowering their numbers in the child welfare caseload and skewing the criminal justice figures toward female victims.

AGE

The children whose cases reached prosecutors' offices in these eight jurisdictions ranged in age from one month to seventeen years (see Figure 4.2). The discrete ages most represented were 5, 10, and 13 years old, with the mean being 9.3 years and the modal age-range category being 9–12 years. This reflects the incidence pattern, as well. Although children are most often abused between nine and twelve years of age (Russell, 1983; Finkelhor, 1984; Wyatt, 1985), they most often resist and/or report sexual abuse when they reach puberty, even if the abuse has been taking place for years. Consider the following not-so-unusual case from one of the study jurisdictions.

> *The defendant is the thirty-year-old father of the victim. The victim was seventeen years old at the time of the trial. Outcry had taken place when the victim was fifteen years old, for sexual abuse by the father over a period of four years when the victim was eight to twelve years old.[1] The charge in this case was that the defendant had fondled the child's genitals ("indecency with a child," in this particular jurisdiction). There was medical evidence of sexual intercourse occurring over many years that was used in court, although it could not be shown that this evidence was attributable to the defendant. The victim gave testimony. Her twelve-year-old sister also gave testimony: she walked into the bedroom and saw the defendant kneeling over the child who was undressed. The child allegedly had intercourse with the father from age nine to twelve, then she fought too much. Father admitted to "examining" her vagina on three separate occasions. He was worried about her having intercourse with others or with her brother.*

There were, however, a substantial number of cases in which the child victim was very young: over 18% of the sample consisted of children five years old or younger (see Figure 4.3). This constitutes a difference in the criminal-justice sample from general incidence. David Finkelhor summarized the findings regarding age of victims of six prevalence studies in his 1986 *Sourcebook on Child Sexual Abuse*. Extrapolating from the vulnerability ratings he calculated, it appears that only 9% of the children in all these studies were under six years old. That is only half the proportion of victims who were in this age group in the criminal-justice sample of this study.

Cases in which the victim is very young may be perceived as being more serious precisely because of the victim's age, and may therefore be disproportionately represented in the criminal

FIGURE 4.3
Age of Child Victim

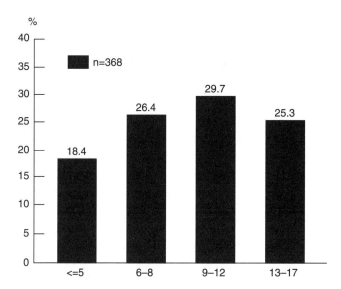

justice system. If this were so, however, it would constitute a departure from the usual reasoning behind selection for this system, that is, whether the case is "prosecutable." Cases where the child victim is five years old or younger are notoriously difficult to prosecute effectively, due to credibility problems with the child witness. In addition, while a third of these cases with young victims included definite or suggestive medical evidence, this was not a higher percentage than for cases with older victims. We are left regarding the considerable number of criminal cases with particularly young victims as an aberration of the sample, a trend over time, or a completely spurious outcome.

The age-related pattern for girls and boys in this study was somewhat different, although not strikingly so considering the much smaller number of boys (see Figure 4.4). There is no difference in mean age of victimization (9.3 years) attributable to gender, and the median is only different by a year (median for girls was ten, for boys, nine), but there are two modal ages for boy-victims in this sample that do not appear for girl victims: five and thirteen. Many other investigators have found differences in the age of male and female victims. It is often reported that the

FIGURE 4.4

Age of Male and Female Victims

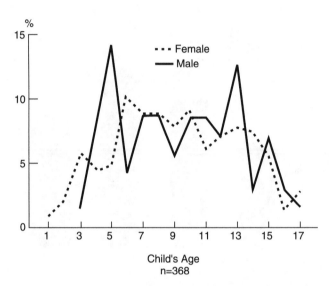

Child's Age
n=368

boys are abused younger than the girls (American Humane Association, 1983), though there are actually more data to support the opposite (Mohr, Turner & Jerry, 1964; Gebhard et al., 1965; Frisbie, 1969; Finkelhor, 1979; Faller, 1989). As far as the two distinct peaks in incidence at five and thirteen years of age for boy victims is concerned, the work that others have done neither corroborates nor contradicts this, as the age of the children is usually reported as an average in these studies. We might propose precipitously greater access by strangers to beginning school attenders and then again to early adolescents as an explanation for this pattern, but entirely other factors could be at work to produce these figures.

RACE

Most of the victims in these criminal cases were white, but the number of cases with black victims was disproportionate to the percentage of blacks in the jurisdictions represented ($\chi^2 = 119.4$, $p < .001$, see Figure 4.5). Using the 1984 racial-composition figures that can be found in the *County and City Data Book* (U.S. Bureau of the Census, 1988) for each of the counties represented

FIGURE 4.5
Race of Defendant and Child

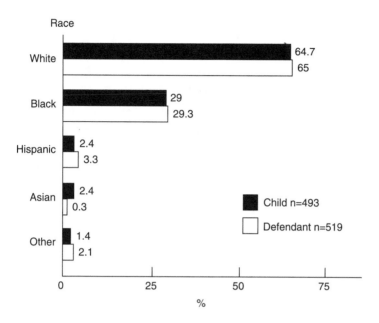

by the jurisdictions, and adjusting for the proportions of our sample each jurisdiction contributed, it can be calculated that 16.6% of the sample should be nonwhite (an even smaller proportion would be black) if there were no bias in 1) incidence of abuse, 2) reporting of the allegations, 3) presentation to the prosecutor, or 4) acceptance into the criminal system. Instead, 29% of the children in this criminal-system caseload are black. While outdated census figures may, in part, account for this discrepancy, it is very unlikely that they explain it completely.

This fact presents us with an interesting dichotomy. Although a disproportionate number of black alleged perpetrators make their way into the criminal-justice system presumably due to institutional racism (see discussion of perpetrators, following), this also means that a larger percentage of black *victims'* cases are prosecuted (since almost all—89%—of the abuse happened within racial groups in this sample), constituting a benefit for these black children if we believe that criminal prosecution is desirable.

THE PERPETRATORS[2]

Individuals accused of child sexual abuse and entering the criminal system because of this charge may or may not differ from the larger group of child sexual abusers. Lower-class families come into contact with public income maintenance and child welfare agencies more often and may begin a chain of events that culminates in referral to the criminal justice system for child sexual abuse that might otherwise go unrecognized. Also, certain individuals and classes of individuals may be more prone to the scrutiny of the police and court. The existence of prior offenses or charges, for example, might make one vulnerable to being charged again, particularly during the probationary period. These potential differences cannot be ascertained with any certainty because the data on child molesters who avoid detection is so scant, but the accused individuals who were criminally charged in these particular jurisdictions can be described as follows.

GENDER

The great majority of perpetrators in this sample were male (97%). Most cases (79%) involved male perpetrators and female victims. Second most common were male perpetrators and male victims (19%). Few cases involved female perpetrators and female victims (2%), and a negligible number involved female perpetrators and male victims (1%).

AGE

The perpetrators ranged in age from seventy years old, to fifteen, but there was a distinct pattern to the age array (see Figure 4.6). There were more defendants between twenty-seven and thirty-seven than any other ten-year age span, and there is a clear peak around age thirty-five. Incidence of child sexual abuse in general, regardless of criminal system involvement, also peaks around age thirty-five, according to some studies (Finkelhor, 1986, mentions eight separate studies that show most offenders to be between thirty-five and forty years of age), although there are also studies showing a slightly younger modal

FIGURE 4.6
Age of Defendant

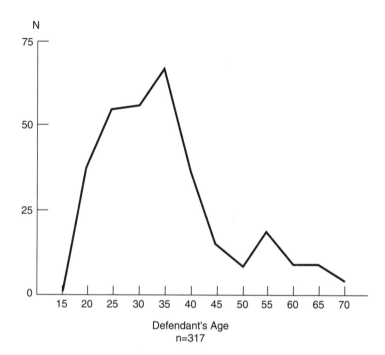

Defendant's Age
n=317

age (Freund et al. 1972; Quinsey et al., 1979, 1980). In a study of convicted sex-offenders and their offenses in 1965, Paul Gebhard and his colleagues found the average age of the child molesters to be thirty-five, within a narrow range of ages; only one-sixth of the offenders were over fifty (MacNamara & Sagarin, 1977). The age distribution found here would appear to be due to a coinciding pattern of opportunity. That is, if individuals are generally about 20 years older than the children for whom they are parents or parent figures, then the fluctuations in incidence for perpetrators from twenty-five to thirty-seven would be similar to the fluctuations in incidence for victims age five to seventeen (see Figure 4.7). While these patterns are not a perfect match, they are reminiscent of each other.

FIGURE 4.7
Relationship of Defendant's Age to Child Victim's Age

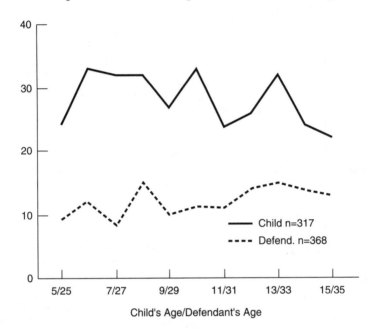

Child's Age/Defendant's Age

EDUCATION

The largest number of defendants had less than a high school education (41.3%, see Figure 4.8), followed by nearly as many who graduated high school (37.6%). The rest attended college or graduated from college, but together they accounted for less than a quarter of the defendants. The total group of defendants is certainly less educated than the population of the sample counties at large, as any sample taken from the criminal-justice system would be (see Table 2.2), but the deviation from national figures regarding education is somewhat narrower (almost 60% with at least a high school degree in this sample versus 76% of persons twenty-five years of age and older with this educational level in the general population [U.S. Bureau of the Census, 1989]).

While there is no reason to connect child sexual abuse with educational level, per se, there were, in early prevalence studies, some indications that sexual abuse is related to social class (Finkelhor, 1984). Later review of multiple studies (Finkelhor,

FIGURE 4.8
Education of Defendant

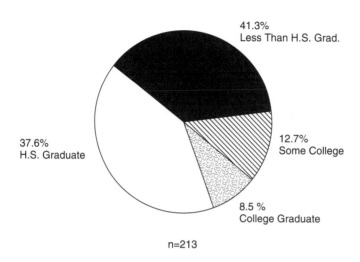

41.3%
Less Than H.S. Grad.

37.6%
H.S. Graduate

12.7%
Some College

8.5 %
College Graduate

n=213

1986) suggests that sexual abuse and social class are unrelated. *Being reported to public agencies* for abuse is not unrelated to social class or education, however, and may account for some of this discrepancy between prevalence and criminal statistics, giving credence to bias against those with less education on the part of the law enforcement and criminal justice systems as an explanation for the deviation.

CRIMINAL RECORD

Reliable composite indicators of social class were not available from prosecutor's records, and hence are not dealt with here. However, information was available for one very telling measure of social functioning that is particularly relevant for this study, and that is prior experience with the criminal-justice system. Less than half (43%) of the defendants had no criminal charges filed against them prior to this instance, 35% had charges in their past for other than sex crimes, and 22% had been charged with sex crimes in the past. Fifteen percent had at least one sex crime charge, 27% had at least one felony charge, and 22% had at least one conviction. Of those with prior charges, 16% had felony convictions for nonsex crimes, 16% had misdemeanor convictions for nonsex crimes, 13% had felony convictions for sex crimes, and 3% had misdemeanor convictions for sex crimes. The relatively small percentage of misdemeanor convictions for sex crimes may reflect the unrecognizability of certain misdemeanor charges as being sexually related. An example of this would be "contributing to the delinquency of a minor." The general criminality of the sample, particularly the number of defendants with felony criminal records for crimes ostensibly unrelated to sexual abuse of children, is surprising, given our current understanding of child molesters as being functional and normal in other aspects of their lives (Finkelhor, 1984), but may reflect the greater scrutiny to which already identified criminals are subjected.

RACE

As shown in the discussion of victims, above, there is a large percentage of black perpetrators in this criminal sample (29.3%, Figure 4.5), but not in the jurisdictions the sample represents. This is not likely due to a higher prevalence of sexual abuse in this racial group. Peters, Wyatt, and Finkelhor (Finkelhor, 1985) summarize existing research data on this subject as follows. "There is growing evidence that the prevalence of sexual abuse is no higher among Afro-Americans than among the white population. The results of five community surveys, conducted independently in diverse locations, consistently show similar prevalence rates for Afro-Americans and whites." (Keckley Market Research, 1983; Kercher & McShane, 1984; Wyatt, 1985; Russell, 1986). Therefore, there is reason to believe that racial bias was operating in determining whose cases crossed the threshold into the criminal justice system for child sexual abuse in these study counties. We should keep in mind, however, that this bias has been noted in studies of the criminal system in general, particularly the disproportion that ensues from the indirect effects of race and income that operate through their relationship to other such variables as defendant's prior record (Zatz, 1984; LaFree, 1985). (See Chapter 5 for a discussion of the relationship of race to case processing in this sample).

FIGURE 4.9

Proportion of Intra-Family and Extra-Family Abuse

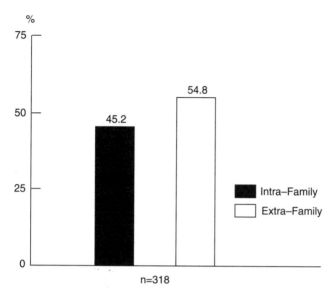

n=318

RELATIONSHIP TO VICTIM

The abusers were people known to the children, for the most part; only slightly fewer were actually family members (45.2) than the proportion who were outside the family (54.8, see Figure 4.9). This is a very high rate of intra-family abuse, compared to the prevalence studies of other researchers.[3] It is closest to Finkelhor (1979), who found that 43% of the female college students he surveyed had been abused sexually by members of their own families. However, Russell, Haugaard, Kinsey, and the Canadian Population Survey all found that between 20 and 30% of their respondents were abused by family members (Haugaard & Reppucci, 1988).

Why would the rate of intra-family cases be so high in a criminal justice sample? Once again, most of the cases in this system come from the child welfare agency, either by way of the police or directly. Cases in the child welfare system occur within families by definition. However, many cases come through the police with no civil component to them. Unfortunately, the proportion of such cases is not discernible from the data obtained for this survey. The referral source that was recorded is the proximate agency that sent the cases to the prosecutor's office, regardless of the involvement of other agencies. Because that agency was so often the police—sometimes by virtue of locally mandated procedures—the cases erroneously appear to have come mostly from the police. Nevertheless, it is a child welfare caseload the criminal courts are dealing with, for the most part. The fact that the cases are being referred by child welfare to criminal justice represents a shift in perception regarding the seriousness and treatability of these situations.

We do know the specific relationships involved in this seemingly disproportionate number of family cases in the criminal justice system. Much of the intra-family segment of criminal cases can be accounted for by the larger percentage of fathers and father figures than other investigators have found among perpetrators of child sexual abuse at large. In this study sample, the victim's stepfather was the accused perpetrator 15.7% of the time, while biological fathers accounted for another 13.4% of the cases. (Biological mothers represented less than one-half of 1% of the accused in these cases.)

The data from other researchers regarding stepfathers versus biological fathers is very interesting. While many have found stepfathers to be the most prevalent abusers of all (Giles-Sims & Finkelhor, 1974; Sagarin, 1977; Russell, 1984), some feel that this finding is just an artifact of study design and interagency referral patterns (Vander Mey and Neff, 1986), and that if these mediators were neutralized, it would be natural fathers who would be shown to be the more prevalent abusers.[4]

Noncustodial acquaintances make up the largest single group of alleged abusers in this study (26.5%, see Figure 4.10), although this is most likely related to the fact that "noncustodial acquaintances" is a more inclusive category than others. This category included neighbors, friends, and acquaintances of the victim's parent(s), as well as a few individuals unknown to the parents, but known to the child.

The accused abusers were custodial acquaintances of the victim—babysitters, day-care workers, and so on—only 7.1% of

FIGURE 4.10
Relationship of Abuser to Victim

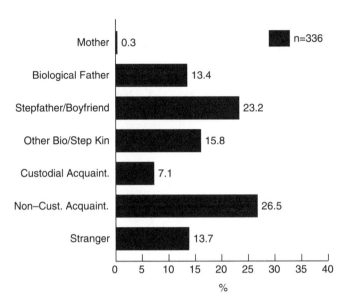

the time. They were strangers to the child 13.7% of the time. This is a figure similar to what others have found when they limit their definition of abuse to contact offenses (Russell, 1984, 11%; Fromuth, 1986, 11%; Haugaard, 1987, 12%), indicating that stranger cases are not sent to the criminal system disproportionately, contrary to what we might expect. Although, we shall see that once there, they are prosecuted differently, and often not at all.

In this study of cases referred for criminal prosecution, perpetrators with different relationships to their victims abused children of different ages (see Table 4.1). In general, the pattern that emerged is that most biological and step-relatives abused children ten years old and younger. Custodial and noncustodial acquaintances abused younger and older children in close-to-equal proportions; strangers abused children eleven and older, much more often (see Figures 4.11 and 4.12). This pattern mirrors what we know in general about the prevalence of sexual abuse within different relationships, and seems clearly related to the offender's access to the child. Children are most likely to be molested by those with greatest access to them. Strangers are

FIGURE 4.11
Intra-family and Extra-family Abuse by Age of Victim

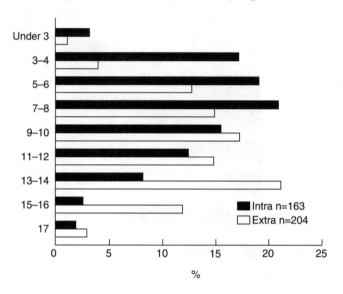

FIGURE 4.12
Proportion of Intra-family and Extra-family Abuse of Younger and Older Children

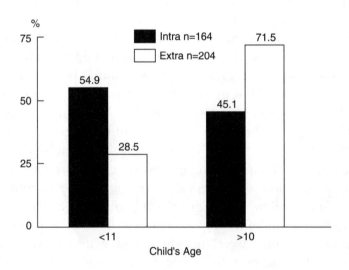

TABLE 4.1
Relationship of Defendant to Child by Age of Victim

Child's Age	Relationship of Defendant						
	Mother %	Biological Father %	Stepfather/ Mother's Boyfriend %	Other Biological/ Step-relation %	Custodial Acquaintance %	Non-custodial Acquaintance %	Stranger %
Under 3		6.7		4.8			
3–4		40.0		14.3	7.7	1.9	3.8
5–6			11.1	19.0	7.7	15.4	15.4
7–8		20.0	18.5	28.6	23.1	19.2	7.7
9–10	100.0	13.3	29.6	23.8	15.4	9.6	
11–12		6.7	11.1	4.8	7.7	15.4	19.2
13–14		6.7	18.5	4.8	30.8	30.8	23.1
15–16		6.7	7.4		7.7	7.7	19.2
17			3.7				11.5

more likely to come into contact with older children who have more freedom of movement in the community.

THE OFFENSES

It would be expected that the cases that reach the criminal system—as opposed to going unredressed at all—being handled privately, or being attended by the child-welfare and family-court system, would be those with more serious offenses alleged, but again, data do not exist to determine this with confidence. The offenses alleged in these criminal cases span a wide range of behaviors. Most cases contained accusations of several of the abusive acts that were specified on the case history documentation forms used in the study. The most prevalent of these was fondling. This behavior was recorded in over half the 410 cases that made up the core study sample (57.3%), but was probably present in far more of the cases, as we might expect that the less serious behaviors were not noted when more serious acts were present. Intercourse was alleged in just over a quarter of the cases (25.1%), and said to have been attempted in about 17% more. Physical abuse was a component in under 8% of the cases. So-called ritualistic abuse (defined as involving the occult, supernatural, or satanic) was noticeably absent from these caseloads (.3% of the sample), given the publicity devoted to this kind of abuse during the study period.

How these figures correspond to noncriminal incidence and prevalence figures regarding specific acts is not altogether clear because of differences in categorization, but some comparisons can be noted with caveats. Fondling statistics for this criminal-justice sample are similar to those reported by Kinsey (58%) and Haugaard (52%), and somewhat higher than those reported by Finkelhor (40%) and the Canadian Population Survey (36%) (Haugaard & Reppucci, 1988). According to Haugaard & Reppucci's compilation of studies, so-called noncontact experiences usually made up about 20% to 30% of the cases. This corresponds closely to the combined percentages of exposure and sexual photos in this criminal sample. Where the criminal sample was unique was at the more damaging end of the behavior continuum. Intercourse was considerably higher for this court sample at 25.1% than for Finkelhor (4%), Haugaard (5%), or Wyatt (11%) (Haugaard & Reppucci, 1988). However, the percentage of cases involving intercourse (27.6%) referred to a treatment program at Tufts New England Medical Center in Boston (The Family Crisis Center) was similar to the percentage in the criminal-justice sample (Gomez-Schwartz, Horowitz, & Cardarelli, 1990).

It should be recognized that the checking-off of discrete behaviors can sometimes fail to capture the nature of these offenses. Take, for example, a case of a teenage girl whose father was accused of having intercourse with her. The volunteer recorded the following sketch of the case:

> *Defendant is thirty-five years old and the natural father of the victim, although he has been divorced from the victim's mother for many years. He is a "business owner" with no prior convictions. [The victim] did not know her father until her recent move to [city], because her parents were divorced when she was very young. The father began sexually abusing his daughter in December 1986, when she was twelve. The victim began to try to avoid contact with father in January 1987. She quit eating, began losing weight, started missing school, vomited for no reason, became nervous and generally showed numerous signs of distress. The victim finally told a friend, who then told the victim's mother. The victim recounted many instances of abuse including oral sex, masturbation, and intercourse.*
>
> *For the purposes of this case, the prosecutor focused on one event. The father was supposed to take the victim and her brother out to lunch for the victim's birthday. Instead, he told the brother there was no room in the car and he could not go with them. He took the victim to his apartment where he forced her to have intercourse.*

CASE TYPES

For what it is worth, certain abuse behaviors often cluster together, making for several types of cases (see data-analysis portion of Chapter 2 for discussion of factor analysis that resulted in identifying these types). Without making judgments about the severity of the cases, the types can be described as follows in descending order of the strength of the characterization (factor) in explaining differ-

FIGURE 4.13
Children Receiving Medical Examination

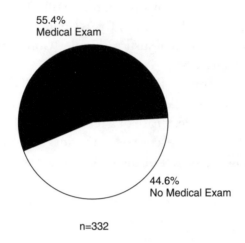

55.4%
Medical Exam

44.6%
No Medical Exam

n=332

ences among cases. There is a type of case that consists primarily of nontraditional sexual assaults, including oral-genital contact and penetration offenses including penetration of the vagina or anus by fingers or objects (Type 1, 51 cases).[5] Another type consists of fondling behaviors (Type 2, 153 cases). A third type can be characterized as nontouching offenses (Type 3, 105 cases). Included in this third group are exposure by the defendant, the taking of photographs of the victim, and masturbation by the defendant in the victim's presence. The final category includes penile/vaginal intercourse and attempted intercourse (Type 4, 64 cases). As it turns out, these case types are related to the child's age, and the race of the individuals in the case, at least in the jurisdictions studied here. These interrelationships, as they affect case disposition, are explored later.

FREQUENCY, DURATION, AND DISCLOSURE

The abuse was alleged to have occurred once, several times, and many times in about equal proportions of the cases (39%, 34.8%, and 25.8%) over a period of less than a year to 11 years in one case. The victim was told by the perpetrator not to tell anyone about the abuse, and threatened with consequences if she did tell, in almost 33% of the cases. Nevertheless, the child disclosed the event before

FIGURE 4.14
Evidence from Medical Examination

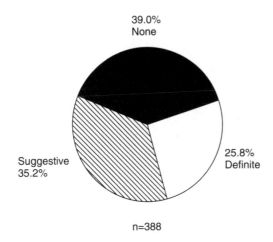

39.0%
None

25.8%
Definite

Suggestive
35.2%

n=388

questioning in about two-thirds of the cases, and about two-thirds of these were children who had been threatened. Over half the time (57.1%), this disclosure was to the biological mother; next most often (12.2% of the time), it was to another biological relative.

CORROBORATING EVIDENCE

The child was medically examined in over half of these cases (see Figure 4.13). Although slightly more of these examinations showed no evidence (39%), the cases that showed suggestive evidence and the cases that showed definitive evidence were not different in number (35.2% and 25.8%, Figure 4.14). These figures do not conflict with known statistics (many studies have shown that about 30% of medical examinations conducted for this purpose fail to detect abnormalities [Muram, 1989]), but there is an uneven state of medical professional expertise in performing and interpreting these examinations (Krugman, 1989).

There was an eyewitness to the event in under 19% of the cases (see Figure 4.15). This was another child or adolescent in almost all cases. Over 19% (19.3%) of the time, the witness was the brother of the child; another 19.3% of the time, the witness was a sister. Only about 10% of these witnesses ended up testifying in court.

In the majority of the cases, there was no medical evidence, or

FIGURE 4.15
Cases with Eyewitnesses

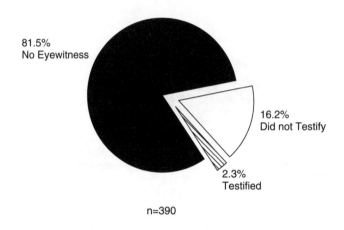

81.5%
No Eyewitness

16.2%
Did not Testify

2.3%
Testified

n=390

there was no eyewitness to the events at issue (63.9% and 83.4%, respectively). In 53.2% of the cases, there was neither.

THE DISPOSITIONS

LENGTH OF TIME IN SYSTEM

Although this information was not available for many of the cases studied as the date of the final disposition was not always recorded for nontrial cases, it is possible to estimate the duration of involvement in the criminal system from those cases with the information. It should be noted that this will be an underestimate for the trial cases, because for these, the date that the trial commenced was used, as it was more faithfully recorded than the date the trial ended. The study jurisdictions show notable differences (see Table 4.2). In Clay, Nassau, and Duval counties in Florida, the average case took approximately 71 days from initial presentation to prosecutor to initiation of trial or other disposition, in St. Louis County, it took 297 days. Because some very lengthy cases appear to be pulling the means upward, medians may be better indicators of duration. Using these measures, there is even more variation: from a median duration of 41 days in the Florida jurisdictions to a median of 301 in St. Louis.

TABLE 4.2
Duration of Cases from Presentation to Trial or Other Disposition

Site	N	Mean (days)	Median (days)
San Francisco County	28	96	80.5
Jacksonville (Clay, Nassau, & Duval counties)	72	71	41
Louisville (Jefferson County)	10	194	153
New Orleans (Orleans Parish)	14	203	153
Kansas City (Johnson County)	7	111	118
St. Louis County	9	297	301
Baltimore County	28	145	116
Dallas County	2	149	149

This protraction of the criminal proceedings has been cited by several child advocates as one of the most damaging aspects of prosecution to the child victim witness. Desmond Runyan of the University of North Carolina at Chapel Hill School of Medicine found that "the child is adversely affected by lengthy delays in the resolution of criminal prosecution of child sexual abuse. This finding appears to be robust, persisting after control for age, type of abuse, relationship to the perpetrator, and duration of abuse. Protracted involvement with the criminal justice system, especially when a trial is pending, may increase feelings of powerlessness and subject the child to stigmatization by family, the public, and self. The reduced improvement may represent either a delay in the resolution of the adverse effects or an actual exacerbation by the intervention process" (Runyan et al., 1988).

Because not all jurisdictions collected data on all types of cases, a cross-sectional sample representative of the full spectrum of dispositions including not filed, dropped after filing, incompetent to stand trial, pled to original charges, plea-bargained, and tried cases is not attainable. Several groupings of jurisdictions can be reported to illustrate certain sections of the process here, however, and one jurisdiction, the counties surrounding Jacksonville, Florida, supplied complete data on cases from all of these categories, which is used alone for certain analyses.

Some percentage of the cases that come to the attention of the prosecutor's office do not go forward, as no charges are filed. This proportion varies from place to place due to the differences in screening and referral, but it is often substantial (for instance in Clay, Duval, and Nassau counties, over 38% of the presented cases are not filed).[6] When charges were not filed, the reasons noted in the record for not filing were many, but they can be reduced to only a few that were given repeatedly (see Figure 4.16). By far the most often cited was lack of corroborating evidence (48.2% of the case records contained a notation to that effect). This is the catch-22 of child sexual abuse cases. Often, there is either inconclusive medical evidence, or a child is not taken to a doctor so that medical evidence can be gathered (semen) or noted (injury). Furthermore, sexual abuse is a secret crime; it is very unlikely that there would be a witness to the event. Whether there was a lack of *any* corroborating evidence in these cases, such as behavioral changes, or statements to others, is unclear from the prosecutor's notes, but it can be assumed that, at least in some cases, lack of medical evidence or a witness was considered sufficient not to file the case.

The next most often cited reason for not filing was that the victim changed her story (21.9%). This could include simply inconsistent accounts of the abuse, or outright refutation of the original claim. While this obviously poses a serious problem for the prosecutor, it is not an unusual occurrence. Billie Wright Dziech and Judge Charles B. Schudson discuss recantation in *On Trial*. They point out the predictability of the child's reversing

FIGURE 4.16
Reasons Charges Were Not Filed

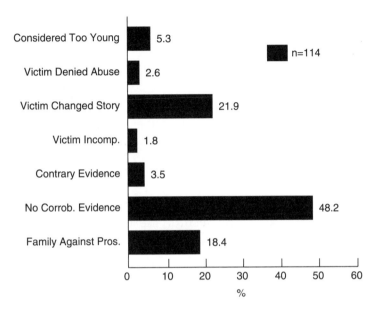

her story after she has disclosed abuse. They say, as any therapist who works with child victims of sexual abuse will attest, that the child has a self-protective impulse to "forget" the events, in order to go on with her life. Even if she does not repress the abuse, she may recant to assuage her guilt for disrupting her family, or in response to an actual threat by the perpetrator. "If a child is terrified of an abuser," they point out, "denial is a way of saying, 'I kept my promise. I didn't tell, not really.' If disclosure has disrupted a child's life and created pain, anger, or chaos in the home, denial is a means of banishing the trouble" (1989, pp. 56–57).

In the case of recantation, unless there is some admissable evidence regarding the sexual abuse, the prosecutor cannot proceed. If a child recants and denies, the prosecutor has to have some "proof" of the abuse to put forward in order to make his or her case. This means that there would have to be a prior statement of the child describing the abuse that fits a hearsay exception, or another witness. The first of these is not always available, and the second is rare.

Many times (18.4% of the sample), the family resisted prosecution of the offender, and this was noted in the record as a reason for not filing. The perpetrator may have been the grandfather of the victim, an old man who is believed by his children, the victim's parents, to be senile and not responsible for what he did, or too frail to undergo the trial or the punishment. They may have felt they could control his behavior in the future. The family was sometimes seeking to protect the victim from the trauma they believed she would suffer in court. Conversely, the mother of the victim and wife of the abuser may have been protecting her husband, out of fear for her safety, or fear of losing him.

Declining to file because the family of the victim is against it is problematic because the prosecutor must represent the entire community, not just the victim and her family. A prosecutor must be concerned about the potential risk an abuser poses to other children in the community, and while the individual child's interests often coincide with this, it is not always the case. Also, as Patricia Toth of the American Prosecutors Research Institute points out, it is not fair to the child victim to use standards that put the responsibility on her for going forward with a case (personal communication, August 1992). Even though empowering the victim can be one result of prosecuting her abuse, and that is desirable, she needs to know the decision is not completely up to her. That is simply too heavy a burden for a young child. The message that the community (and not just she and her family) is interested in seeing the harm that was done to her redressed, however, is one that may offer some support.

Of course there are many reasons for not filing that come down to the credibility of the child as a witness in her own case—often the only direct witness. She simply may have been judged too young (around 5%) or otherwise incompetent to testify (about 2%).[7] She was sometimes afraid to testify (another 1%). Or, she may never have disclosed abuse (approximately 4%); it may be that someone else initiated the case in the belief that she was abused.

FIGURE 4.17
Reasons for Filing Charges

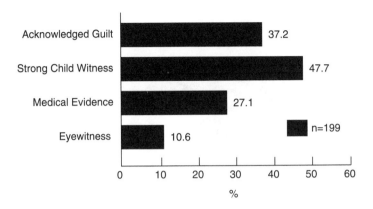

FILED CASES

When the case was filed (Figure 4.17), it was usually on the basis of a judgment that the child would make a strong witness (almost 48% of the time this was noted in the record of filed cases). Almost as often, however (about 37% of the time), the defendant acknowledged guilt, and the prosecutor proceeded on that basis. In 27.1% of the filed cases, the fact that there was some medical evidence facilitated the decision to file, and in 10.6% the existence of an eyewitness prompted the filing decision.

For the jurisdictions that did not have diversion programs in this sample (St. Louis, Louisville, New Orleans, and Baltimore County), after those cases that were dropped after filing were culled out, 37.5% of the defendants pled guilty to the full set of original charges brought against them. Another 51.7% negotiated some lesser charge or charges. Just under 11% (10.8%) of the final caseload went to trial in these jurisdictions where diversion was not an option (see Figure 4.18).

DIVERTED CASES

Diversion to treatment is a controversial prosecution tool. Technically, diverted cases are not prosecuted. If the defendant complies with the order to accept counseling, the charges against him are dropped from the record. Diversion has several pur-

FIGURE 4.18

Filed/Not Dropped Cases in Jurisdictions Without Diversion Programs

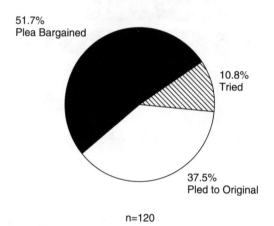

51.7%
Plea Bargained

10.8%
Tried

37.5%
Pled to Original

n=120

poses. One is to reroute cases considered to be more appropriately treated, rather than prosecuted, into the therapeutic system. In jurisdictions such as Johnson County, Kansas, where only incest cases are eligible for diversion, this is presumably the predominant rationale. There are a host of rules that have to be satisfied in that jurisdiction in order for a defendant to qualify for pretrial diversion. These offenders cannot have used threat or force in committing the abuse, have to be deemed treatable by a therapeutic professional, and have to move out of their own home during treatment. It is presumed that these rules increase the chances that the treatment will be effective. In the three-county jurisdiction that includes Jacksonville, Florida, diversion is perceived as a desirable option to use, when possible, as a way of keeping families intact. There, according to an assistant prosecutor, cases are most often diverted when the offender has a history of being a reliable source of financial and emotional support to the family. Furthermore, Jacksonville has a special program that refers diverted cases to professionals who are experts in the treatment of child sexual abuse offenders. Professionals in the program report back on the progress of the offender and whether or not they are meeting the terms of their probation.

Unclogging the criminal calendars is the other reason that diversion to treatment is used, however. Complicating this decidedly pragmatic motive is the lack of standardization regarding the type of treatment that qualifies for diversion. Unlike the three Florida counties studied, in many jurisdictions this treatment does not have to be rendered by a specialist in sexual disorders of this kind, or at a facility that specializes in this type of treatment. The belief in some quarters is that any psychotherapist will do, or even that the attention of any helping professional will suffice. In this sample, of the 61 diverted cases, most of which were from Jacksonville, 71% of the defendants were directed to professionals or centers designated as specializing in sexual deviance. The situation was worse for court-ordered treatment in conjunction with probation. In one case where there was an order for counseling, the assistant district attorney informed the volunteer data collector that the counseling the defendant had received was from a Doctor of Naturopathy, who treats disease by diet, exercise, and heat, and that because of the way the system was set up, there were no sanctions even when the defendant dropped out of that. Furthermore, treatment during incarceration or other residential treatment is virtually unheard-of in these cases, at least in the jurisdictions studied.

In the jurisdictions in which diversion *was* an option—at least for some categories of cases (San Francisco; Clay, Duval, and Nassau counties in Florida; and Johnson County, Kansas)— almost 23% of the filed cases were diverted to treatment. In these jurisdictions, 9.2% of the cases were dropped, and 1.1% of the defendants were found incompetent to stand trial. Over 27% of the defendants pled guilty to the original charges brought against them, but 36% plea-bargained. Trials resulted from 8.4% of these cases.

Even if the dropped cases were disregarded to allow for comparison with nondiverting jurisdictions (the jurisdictions without diversion programs in this sample did not all collect information on dropped cases), a particular pattern remains. In jurisdictions that diverted cases to treatment, cases pled to original charges were 30.2% of those cases handled, cases plea bargained were 35.1%, and the portion of the caseload that was

FIGURE 4.19
Filed/Not Dropped Cases in Jurisdictions with Diversion Programs

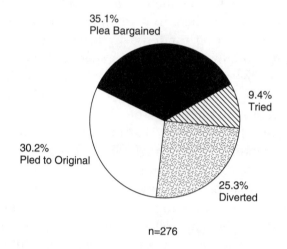

n=276

tried in court was only 9.4% (see Figure 4.19). This lack of meaningful difference in trial statistics for cases in jurisdictions with a diversion program and those without such a program (10.8% versus 9.4%) indicates that while diversion is routing people out of "the system," it is not keeping people out of the courtroom in great numbers. It would appear from the statistics that diverted cases would otherwise be plea-bargained.

CASES ADJUDICATED THROUGH GUILTY PLEAS

Regardless of whether there is a diversion program in place or not in the study jurisdictions, most of the cases resulted in guilty pleas. In this regard at least, the handling of child sexual abuse cases by these jurisdictions is typical of general criminal practice. In jurisdictions with diversion, 65.3% of the prosecutors' final sexual-abuse caseload pled guilty, either to original charges or to negotiated charges. In jurisdictions that do not divert cases from the system, the proportion is 72.9% of the filed and not subsequently dropped cases.

TRIED CASES

Very few of the cases that were filed during the data-collection year in any of the jurisdictions went to trial (see Table 4.3).[8] Because we do not know the number of cases not filed and/or dropped after filing in many of the sites, the exact percentage of *all cases presented to the district attorney's offices that went to trial* (which would, of course, be even lower) cannot be calculated.[9] But we have seen that, regardless of the structure of the system in a particular jurisdiction, approximately 10% of the filed and retained cases are tried in court. Of those cases that do progress to judge or jury trial, 75% result in convictions (42 cases of the 56 trials in this sample).

Plea-bargaining, pleading guilty to original charges, and being convicted at trail are not case outcomes, ultimately, but a means to reaching the final disposition: the sentence. If these sentences are not very different, then it could be argued that the method of case processing is meaningful *only* as an expedient, and should not be assigned any fundamental significance. This turns out to be the case: sentences were not significantly differ-

TABLE 4.3
Cases Proceeding to Trial

Site	Number
San Francisco	5
Jacksonville	10
Louisville	3
New Orleans	5
Kansas City	8
St. Louis	2
Dallas	20
Baltimore	3

FIGURE 4.20

Length of Prison Sentence in Pled, Plea-Bargained, and Tried Cases

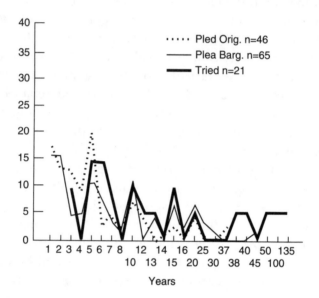

ent for cases processed differently. Eighty-three percent of the defendants who went to trial were sentenced to serve some jail or prison time, as against 62% of those who plea-bargained and 65% of those who pled guilty to initial charges filed against them. In 6% of the tried cases, 4% of the plea-bargained cases, and 3% of the pled cases, the defendant was sentenced to probation. Treatment was ordered for 11% of the tried cases, 34% of the plea-bargained cases, and 32% of the cases with guilty pleas to original charges.

When the prison sentences of the cases that were prosecuted via these three routes are plotted against each other (see Figure 4.20), their essential similarity is evident. The three trajectories *are* quite different at the ends of the continuum. Not surprisingly, people who are tried in court and convicted are not likely to get a sentence of less than 3 years. Likewise, tried cases are the only ones that receive sentences of more than 45 years. Defendants who pled to the original charges against them were more likely to be sentenced to less than a year in jail, perhaps because people are more likely to plead to the original charges if those charges are relatively minor. But, for the bulk of the cases—those that receive sentences of between 3 and 37 years—the sentencing patterns for cases that were tried, plea-bargained, and pled to original charges were remarkably alike, with the general trend being one of decreasing percentages of cases receiving longer sentences. However, there were peaks at the 5-, 10-, and 15-year marks, reflecting the sentencing convention of using 5-year increments.

SUMMARY

We have seen that the criminal system in these study jurisdictions received cases with characteristics that for the most part paralleled the profile of child sexual abuse in the literature. However, the cases that reach the criminal justice system are unique in some ways. For example, in 1986–87, courts in these jurisdictions received four cases with girl victims for every case with a boy victim. General estimates of victimization by gender would indicate that the criminal system, then, is slightly skewed toward cases with female victims. This disparity is unfortunate for the young males who are sexually abused and have no means of retribution. It means that many abusers of young boys are spared disclosure and are free to abuse again. It means, furthermore, that the victims themselves may not get the services they need to help them avoid becoming child molesters in turn, as many male victims in particular, do (Gebhard et al., 1965; Finkelhor, 1979; Groth, 1983; Abel, Becker & Cunningham-Rather, 1984; Finkelhor, 1984, and others are afraid they will (Bruckner and Johnson, 1987). But to suggest as some have (Kempe & Kempe, 1984), that sexual abuse is "harder on boys" may be the result of sexist stereotyping. It implies that victimization is somehow more "natural" for females, and therefore less destructive to their identity.

Most of the victims were white, but the number of black victims and defendants was disproportionate to the percentage of blacks in the jurisdictions represented. One key to the disparity seems to be the fact that the black defendants in these jurisdictions allegedly committed more serious offenses, and more of the black defendants had a criminal history. Both of these "facts" require further exploration, as they hint at racial bias at an earlier point in the system without shedding light on the exact location of that bias.

Patterns of age and victim-abuser relationship seem to be related primarily to access to the children. Theoretically, there is increased access to children of vulnerable age during the ten-year period (ages twenty-seven to thirty-seven) that includes most defendants. Furthermore, the abusers were people known to the children. Noncustodial acquaintances made up the largest single group of alleged abusers. Second in preponderance to acquaintances were the victim's stepfather or her mother's boyfriend. In general, most biological and step-relatives abused children under eleven years old. Custodial and noncustodial acquaintances abused younger and older children in nearly equal proportions, and strangers abused children eleven and older much more often.

Although there are countless permutations of the separate abusive behaviors that occurred in these cases, four simple case types were developed for analytic purposes, and these show some patterns. In general, younger children are those most often fondled only, and older children are most often the victims of intercourse only. Oral-genital contact and anal penetration offenses, as isolated behaviors, occurred much more often to the younger than the older children.

Case types are strongly related to the relationship of the perpetrator to the child. Biological and step fathers tend to be associated with the cases of fondling; custodial and noncustodial acquaintances, with intercourse and attempted intercourse; and strangers, with the nontouching offenses. Case type was also related to race in this sample. Over half the black defendants were alleged to have committed intercourse or attempted intercourse, but less than a quarter of the white offenders were accused of attempting or effecting intercourse with their victims. The predominant case type associated with white offenders was fondling. This is another place where suspicion of institutional bias is warranted and should be explored.

There is no discernable pattern to the length of time sexual abuse occurred before it was brought to the attention of the prosecutor's office, which ranged from one day to eleven years. Child disclosure was usually the precipitant of referral to the courts and this disclosure was more likely to take place at puberty than other points in a child's life, regardless of the duration of the abuse.

Handling of these cases is somewhat different by jurisdiction. One difference is the length of time cases take to traverse the system in the jurisdiction: from a median duration of 41 days in the Florida counties to a median of 301 in St. Louis. These cases did not pose an easy task for the prosecutors from a legal standpoint. In the majority of the cases, there was no medical evidence, or there was no eyewitness to the events at issue. In over half the cases, there was neither. Charges were not filed on over a third of the cases presented to district attorney's offices for prosecution.

Diversion programs were in place in about half of the study jurisdictions and over a quarter of the retained cases in these jurisdictions were diverted to treatment. Various assumptions are in evidence in the policies and requirements surrounding decisions about diversion in these jurisdictions. Some of these are that intra-family abuse is more treatable than extra-family abuse, that emotional coercion to sexual abuse is less serious than physical coercion, and that heads of households are more deserving of—or more likely to benefit from—psychological services. It is possible, however, although not adequately testable with these data, that diversion is actually "widening the net" of the criminal-justice system, which is accepting responsibility for these case and diverting them when they otherwise would not even reach the threshold of acceptance.[10] Trials resulted from 9.4% of the retained cases in jurisdictions with diversion programs, and 10.8% in jurisdictions where diversion was not an option. Evidence from one jurisdiction suggests that if all cases presented to the prosecutor for consideration are counted, only around 3% are eventually tried. Most of the cases were pled, either to original charges, or—slightly more often—to negotiated charges. Prison sentences were given to the overwhelming majority of tried cases and over 60% of the pled cases, whether the plea was negotiated or not. These sentences ranged from 3 to 37 years, with the most likely sentence being 5 years.

5

Which Way to Go?
Factors Related to
Case Processing

Once it is determined that various proportions of referred cases are handled in particular ways, the question emerges of why and how these decisions are made. Answering this question in full is far beyond the scope of this study, but looking at what case and individual factors are associated with these different decisions suggests something of the underlying structure of decision making in this area.

Before turning to later processing decisions, it makes sense to look at which situations of alleged sexual abuse result in filed charges. Every prosecutors' office has standards governing the manner in which filing decisions are made, and these standards are designed, in part, to be safeguards against arbitrariness and bias (Toth and Whalen, 1987). In Chapter 4, we saw that the factors most noted in prosecutors' records as influencing the decision to file charges were those pertaining to the legal case (strength of the child witness, acknowledgment of guilt by the defendant, medical evidence, or the existence of an eyewitness). To see if there were factors other than those noted by the prosecutors in the case records that accounted for whether or not charges were filed, the characteristics of both groups of cases were examined against each other. (The three-county jurisdiction centered in Jacksonville is the only location in this study where this could be done, as there, information was available on all charged and not charged cases that went through the prosecutor's office).

Two additional factors were identified: the criminal history of the defendant and the age of the child victim. Not surprisingly, the accused perpetrators with criminal histories were more often charged. Seventy-five percent of accused perpetrators with prior charges filed against them were formally charged, and only 56% of those with no criminal record ($\chi^2 = 8.8$, $\rho < .01$). While there may be certain protections against admitting information regarding previous related crimes into the proceedings at trial, the earlier decision of whether to file charges or not, is naturally influenced by "priors."

Less obvious, but also "explainable" is the fact that the cases where the child victim was ten years old or younger were more likely to be filed (70.1%) than when the child was at least eleven years old (54.5%; $\chi^2 = 5.5$, $\rho < .05$). Children eleven years old and above are often seen as at least partially "responsible" for being the objects of sexual behavior, making the case more difficult for the prosecutor. Because they are reaching puberty, these girls are perceived by some as being seductive, and their victimizers are commensurately excused for their acts. Another dimension of the situation in Jacksonville particularly is the high number of runaways, many of whom are drawn to the areas of town where servicemen congregate. These teenage and preteenage girls sometimes become involved with the sailors and consequently provoke little sympathy among jurors when a charge of sexual molestation is brought.

AGE OF CHILD

One factor that is clearly related to case processing is the child victim's age. Cases proceed to trial at very different rates, depending on the age of the child victim. Disregarding dropped and diverted cases, a larger proportion of the cases where the victim is five or six years old versus any other two-year age span, younger or older, went to trial (31.4%; $\chi^2 = 26.7$, $\rho < .05$; see Table 5.1). It is not clear why. This age may be perceived by the prosecutor as optimal for convincing testimony, or it may be that these cases cannot be handled in other desirable ways such as eliciting a guilty plea from the defendant. (While many cases in this age group were plea-bargained, few abusers of five- or six-year-old children in this sample pled guilty to original charges.) The defendant may have been more willing to take his chances in court when the child victim was in this age group, thinking five- and six-year-olds in particular would not be believed, although why this conclusion would be drawn only for this two-year age group is not clear. Or, plea negotiation may have been refused by the defendant, and if the case was deemed prosecutable, the prosecutors may have had no choice but to go to trial.

TABLE 5.1
Child's Age by Case Processing

Child's Age	Prosecution Route ($n = 302$)		
	% Tried	% Plea Bargained	% Pled to Original Charges
Under 3	16.7	16.7	66.7
3–4	24.1	55.2	20.7
5–6	31.4	47.1	21.6
7–8	16.7	43.3	37.0
9–10	8.7	58.7	32.6
11–12	20.0	44.0	36.0
13–14	9.8	43.9	46.3
15–16	4.8	47.6	47.6
17	0	25.0	75.0

The age-related pattern with regard to pleas to original charges is varied, as well. Between 20% and 50% of defendants abusing children in most age groups pled guilty to the original charges against them. However, over 66% of the cases where the child was under three years old were settled with pleas to the original charges, whereas only 20.7% of cases where the child victim was in the next highest age group—three or four years old—resulted in pleas to the original charges. To some extent, this can be accounted for by the extremely small number of cases with victims in the youngest age group ($n = 8$). But even allowing for this, these cases are processed in strikingly different ways from cases in adjacent age groups.

The explanation cannot be that in the cases with child victims under three there was compelling evidence, such as medical examination results, to encourage admission of guilt. There were no differences in medical evidence, nor were there any apparent differences in the presence of other kinds of evidence. Likewise, the character of the crime was similar in the two age groups, but with one notable difference. In both age groups the primary behavior alleged was fondling, but with the youngest children (under three), exposure by the defendant was common. This behavior nearly disappears with the older children (three–four), and oral-genital behavior increases somewhat.[1] The relative benignancy of the act committed by abusers of children less than three years old may be what leads them to plead guilty to the charge and take the consequences, rather than engender the increased exposure of a trial.

Interestingly, besides the under-three groups, the only other category of case in which the predominant disposition is the defendant's pleading guilty to original charges occurs when the victim is an adolescent. For the cases with victims between three and thirteen years of age, plea-bargaining to lesser charges is employed more often than any other means of settling the case.

In spite of this discrepancy between the cases with victims under three years old and those with three-to-five-year-old victims, the relationship of victim age to case processing can be summarized by looking at the paths taken for cases in which the child victim is ten years or younger, versus those in which the child is eleven years or older (see Figure 5.1). The differences are

FIGURE 5.1
Prosecution Routes by Age of Child Victim in Jurisdictions With
Diversion Programs

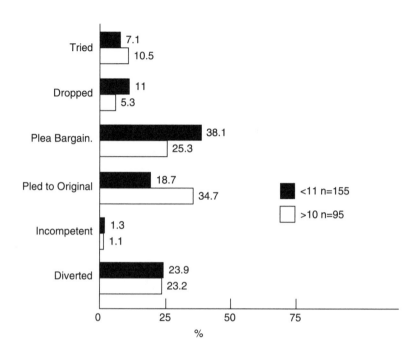

striking ($x^2 = 11.5$, $p < .05$). Cases with younger victims more often were dropped or plea-bargained. These cases less often were resolved with guilty pleas to original charges and proceeding to trial. Diversion of the defendant's case out of the criminal system and into treatment, on the other hand, was apparently unrelated to the victim's age. Again, we see that the decision to offer diversion on a case has little to do with the victim or the crime, but rather rests on who committed the offense and some estimate of the likelihood of his committing such a crime again.

RACE OF DEFENDANT

Case handling also varied by the race of the defendant (and child victim). This is true, however, only for jurisdictions with diversion programs. In these jurisdictions, although three prosecution routes—dropping the case, finding the defendant incompetent to

FIGURE 5.2
Prosecution Routes by Race of Defendant in Jurisdictions with
Diversion Programs

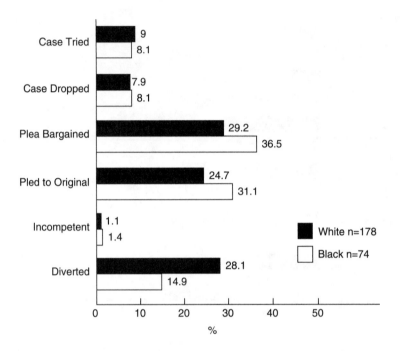

stand trial, and proceeding to trial—accounted for very similar
percentages of white and black defendants, and the percentage of
defendants who pled guilty to original and reduced charges was
not significantly different by race, black defendants were diverted
to treatment at only about half the rate of white defendants (14.9%
versus 28.1%, $\chi^2 = 5.8$, $\rho < .05$, see Figure 5.2). Because diversion
was officially available as an option only in Johnson County in
Kansas, and Clay, Duval, and Nassau counties in Florida (counties
with a particularly low black population), we explored the possibility that this finding was an artifact of the sample. We found that the
actual percentage of blacks in the criminal system in these jurisdictions was not significantly less than in the sample as a whole, and
this percentage was disproportionately high for the racial makeup
of the counties involved, at least in Florida. While, fewer than 3.1%
of the defendants from Johnson County, Kansas, and fewer than
15.6% of the defendants in the Florida counties would have been

black, if not for the bias found earlier in the overall sample, the percentage of the sample that was black was in fact 5.5% and 33.5%, respectively—suggesting that there is bias regarding who enters the system in the Florida counties ($x^2 = 83.5$, $p < .001$), but not necessarily in the Kansas county (*chi* square test, not significant).

Although differential rates of diversion for blacks and whites were not found to be artifacts of the sample, they were found to be related to different rates of prior charges for blacks and whites in these jurisdictions ($x^2 = 4.1$, $p < .05$). When only defendants without prior criminal charges were considered, the race-related differences in diversion disappeared. When only defendants *with* prior criminal histories were considered, the relationship between race and diversion rates persisted ($x^2 = 7.3$, $p < .01$) Fewer black defendants with prior criminal charges in their background were diverted to treatment than were white defendants with similar backgrounds ($x^2 = 4.9$, $p < .05$), again suggesting bias. In fact, of the cases for which all of these variables are known, only one black defendant with a prior record was diverted to treatment in either of these jurisdictions (see Table 5.2).

TABLE 5.2
Rates of Diversion by Race and Prior Charges

Whites ($n = 140$)		Blacks ($n = 59$)	
No Prior Charges	*Prior Charges*	*No Prior Charges*	*Prior Charges*
Diverted			
34 (51.5%)	16 (21.6%)	10 (50.0%)	1 (2.6%)
Not Diverted			
32 (48.5%)	58 (78.4%)	10 (50.0%)	38 (97.4%)

RELATIONSHIP OF DEFENDANT TO CHILD

When the relationship between the defendant and the child is dealt with, in all of its discrete categories (13 separate relationships in all), there is no apparent effect of relationship on case processing. However, when categories of relationship are grouped as intra-family relationships and extra-family relationships, there is a significant effect (χ^2 = 11.9, ρ < .05).[2] Only guilty pleas to original charges and cases where the defendant was found incompetent to stand trial are unaffected by relationship. Fewer extra-family cases were dropped, only about half as many extra-family cases were diverted to treatment, more extra-family cases were plea-bargained, and twice as many extra-family cases went to trial (see Table 5.3). Clearly, where the abuser is outside the family, cases are handled more aggressively by the legal system.

TABLE 5.3

Case Processing by Intra-Extra-family Status of Defendant

	Defendant Member of Family	Defendant Outside of Family
Case Dropped	7 (4.2%)	20 (9.6%)
Defendant Incompetent	1 (.6%)	2 (1.0%)
Case Diverted	42 (25.0%)	29 (13.9%)
Plea Bargained	56 (33.3%)	86 (41.3%)
Pled to Original	45 (26.8%)	53 (25.5%)
Tried	7 (4.2%)	20 (9.6%)

Note: Figures pertain only to jurisdictions that had diversion programs and information available on dropped cases.

It is clear that the intra- or extra-familial status of the offender is of major importance in the criminal justice system's consideration of child sexual abuse cases. This may stem, in part, from the prevailing view (until recently) that sex criminals and sex crimes are classifiable into "types" of offenders and acts, easily distinguishable from one another, and furthermore, that someone who abuses his own child is unlikely to abuse others and hence represents a lesser danger to society (Kinsey, 1949). But the latest information from those who treat sexual offenders is that when more extensive case histories are extracted from offenders, the categories are crossed and crossed again (Abel et al., 1981; Murphy et al., 1986; Salter, 1988). This differential treatment of in-family and out-of-family cases may also stem from the influence of social workers on legal policy regarding child sexual abuse (Weisberg, 1984), but, as we have seen, the therapeutic approach to intra-family cases of child sexual abuse—at least in the child welfare system—has not been very successful. Perhaps this differentiation between cases with defendants internal to the family of the victim and those with defendants external to the family of the victim is anachronistic and should be rethought in light of new evidence.

CASE TYPES

It is very difficult to untangle the relationship between the types of offenses committed, the way the case was processed, and the eventual sentences received. One reason is that these cases obtain overlapping combinations of many abusive behaviors. The simple presence or absence of a behavior or set of behaviors would not be a meaningful distinction between cases, as other behaviors may or may not be present. It is helpful, therefore, to conceptualize the cases as "pure" types, containing related behaviors and not containing unrelated behaviors. This eliminates all "mixed" cases from the analysis and, as a result, some measure of statistical power is lost due to the reduced number of cases. What is lost in statistical power, however, may be gained in understanding.

As explained earlier, the case types derived from the data in this study were four (see "Methods" section for technical discussion of factor analytic procedure): Type 1, cases of anal penetration or

FIGURE 5.3
Case Type by Relationship of Defendant to Child

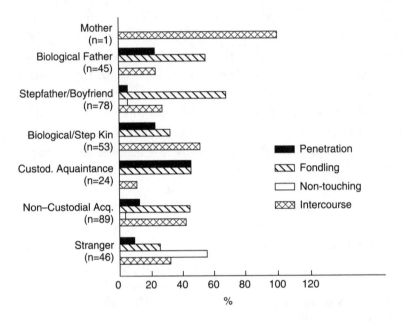

oral-genital contact in either direction (the defendant initiates oral contact with the child's genitals or forces the child to engage in oral contact with his genitals); Type 2, cases of fondling behavior only; Type 3, cases involving sexual offenses that do not include touching the child (exposure of genitals to the child, masturbation in the presence of the child, or taking nude or otherwise erotic photographs of the child) and Type 4, cases where (vaginal/penile) intercourse or attempted intercourse were the predominant behaviors.[3] It is recognized that cases belonging to a type may be very different, even though they are similar in this one way.

Another reason it is so difficult to relate case types to final case disposition is that there are so many intervening variables. Case types are strongly related to the relationship of the perpetrator to the child in this criminal justice sample. Biological fathers and stepfathers tend to be associated with the cases of fondling; custodial and noncustodial acquaintances, with intercourse and attempted intercourse; and strangers, with the nontouching offenses (see Figure 5.3, $\chi^2 = 83.9$, $p < .05$). Although not broken down in

FIGURE 5.4
Case Type by Race of Defendant

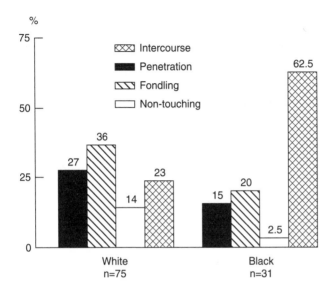

the same way, these figures jibe in direction with Russell's (1984) findings of differences between extra- and intra-familial abuse in the general population, and once again suggest a conditioning continuum of the victims by perpetrators closest to them (see endnote 1).

Interestingly, case type was also related to race in this sample (see Figure 5.4, $\chi^2 = 57.3$, $p < .001$). Over half the black defendants were alleged to have committed intercourse or attempted intercourse, but less than a quarter of the white offenders were accused of attempting or effecting intercourse with their victims. The predominant case type associated with white offenders was fondling. For whatever reason, the black defendants in these criminal systems are there for more serious crimes than the white defendants. What accounts for this? Treating educational attainment as an indirect measure of social class, we can get some idea as to whether the difference was really one of class, rather than race. Differences in educational attainment between blacks and whites did not account for the differences in the severity of allegations (and, hence, criminal charges) between these groups. Only at the highest education levels (at least some college) did these race differences disappear. Other hypotheses are not testable with these data, unfortunately. Again, it would be important in future research to assess the nature and extent of racial bias in the entry into the criminal justice system for child sexual abuse and in how alleged perpetrators are charged.

These four case types are related to the age of the child, as well ($\chi^2 = 71.5$, $\rho < .05$, see Table 5.4). In general, younger children are

TABLE 5.4
Types of Abuse by Child's Age
N = 243 ("pure" cases only)

Child's Age	Abusive Behaviors			
	Penetration and Oral/Genital Behavior (%)	Fondling Behavior (%)	Nontouching Behavior (%)	Intercourse and Attempted Intercourse (%)
1	–	100.0	–	–
2	–	–	60.0	40.0
3	33.3	44.4	–	22.2
4	29.3	54.5	9.1	7.1
5	43.8	25.0	18.8	12.4
6	–	35.0	60.0	5.0
7	16.7	38.9	27.8	16.6
8	14.3	47.6	14.3	23.8
9	9.1	36.4	40.9	13.6
10	15.0	45.0	25.0	15.0
11	20.0	40.0	33.3	6.7
12	20.0	25.0	25.0	30.0
13	11.1	37.0	25.9	25.9
14	8.3	25.0	16.7	50.0
15	18.8	50.0	6.2	25.0
16	60.0	–	–	40.0
17	20.0	–	60.0	20.0

FIGURE 5.5

Prosecution Routes by Case Type in Clay, Nassau, and Duval
Counties

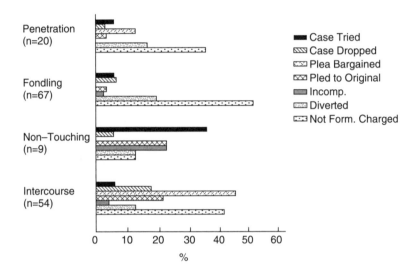

those most often fondled (only), and older children are most
often the victims of vaginal/penile intercourse or attempted
intercourse (only). Oral-genital contact and anal penetration
offenses as predominate behaviors occurred much more often to
the younger than the older children. The cases where nontouching behaviors were the only offenses were rare among both age
groups.

Recognizing that the interrelationship of case type, kinship,
defendant race, and victim age muddies the analysis somewhat,
the routes to prosecution of these cases nevertheless were examined by case type (predominance of one particular abusive
behavior) to see what patterns emerged. Because the Jacksonville sample is a complete sample of all cases referred for
prosecution, including those where no charges were filed, the
relationship between case types and how the cases are handled
can be seen particularly well there ($\chi^2 = 29.2$, $p < .05$, see Figure
5.5). These are considered first.

In a larger proportion of the nontouching offense cases than
in other cases in the 276-case Florida sample, defendants pled
guilty to original charges (45%) or ended up in court (13%),

although the absolute number of cases based on nontouching offenses is small. Although there has been no sexual contact between defendant and child in these cases, the behaviors are often particularly exploitative, and sometimes bizarre, such as staging sexual acts and forcing the child to watch. This may account for the cases being taken to court so disproportionately. Over half of the fondling cases were not charged at all. When they were, they were diverted to treatment and dropped more than other types. Intercourse and attempted intercourse cases were more often plea-bargained than noncontact or fondling cases, but type 1 cases (anal penetration or oral-genital contact) were most often plea-bargained. A larger percentage of these cases are settled with guilty pleas to original charges than the percentage of several other types, but even more fondling cases are handled in this way. Although there are few cases where the defendant was found incompetent to stand trial, this disposition was given in over 20% of the cases based on nontouching offenses. Perhaps most striking of all in the Florida jurisdiction (but not testable in the others) is the fact that over 40% of the alleged intercourse and attempted intercourse cases presented to the prosecutor were not charged and nearly as many anal penetration or oral-genital contact cases (35%) were not charged.

Looking at the larger, eight-jurisdiction sample, and considering only the cases that were filed and not subsequently dropped, there were also significant differences in how the prosecutors proceeded with cases of the different types (χ^2 = 15.9, p < .01, see Figure 5.6). Of the oral-genital contact and anal-penetration cases that remained in the caseload, the vast preponderance were plea-bargained. Of the fondling cases remaining in the system, disposition was fairly evenly split between guilty pleas to original and to negotiate charges. The pattern was similar for the nontouching offense cases. And even the intercourse and attempted intercourse cases are divided in this way, although with these, a slightly larger proportion was plea-bargained.

Case type was also cross-tabulated with sentence categories. Although results were, in general, equivocal, one relationship is

FIGURE 5.6
Case Type by Prosecution Routes

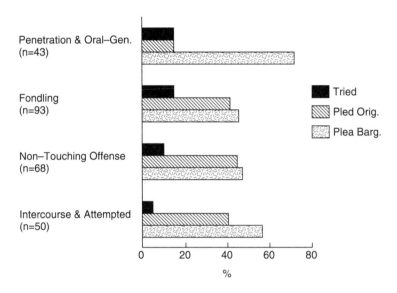

very clear. Defendants who pled guilty to, or were convicted at trial of, intercourse or attempted intercourse were more likely go to jail. Nearly 62% of the defendants who were convicted of intercourse or attempted intercourse were incarcerated, as against 43% who were convicted of other types of offenses ($\chi^2 =$ 4.39, $\rho < .05$, see Figure 5.7).

MEDICAL EVIDENCE

Not surprisingly, the existence of medical evidence affected what happens to cases of sexual abuse in the legal system in these jurisdictions. However, this effect was not on case processing decisions, but on sentence categories. When all sentence categories are considered, lack of medical evidence, suggestive medical evidence, and definitive medical evidence are associated with significantly different levels of each option ($\chi^2 = 29.6$, $\rho < .001$), but again the difference lies primarily in incarceration levels. When there was no evidence found in medical examinations, 42.1% of the defendants were sentenced to at least some jail time. When an examination uncovered suggestive evidence of abuse, 77.6%

FIGURE 5.7

Incarceration Rates for Defendants Convicted of Intercourse and Other Offenses

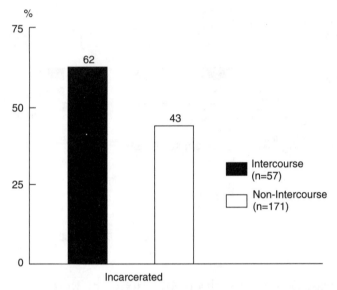

of the defendants went to jail. When there was definitial evidence of abuse, 82.1% of the defendants went to jail (see Figure 5.8, $\chi^2 = 12.0$, $p < .01$).[4]

Somewhat less obvious than the relationship of medical evidence to case disposition and sentencing, is why the mere presence of a medical examination should predict case outcome, especially given that almost two-thirds of these exams show no evidence of trauma. Nonetheless, there were statistical differences in sentencing between those cases where the child received an examination and those in which she did not (see Table 5.5). Perhaps this fact can in part be explained by hindsight bias. That is, if someone was concerned enough at the time of the allegation to take the child for an exam, then the jury or judge reasons in retrospect that the exam must have been warranted, regardless of outcome. The major difference between cases with an exam and those without is in levels of incarceration. Seventy-five percent of defendants whose victims received medical exams were sent to jail, but only 55.4% of the defendants whose victims received no exam were sentenced to jail ($\chi^2 = 8.7$, $p < .05$).

FIGURE 5.8
Incarceration For Cases With and Without Medical Evidence

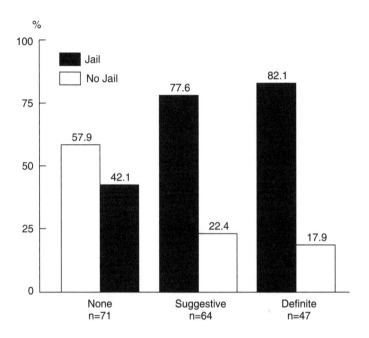

TABLE 5.5
Incarceration Rates for Cases With and Without Medical
Examination *(n = 228)*

Examination	Incarceration %	
	Yes	*No*
Yes	75.0	25.0
No	55.4	44.6

TABLE 5.6
Prison Terms for Different Prosecution Routes (n = 68)*

Term (years)	% Pled Guilty to Original Charges	% Plea Bargained	% Tried
>5	72.0	43.6	33.3
5–10	16.0	25.6	–
10–15	8.0	12.8	–
15–20	–	10.3	–
20–25	–	2.6	–
25–30	–	2.6	–
30–35	–	–	–
35–40	4.0	–	–
40–45	–	2.6	–
>45	–	–	66.7
Total %	100	100	100

*Prison Term information was unavailable for most cases, either because it was not recorded in the prosecutor's record, was determined at a separate hearing not attended by data collectors, or because the case had not terminated when data collection for this study ended.

Although the path that was followed in prosecuting these cases—whether they were charged, plea-bargained, decided with guilty pleas to original charges, or tried—was not significantly related to the type of sentence conferred, if incarceration was included in the sentence, the prosecution route taken *was* related to the actual duration of the prison term (see Table 5.6).

CRIMINAL HISTORY

The factor that is most related to different patterns of case handling is a history of prior criminal charges against the defendant (x^2 = 22.7, p < .001, see Figure 5.9). (While this history may include other child sexual abuse crimes, all crimes for which the defendant had been charged and the charge

FIGURE 5.9

Prosecution Routes for Defendants With and Without Criminal Histories

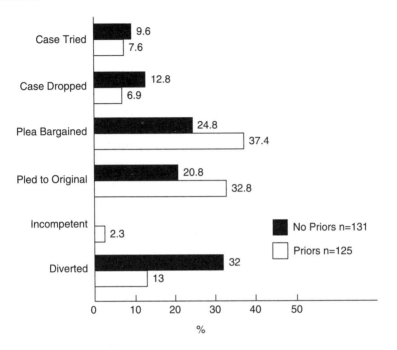

reflected in the prosecutor's case record were included in this initial analysis. Information was not always available, but it appears that about three-quarters of these prior charges resulted in convictions). This link with prior crimes raises the issue of formal versus informal judicial philosophy and procedures. In the criminal justice system, the criminal history of the defendant is to be taken into account in sentencing, but "prior bad acts," including prior convictions, are generally limited in their use at trial (Liles & Bulkley, 1985). The extent to which they are admissible varies from state to state. Some states do allow such evidence under some circumstances, though the fact-finder (judge or jury) is not supposed to assume that a defendant is likely to have committed the current crime based on past criminal history. In addition, some prosecutors will say that a prior criminal record influences their willingness to plea-bargain with the defendant and vice versa.

Among the data from this study, however, the association between prior criminal history and current case processing is strong. With the exception of trials and incompetent defendants, (in the percentage of cases proceeding to trial, there was only a small difference between cases in which defendants had a criminal history and those in which they did not—7.6% versus 9.6%—and only three defendants found incompetent to stand trial), all other avenues of prosecution were applied disproportionately to the two groups of defendants.

Some of these differences have validity, at least on their face. For instance, far fewer cases were diverted to treatment when the defendant had criminal charges in his past (13% versus 32%). Only 5.7% were diverted when the prior charges were related to child sexual abuse, and even fewer when the prior charges were felonies. The apparent chronicity of the abusive behavior mitigated against a disposition of treatment over prosecution, as might be expected. Also, fewer cases were dropped when there was a criminal history (6.9% versus 12.8%), indicating either that these cases were more clear-cut, or perhaps that the prosecutor tried harder to make the case when there was a history of criminal charges. However, a closer look reveals that 7.5% of the defendants with sex-related charges had their cases dropped versus only 6.3% of the defendants with other charges in their past. This difference, though small, is in an unanticipated direction. It is likely that there were unusual factors involved in these cases, but it is disturbing to believe that repeat child sex abuse offenders may be dropped from the criminal justice system under any circumstances.

Far more cases involving defendants with prior charges than those without previous charges were disposed of with guilty pleas to original charges (32.8% versus 20.8%). These figures lend credence to the hypothesis that the cases against second and subsequent offenders in this data set were stronger than those against first-time offenders. The situation was similar in some respects for negotiated pleas (37.4% of those with prior charges pled guilty to reduced charges versus 24.8% of those with no criminal record). The speculation that the nonsex crimes were regarded as particularly serious does not hold up as we progress with the analysis, however, if we assume that certain decisions, such as whether to plead guilty, are driven more by system characteristics than defendant characteristics. While 40% of those charged for other than sex crimes plea-bargained and only 34% of those previously charged with sex crimes plea-bargained (nonsex crime charges in one's past led to the highest rate of plea-bargaining), the percentage of cases in which the defendant pled guilty *to the full set of charges* was considerably higher for defendants with previous sex-related charges (41.5%) than for those with other charges (27.5%). An explanation for this is that defendants with prior convictions, especially for sex crimes, can expect lengthier sentences, especially if they go to trial. Prosecutors may be able to, and often do, in some jurisdictions, amend charges to add more if a defendant does not plead guilty as charged. Thus, there is often greater incentive for a defendant with prior convictions to plead guilty and not risk receiving an even longer maximum sentence.

We see that suspected repeat offenders' cases are not dropped or diverted readily, and very few cases of any description go to trial. These cases must, then, be "pled out." If the state cannot obtain a plea to the original charge, it will negotiate. It is notable, however, that the differences between the three groups (no prior charges, charges for other than sex crimes, and charges for sex crimes) are as significant ($\chi^2 = 28.5$, $p < .001$), as those between defendants with prior charges and those without. This finding hints at the intricacy of prosecutor discretion in these cases.

A history of "priors" also affected the type of sentence received by the defendants, as is intended by the legal system. (In jurisdictions with determinate sentencing, some of these differences are required.) Virtually all the possible types of sentences were given disproportionately to defendants with a criminal history, but telescoping the data into two factors—whether the defendant was ordered to treatment or not, and whether he went to jail or not—shows the differences most clearly. Approximately half the convicted defendants with no prior affiliation with the criminal system went to jail (50.4%). However, over three-quarters of the defendants with criminal histories (78.4%) were incarcerated ($\chi^2 = 20.7$, $p < .001$; see Figure 5.10). Con-

FIGURE 5.10

Incarceration for Defendants With and Without Criminal
Histories

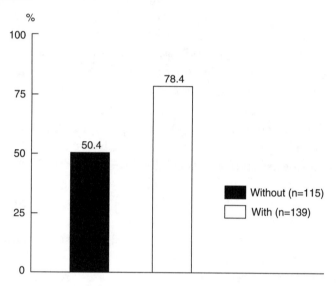

versely, 45.2% of those without previous contact with the criminal justice system were ordered to treatment, while only 29.5% of
those with prior contact were sent to treatment ($x^2 = 6.04$, $\rho <$
.05; see Figure 5.11). Only the outcome of the jail versus no-jail
factor was significantly different when prior charges were di-
chotomized into sex crimes and all other charges ($x^2 = 16.6$, $\rho <$
.001). The differences are in the expected direction. Those going
to jail were 36.4% of those without previous charges, 44.6% of
those with nonsex–related charges in their past, and 66.7% of
those with previous sexual abuse charges on their records ($n =$
269). Within the group that went to jail, however, there were no
significant differences between those without prior charges,
those with sexual abuse charges, and those with other charges in
the amount of time they were sentenced to serve. All these
subgroups were within short range of the overall mean prison
term of 9.79 years.

FIGURE 5.11
Proportion Sentenced to Treatment: Defendants With and
Without Criminal Histories

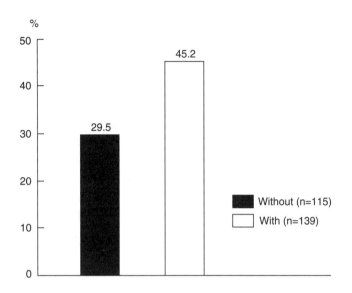

SUMMARY

Prosecutor discretion is evident in the processing decisions made
on the cases in these eight jurisdictions. In general, cases where
the victim was older were taken further in the legal system. They
were more likely to be retained after initial referral, and to be
resolved by guilty pleas to the all charges, (although less likely to
go to trial). However, cases diverted out of the criminal system
were disposed of in this manner for reasons other than the
victim's age.

Decisions regarding case processing were related to the race
of the defendant, with black defendants' cases on average receiving harsher treatment, particularly black defendants with a prior
criminal history. These decisions were associated with the relationship between the offender and his victim to the extent that
extra-family abusers were retained in the system more often and
longer, and their cases tried with more frequency.

The type of case, although related to abuser-victim relationship, race of the defendant, and the victim's age, was also related
to case processing in somewhat predictable ways, the more

serious offenses receiving the most extreme processing. However, the preponderance of "serious" cases among the not-filed group is a concern.

This discretion appears to operate on at least three "tracks." Prosecutors are making some decisions based on a justice criterion. Here, the question is asked: "Does the societal response fit the alleged crime?" Evidence that this standard comes into play is the fact that case processing seems to be related, at least in part, to the details of the case: the type of abuse committed, for instance. The relationship of the victim's age to case processing does not support this criterion, however, as the general pattern of more attention given to cases with older children would go against a common notion of abuse of young children being more devastating than abuse to older children. Instead, the pattern with regard to victim age seems a point to a second criterion for discretionary choices—the legal case, that is, the likelihood that the case can be successfully prosecuted. Also supporting this as a criterion are the findings regarding medical evidence and prior charges (although this last category is more problematic). Consideration of criminal history, however, begins to bleed into the third criterion for discretion: prediction of future offense. Another factor shown to be related to prosecutor decisions that suggests this utilitarian motive is the relationship between victim and perpetrator—particularly the intra-/extra-family status of this relationship. As mentioned earlier, however, this reasoning may reflect more bias than fact.

6

The Trials:
What Did Jane Q. Public
See from the
Courtroom Pew?

It originally seemed that chronicling the innovative procedural reforms that were used in jury trails would tell the "real
story" of child sexual abuse cases in the criminal justice system.
There was much interest in these innovations at the time the
study began (Whitcomb, Shapiro, and Stellwagen, 1985; Eatman
and Bulkley, 1986). The general belief was that many prosecuted
cases went to trial and even, perhaps, that more should. Many
concerned citizens thought that children must be protected from
the almost certain trauma of the adversarial process as it was
then constituted. Participating in a process designed for adults,
being asked questions that they don't understand, being taken to
task for their developmentally appropriate answers, having to
recount painful details of their abuse, and—most important—
having to do all of this in the presence of the person who

victimized them were cited over and over again as re-abuse of the child, and child advocates of many disciplines seized on these courtroom reforms as the answer to this "travesty." But just as the legal system knew little about children prior to the influx of child sexual abuse cases, so did the child advocates know little about the legal system. With some important exceptions, what the child supporters and even some lawyers in the prosecutors' offices would agree are progressive, humane, and essential accommodations of the judicial system to the needs of child victims, were requested rarely, used minimally, and generally distrusted in practice.

PROCEDURAL REFORM

Although in slightly different combinations, each jurisdiction in the study site already had, prior to the data-collection year, statutory provisions for most of the innovative prosecutorial techniques that have been advocated across the country in recent years. Of those techniques for which the jurisdictions have statutory authority, however, they reported using only some of them. By 1987, when data collection for the full study began, even fewer of these procedural reforms were generally thought to be useful and were in frequent use, at least in the jurisdictions studied in this research.

For instance, the wording of the truthfulness oath that witnesses must take can be modified for child witnesses on a case-by-case basis to ensure their comprehension, and this has been called for by many reformers (Dziech & Schudson, 1989). An example of this modification is that the child witness would be asked to "promise" to tell the truth, rather than "solemnly swear," which could either be not comprehended by the child at all, or misconstrued if she had been taught not to "swear." However, this modification was carried out in observed trials in only three jurisdictions: in from 30% to 66% of the cases for which the information was recorded (see Table 6.1 for data on reforms used in each jurisdiction). Except in San Francisco, the courts made this exception not as a matter of course for young witnesses, but only when they felt it was especially needed.

Videotaped and closed-circuit televised testimony are practices that were and are receiving a great deal of attention across the country, and in some circles they had come to be thought of as the main reform necessary to protect child witnesses from system-induced trauma. Battles have been fought over the constitutionality of separating the accused from the accuser, which is the intent of electronically transmitted testimony. The reasoning behind advocating for these technological aids is that for the child, being witnessed by others in the courtroom, particularly the defendant, is the intimidating feature of testifying. Six of the eight jurisdictions surveyed for this study had produced legislation allowing closed-circuit testimony (usually taking place in the judge's chambers) and seven had laws allowing videotaped testimony (St. Louis did not allow closed-circuit TV testimony, and Dallas allowed neither). However, a videotaped deposition was taken in only one case during the entire data collection year. This took place in Dallas, where 11 other trials were observed in which no videotaped depositions were included in the proceedings. Similarly, closed-circuit television was used only once in eight jurisdictions during the entire year, as well. This happened in Johnson County, Kansas, where the particular arrangement was one-way closed-circuit testimony; that is, the defendant was not visible to the child during this testimony. (There is a provision in use in some jurisdictions in which the child can see the defendant on the monitor, sometimes referred to as two-way closed-circuit testimony.)

Why videotape and closed circuit television are used so infrequently is not entirely clear. Whenever they are proposed, these techniques are virtually certain to be challenged by defense counsel. In *Maryland v. Craig* (*110 S.Ct. 3157 [1990]*), the U.S. Supreme Court upheld the use of "one-way" closed-circuit television testimony of child witnesses, so long as case-specific findings of necessity are made. Nonetheless, several prosecutors in these jurisdictions said closed-circuit televised testimony was a technique of last resort, and that they believed that a "live" witness was far superior to an image on a small screen from another room—or worse, from another time, as is the case with videotaped depositions.

It is widely believed that permitting other witnesses to testify regarding statements made by the child outside of court, i.e., hearsay, is extremely useful in prosecuting child sexual abuse cases. While there is a general prohibition against admitting hearsay in trials, many exceptions have been developed over time. Two categories of hearsay exception are mentioned most frequently as applicable to child sexual abuse cases—excited utterance (or spontaneous declarations) and special statutory hearsay exceptions for statements by children about abuse. A spontaneous declaration is a statement made by a child to another person about what happened to her under the stress of excitement from the event, that is not prompted by questioning. This is also referred to as *outcry, res gestae,* or *excited utterance.*[1] These exceptions are more commonly used, and were allowed by all of the study jurisdictions at the time the study began, since they are long-standing traditional exceptions available for use with witnesses generally. Judge Charles Schudson points out that the courts have recently expanded the traditional excited utterance exceptions in child sexual abuse cases (Dziech & Schudson, 1989). According to Judge Schudson, the requirement of immediacy of the outcry (after the assault) has been relaxed and the child's first disclosure, regardless of temporal distance from the event, is often allowed under this exception. Almost every respondent to the preliminary survey identified the admissibility of spontaneous declarations as the most useful procedural innovation for prosecuting these cases. Special statutory hearsay exceptions specifically for child abuse cases are a more recent development, and generally allow a broader range of statements made outside of court by a child to be admitted into evidence. These exceptions exist in all of the study jurisdictions except Dallas, New Orleans, and San Francisco.

During the actual study period, hearsay was relied upon moderately by the prosecutors. Hearsay in the form of spontaneous declarations was observed in from one to four cases in each of the jurisdictions, representing from slightly under half of the monitored trials per jurisdiction to almost all. Just over half (15/28) of all the observed cases used this type of evidence. Statements admitted pursuant to special statutory hearsay exceptions were used less often, only 8 times in the 30 observed cases.

Several accommodations to the linguistic differences in children's and adult's speech have been widely endorsed by child advocates, and do not require legislative changes in order to be employed. One of these accommodations is that language is scaled down (made less technical or complex) for the child witnesses when they are asked about sexual acts and body parts. The proportion of cases in which this adjustment was made ranged from a quarter of the cases in one jurisdiction to all of the cases in another jurisdiction, but the number of cases that went to trial in these locations during a year's period was so small that the proportions might not hold up over a more extended time. In the data-collection year, 20 out of 36 trials made this linguistic accommodation to the child witnesses. In addition, anatomically complete dolls are sometimes allowed in order to facilitate the child's recounting of the abuse. However, this technique was resorted to only once per jurisdiction, except in New Orleans, where the dolls were used in three out of four cases (where observers were present) and information was recorded on this item. This is curious, as there was so much reliance on anatomical dolls reported at the preliminary survey. Whether the use of the dolls was actually greater during this earlier period, and whether this was due to the enthusiasm attendant to a new technique, or whether the dolls have proved problematic because of defense challenges or other reasons is unclear.[2] It is also possible that preliminary survey respondents were reporting doll use in investigative interviews, rather than trials themselves.

Modifying the physical environment of the courtroom to reduce formality and intimidation—for example, making the witness chair smaller for the child—was permitted in seven of the jurisdictions (all but St. Louis), according to the preliminary survey interviews. During the actual study period, the physical environment of the courtroom was perceived by observers as having been modified to help the child to feel more comfortable in at least one case in every jurisdiction (even St. Louis), resulting in 10 out of 32 cases in which such modifications were made.

By law, seven of the eight jurisdictions in the study did not require children to appear at the grand-jury hearing—all but Johnson County, Kansas—but only one jurisdiction reported always exempting the child, and two said they seldom or never do. According to at least one of the prosecuting attorneys interviewed, however, testifying before the grand jury can be a good experience for the child, allowing her to become comfortable recounting the alleged abuse without the defendant being present. In practice, excusing the child from appearing at the grand jury hearing was not widespread. The child was not required to appear before the grand jury in observed cases only in Louisville and Dallas—four cases out of a total of fourteen.

Another way of lessening intimidation of the child witness is to keep attorneys at a particular distance during questioning. Dallas and Louisville did not do this at the time they were surveyed in preparation for the study, but the other six jurisdictions had established such a distance for some of their cases. In four of the jurisdictions where observers viewed trials, attorneys were kept at a distance of six feet from the children while questioning them. This happened in both of the cases observed and recorded in San Francisco, half of the cases in Kansas City and St. Louis, and—in contrast to the preliminary survey data—2 out of 12 in Dallas. (Observers were not always able to determine whether this practice was in effect or not). In all, only 7 cases out of 32 were noted as honoring this distance.

Using leading questions has been a tool, particularly with young children, to assist them in giving a consistent, detailed, chronologically correct accounting of something that happened to them. Although children have not been shown to be much less accurate or reliable in their accounts than adults, they are not facile at free recall (Goodman, et al., 1987). Therefore, the use of some leading questions on direct examination of the child witness has been advocated. New Orleans reported not permitting this kind of questioning at the time of the preliminary survey, but all of the other jurisdictions allowed leading questions during direct examination of the child witness. This technique was reported in the preliminary survey not to be used automatically, but only when deemed necessary. During the study period, leading questions were allowed on direct examination in at least half of the cases in each of the jurisdictions where trials were observed that is, nearly two-thirds of the total observed cases.

There are many programs that supply attorneys (e.g., Guardians *ad litem*, Law Guardians), trained volunteers (e.g., Court Appointed Special Advocates—CASAs), or other advocates (e.g., Victim Witness Advocates) for child abuse cases. These individuals are charged with guarding the child's rights, and offering support to the child during the proceedings. All jurisdictions except New Orleans and San Francisco had such a program. All the study jurisdictions also allowed an unofficial support person for the child (parent, relative, or therapist) in the courtroom, according to prosecutors interviewed in the preliminary survey to the study, and all reported that there was a support person present in *every* case in their jurisdiction.

In observed trials, however, child victim advocates were used in Jacksonville, Louisville, and Kansas City, only. Although in Jacksonville and Louisville these advocates were used most of the time, in Kansas City they were used only once. Other support persons were allowed more often in these cases. Cases in all the observed jurisdictions except New Orleans had some type of support person for the child present in the courtroom in at least one of their cases, but such support persons were obvious to the observers in a total of only 16 of 34 cases. It is possible that child advocates were present in many other cases and were just not apparent to the observers because they were not seen interacting with the child.

At the time of the preliminary survey, expert witnesses were allowed in all the jurisdictions to testify on selected aspects of sexual abuse in general, to provide developmental information to compare normal behavior patterns with those of a child who was sexually abused, or to provide testimony that explains the child victim's behavior after the event. According to representatives from the prosecutors' offices, experts were not used in every case for all three of these purposes, not for even one of these purposes per case at the time the study began.

In actual practice in the volunteer-observed cases, expert witnesses were indeed used infrequently. In from only one-sixth to almost one-fourth of the cases, were experts used to testify on certain aspects of child sexual abuse, to provide developmental information that would facilitate comparison of normal behavior patterns with those of children who had been sexually abused, or to provide testimony to explain the child's behavior after the event, such as keeping the abuse a secret, or recanting.

When a case of child sexual abuse goes to trial, the child victim's privacy usually can be assured by statute or by the judge, although the Supreme Court held in the Globe Newspaper Case (457 U.S. 596 [1982]) that the constitution guarantees a public trial, and that the courtroom may be closed only upon a particularized showing of necessity. Six of the prosecutors interviewed for this study (those from all jurisdictions except Johnson County and Louisville) stated that excusing spectators from the courtroom during the child's testimony was possible in their jurisdiction, but only three of the jurisdictions reported always closing the courtroom during the child's testimony. Another way to protect the child victim's privacy is to ensure that the media not divulge the child's identity in covering the story. All but two jurisdictions had provisions for ensuring confidentiality, and most said they used this authority all of the time. Where there is no official ability to restrict the media from divulging the child witness' identity, it was reported that the media take it upon themselves to protect the child's identity.

In contrast to reported usage prior to the data-collection year, limiting public access to the courtroom both in general and when the child testifies, and assuring that the media not divulge the identity of the child victim witness, were rarely used in these jurisdictions in the cases the volunteers observed (1 out of 27 cases, 2 out of 25 cases, and 9 out of 27 cases, respectively). An exception is Jacksonville, where the child's identity is kept private by the media in all cases.

Although it might not always have been possible for a volunteer observer to determine that a particular technique was requested or desired by the prosecutor if it was *not* eventually used, this was an area that volunteers were particularly sensitive to, and they therefore made a special effort to collect this data.

Nonetheless, only six instances were recorded in which permission to use an innovative procedure was denied, in only two sites (see Table 6.2), and only one technique was requested and refused more than once (two cases). That request was for the court to order the media not to reveal the identity of the child victim in accordance with available statutory authority. These requests were denied on the basis of technicalities.

It is safe to say that, in these eight jurisdictions, commonly described procedural reforms have made little difference in child sexual abuse cases that go to jury trial. There is considerable discrepancy between the techniques people reported they used and found helpful during the preliminary survey to the study and what they actually used in observed cases. There are several possible reasons for this disparity. Requesting certain of these procedural innovations may require the advance preparation of appropriate motions and supporting memoranda and/or affidavits. Prosecutors may not have the time or assistance from aides or law clerks to prepare these documents. Furthermore, the controversial nature of many of these techniques increases the risk for appeals and reversals of convictions, making them less attractive to the prosecutor. Prosecutors may overestimate the difficulty of getting such procedures accepted by judges in their courtrooms. In this study sample, there were relatively few instances of refusals from judges. Or the problem may be lack of knowledge and experience. For instance, prosecutors may believe they cannot seek admission of hearsay statements without changes in the rules of evidence, when, according to Dziech and Schudson, existing exceptions would allow the evidence, if appropriate arguments were made and foundation laid (Dziech & Schudson, 1989).

Many prosecutors claim that the most effective way to prosecute the cases is the conservative way—no new rules, no "bells and whistles," just convincing testimony by the child, on the stand in the courtroom, possibly bolstered by an expert witness. However, in some study jurisdictions where very young victims are disqualified, and experts rarely allowed, it would seem that procedural reforms are worth considering.

TABLE 6.1
Use of Innovative Prosecution Techniques

Site	N Used/N Observed Cases
Modification of Oath Wording	
San Francisco	2/3
Jacksonville	2/5
Kansas City	–
St. Louis	–
Dallas	3/10
New Orleans	0/3
Louisville	0/4
Baltimore	–
	7/25
Closed-Circuit TV Testimony	
Kansas City	1/4
San Francisco	0/3
Jacksonville	0/6
St. Louis	0/1
Dallas	0/12
New Orleans	0/1
Louisville	0/4
Baltimore	–
	1/31

TABLE 6.1 (Continued)
Use of Innovative Prosecution Techniques

Site	N Used/N Observed Cases

Child Cannot See Defendant on Monitor

Kansas City	¹/₁
San Francisco	⁰/₁
Jacksonville	⁰/₆
St. Louis	⁰/₄
Dallas	⁰/₁₆
New Orleans	⁰/₄
Louisville	⁰/₄
Baltimore	–
	¹/₃₆

Videotaped Depositions and Statements

Dallas	¹/₁₂
Kansas City	⁰/₂
San Francisco	⁰/₂
Jacksonville	⁰/₆
St. Louis	⁰/₁
New Orleans	–
Louisville	⁰/₄
Baltimore	–
	¹/₂₇

TABLE 6.1 (Continued)
Use of Innovative Prosecution Techniques

Site	N Used/N Observed Cases

Permitted Hearsay (Spontaneous Exclamations)

San Francisco	$1/3$
Jacksonville	$4/6$
Kansas City	$4/5$
St. Louis	$1/1$
Dallas	$4/10$
New Orleans	$0/2$
Louisville	$1/1$
Baltimore	–
	$15/28$

Permitted Specific Hearsay Exception for Child Sexual Abuse

San Francisco	$0/3$
Jacksonville	$4/6$
Louisville	$2/4$
New Orleans	$0/1$
Kansas City	$1/3$
St. Louis	$1/1$
Dallas	$0/12$
Baltimore	–
	$8/30$

TABLE 6.1 (Continued)
Use of Innovative Prosecution Techniques

Site	N Used/N Observed Cases

Scaled-down Adult Language Related to Sex Acts and Body Parts

San Francisco	⅓
Jacksonville	3/6
Louisville	¼
New Orleans	2/4
Kansas City	2/4
St. Louis	2/2
Dallas	9/13
Baltimore	–
	20/36

Child Not Required to Appear Before Grand Jury

Louisville	¾
Dallas	⅕
San Francisco	0/2
Jacksonville	–
Kansas City	0/2
St. Louis	–
New Orleans	0/1
Baltimore	–
	4/14

TABLE 6.1 (Continued)
Use of Innovative Prosecution Techniques

Site	N Used/N Observed Cases

Anatomically Complete Dolls Used During Direct and Cross Examination

San Francisco	1/3
Jacksonville	1/6
Louisville	1/4
New Orleans	3/4
Kansas City	1/4
Dallas	1/11
St. Louis	0/1
Baltimore	–
	8/33

Physical Environment Modified to Reduce Formality and Intimidation

San Francisco	1/3
Jacksonville	1/6
Louisville	1/3
New Orleans	1/4
Kansas City	2/4
St. Louis	1/1
Dallas	3/12
Baltimore	–
	10/32

TABLE 6.1 (Continued)
Use of Innovative Prosecution Techniques

Site	N Used/N Observed Cases

Attorneys Kept at a Distance from the Child

San Francisco	$2/2$
Kansas City	$2/4$
St. Louis	$1/2$
Dallas	$2/12$
Jacksonville	$0/6$
Louisville	$0/3$
New Orleans	$0/3$
Baltimore	–
	$7/32$

Allowed Leading Questions on Direct Examination

San Francisco	$2/3$
Jacksonville	$3/5$
Louisville	$2/3$
New Orleans	$2/2$
Kansas City	$4/5$
St. Louis	$1/2$
Dallas	$5/10$
Baltimore	–
	$19/30$

TABLE 6.1 (Continued)
Use of Innovative Prosecution Techniques

Site	N Used/N Observed Cases
Child Victim Advocate Present	
Jacksonville	5/6
Louisville	3/4
Kansas City	1/4
San Francisco	0/3
New Orleans	0/3
St. Louis	0/1
Dallas	0/10
Baltimore	—
	9/31
Other Support Person for Child Present in Courtroom	
San Francisco	2/3
Jacksonville	2/6
Louisville	4/4
Kansas City	2/4
St. Louis	1/2
Dallas	5/11
New Orleans	0/4
Baltimore	—
	16/34

TABLE 6.1 (Continued)
Use of Innovative Prosecution Techniques

Site	N Used/N Observed Cases

Expert Witness Testified on Selected Attributes of Child Sexual Abuse

San Francisco	2/3
Jacksonville	2/6
Kansas City	2/5
St. Louis	1/1
Dallas	5/13
Louisville	0/3
New Orleans	0/3
Baltimore	–
	12/34

Expert Witness Provided Developmental Information for Comparing Normal Behavior Patterns with Those of a Child Who Was Sexually Abused

San Francisco	1/3
Jacksonville	1/6
Dallas	3/11
Kansas City	0/4
St. Louis	–
Louisville	0/3
New Orleans	0/3
Baltimore	–
	5/30

TABLE 6.1 (Continued)
Use of Innovative Prosecution Techniques

Site	N Used/N Observed Cases

Expert Witness Provided Testimony to Explain Child's Behavior After the Event

San Francisco	1/3
Jacksonville	1/6
Kansas City	1/5
Dallas	5/11
St. Louis	—
Louisville	0/3
Baltimore	—
New Orleans	0/3
	8/34

General Access of the Public to the Courtroom Limited

Dallas	1/10
San Francisco	0/3
Jacksonville	0/6
Kansas City	0/4
St. Louis	—
Louisville	0/2
New Orleans	0/2
Baltimore	—
	1/27

TABLE 6.1 (Continued)
Use of Innovative Prosecution Techniques

Site	N Used/N Observed Cases

Access to the Courtroom Limited Only While the Child Testifies

Site	N Used/N Observed Cases
Jacksonville	1/6
New Orleans	1/3
Dallas	0/9
San Francisco	0/3
Kansas City	0/2
St. Louis	–
Louisville	0/2
Baltimore	–
	2/25

Assurance Given That the Media Will Not Divulge the Identity of the Witness

Site	N Used/N Observed Cases
Jacksonville	6/6
Louisville	1/2
New Orleans	1/2
Dallas	1/10
San Francisco	0/3
Kansas City	0/4
St. Louis	–
Baltimore	–
	9/27

TABLE 6.2
Techniques Requested but Not Used

Technique	Site	N
Videotaped deposition and/or statement	Dallas	1
Attorneys kept at distance from child	Louisville	1
Leading questions allowed on direct examination of child	Louisville	1
Use of child advocate	Louisville	1
Assurance given that media would not reveal the identity of the child	Louisville	2

A DAY IN COURT

Sixty-eight days of courtroom observation of nine trials were recorded by the volunteers during which time they heard the testimony of 108 witnesses; victims, family members, eyewitnesses, character witnesses, experts, and defendants. The volunteer data-collectors were asked to rate various aspects of the day's proceedings on five-point scales with the extremes labeled. For instance, they were asked to rate the demeanor of the defendant on a continuum ranging from uneasy to confident, with three points in between. The daily impressions of the volunteer observers are of interest as examples of what average citizens would see if they attended a child sexual abuse trial.

In general, the volunteers painted a picture of sometimes-interrupted proceedings in a nearly empty courtroom, proceedings consisting of a few technical issues, presented by prosecuting and defense attorneys who were both undramatic in their demeanor. The observers did not perceive the two attorneys similarly in all respects, however. On a five-point scale from 1 (unprepared) to 5 (prepared), the prosecutor's mastery of the details of the case was rated 4.3, while the defense attorney's mastery was rated only 3.3. It is likely that this difference is at least partially due to observer bias, as volunteers tended to identify strongly with the child witness and the prosecutor's case. The judge was seen by those observers as midway between passively and actively involved in the arguments of the case. No judicial bias could be detected, on average, in favor of the prosecution or the defense.

The observers' perception of the defendants in these cases were generally unflattering. They saw them as unkempt in appearance, antisocial in character, and rated their social class standing on a scale of 1 to 5 (lower to upper) as 1.5. In general, the defendants' demeanor was rated as uneasy as opposed to confident.

Individual juror attentiveness was recorded by volunteer observers for the testimony of 18 witnesses. Neither male nor female juror attentiveness was significantly related to such characteristics of the witnesses as whether they were adults or children, whether they were called by the prosecution or the defense, or whether they were expert witnesses or not. There was no difference between the attention given to the witnesses by males and that given by females. Overall female juror attentiveness was rated as 1.74 on a three-point scale from 1 (extra attentive) to 3 (inattentive), overall male juror attentiveness as 1.73.

COMPETENCY EXAMINATIONS OF CHILD WITNESSES

Since the landmark Supreme Court case of *Wheeler v. United States* (*159 U.S. 523, 524-26[1895]*), the test for the competency of children as witnesses generally requires the following: a present understanding of the obligation to speak the truth; mental capacity at the time of the occurrence in question such that the child should be able to observe and register the occurrence; sufficient memory to retain independent recollection of the observations made; and capacity to translate memory into words (Melton, 1981). These concerns have been operational-

ized in recent years as the child's ability to distinguish truth from
falsehood and to understand the obligation to tell the truth
(Melton, 1981; Whitcomb, Shapiro, and Stellwagen, 1985).

In this study, the questioning of children to determine competency was observed by the volunteer data collectors in 27 of
the 39 cases that went to trial in the eight jurisdictions.[3] For those
where the content was recorded, exactly half the observations
were made at separate *voir dire* hearings, and half during the trial
itself, just preceding the child's testimony. In this very small
sample, the questioning concentrated on three simple areas of
competence that Berliner and Barbieri (1984) mention. These
are the child's ability to: 1) receive and relate information
accurately; 2) understand the difference between telling the
truth and telling a lie, and 3) appreciate the necessity of telling
the truth in court. In order to test the first of these abilities, all
the children in the sample for which the information was known
were asked their first and last name, their age, their grade in
school, and the school they attended at the time. Ninety-one
percent were asked to name a person in their family, 78% were
asked to name a teacher, and 77% were asked to name a relative.
Fifty-eight percent of the children were asked to name a color,
57% and 56% each were asked to count for the interrogator and
name an item of clothing. In order to test the second and third
abilities related to competency, 87% of the children were asked if
they knew what the truth is, 86% were asked if they knew what a
lie is, and 76% were asked to explain the consequences of telling
a lie. All other questions recorded were asked less than half the
time.

The more technical criteria that are mentioned in some legal
sources—demonstration that the child had the mental capacity
at the time of the occurrence to observe and register the event
accurately, that she had memory sufficient to retain an independent recollection of the event, and that she has a present ability
to communicate this memory (American Jurisprudence, 1960)—
were not as clearly in evidence in the competency questioning of
these children. Given that these criteria are not being assessed
even when there are separate competency proceedings, and given
that most jurisdictions no longer have a child competency law,

but presume competency regardless of age, then this would seem to give credence to Dziech and Schudson's assertion that a more fitting test of competency would occur if child witnesses were simply given the opportunity to testify and the jury were given the opportunity to assess the credibility of that testimony.

Much has been made lately of the necessity of becoming aware of the differences in child and adult communication styles, skills, and even linguistic rules, and of adapting to these differences in order to increase the understanding between the child witness and the questioner (Toth and Whalen, 1987; Dziech and Schudson, 1989; Richardson, 8th National Conference on Child Abuse and Neglect, 1989). However, while this understanding and adaptation may serve the interests of fairness, and therefore the interests of the court and society (represented by the judge and jury), it may serve the adversarial purposes of the prosecution more than those of the defense. This would be true particularly in the competency hearing. There, the prosecution has an interest in the child's understanding the questions asked of her and answering them appropriately, where the defense's interest sometimes can be just the opposite.

In this study, the prosecutor's, defense attorney's, and the judge's style during the competency questioning was rated by the observers as either appropriate for questioning a child or more appropriate for questioning an adult. The prosecutor's style was rated as appropriate for a child 95% of the time; the judge's style was considered to be appropriate 93% of the time. The defense attorney's style was seen as appropriate for communicating with a child only 78% of the time.

The attitude toward the child conveyed by those she encounters in court is a somewhat different matter from that of the linguistic fit between their questions and the witness's age, but these issues are related, in that the child-centered approach benefits the prosecution's case more than it does the defense—or at least, that is what was assumed until recently. John Crewdson (1988) quotes a defense attorney giving advice to his colleagues at a seminar in California several years ago, about handling child sexual abuse cases:

Children are insidious liars, and they're practical liars. They are the best. They can lie at the drop of a hat. In order to effectively discredit a child, you want to know about the child's history. You want to know about people who don't like the child—want to know what those people have to say about the child—subpoena the school records. Then insist upon your right of confrontation, insist that you must be able to cross-examine this child in an adversarial atmosphere. That's what a trial is all about. I find that children do not have real good memories, and to show that these children do not have real good memories, I ask them about specific occurrences in their life, such as their birthday, Valentine's Day, and so forth. I ask them where they were and what they did on that day, and I try to show that they really don't know any of these things. Give wings to the child's imagination, if it's a young child especially. Be prepared to show through your cross-examination that the child has a vivid imagination, that it's very suggestible. Be prepared to lead the child into a situation that could not possibly occur. What you want to project is the feeling that this particular child cannot be trusted to tell the truth. (p. 167)

This attitude was not so unusual at the time these things were said. There is some evidence that defense tactics have softened

FIGURE 6.1
Questioning Style Age-Appropriate to Child During Competency Exam

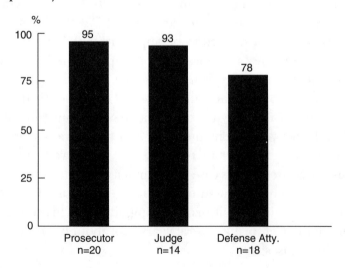

somewhat for fear that their confrontational style would engender sympathy for the child and hurt the defendant's case. Consider these words from one of the defense attorneys in the McMartin Preschool case who, although in his official role would not be considered a child advocate, nevertheless understands the utility of not bullying the witness:

> If you have any experience with kids, you don't have to give a hardened look to get whatever information you want out of them. You don't have to be tricky. It's best to be as straightforward and simple as possible. If you're going to do it in front of the jury, I mean what's the value of attacking the child in front of the jury? You're going to run the risk of angering some jurors . . . when there's no jury, the judge is going to stop you, in most cases. . . . In those cases, in the rare case where it does happen, I would say I'm sure it backfires. (Hechler, pp. 336, 337)

Observers were given four choices of descriptor for the attorney's and judge's manner toward the child during competency questioning in this study. The prosecutor's manner was rated as supportive of the child 75% of the time and businesslike the other 25% of the time. The judge was rated as supportive in 63% of the cases and businesslike in 37% of the cases. The defense attorney's manner was considered to be supportive 61% of the time, businesslike 33% of the time, and condescending 6% of the time. It is interesting that no one but the defense attorney was perceived as being condescending, but the figures for the judge, defense lawyers, and prosecutor are not significantly different.

CHILD WITNESS TESTIMONY

Virtually all the children who underwent competency questioning were allowed to testify (which cast further doubt on the utility of separate competency questioning for children). The testimony of 70 child witnesses in 41 cases was observed by the volunteer data-collectors.[4] They recorded their observations of the conditions surrounding the testimony and the behavior of the child during testimony, both when questioned specifically about the abuse and when questioned about other matters, on a checklist that supplied multiple choices for their response. Although this limited the information gathered, it also standardized it to an extent, and simplified the recording so as to allow for more intense observation.

Most children (91%) testified from the witness stand. They were usually questioned from between half and hour and one hour (63%), although a third of the children were questioned for longer than an hour, and two children testified as long as four hours. In 61% of the cases, there was at least one interruption in the child's testimony (i.e., times that the child left and returned to the stand, or lawyers approached the bench to clarify procedure with the judge).

Observations of the child were made both when the child was questioned about the sexual abuse and when she was questioned about other matters, and separate ratings were made during questioning by the prosecutor and by the defense attorney. The child witness' facial expression during questioning was usually rated as serious. This is true for 68% of the witnesses when they were questioned by the prosecutor about the abuse, and for 62% of the witnesses when they were questioned by the prosecutor about other matters. Even more of the children wore a serious expression when questioned by the defense attorney: 78% of the witnesses when they were dealing with questions about the abuse, and 75% of the witnesses when they were being questioned about other matters.

The child witnesses largely avoided eye contact with the defendant. This was most pronounced when they were being questioned by the prosecutor about the sexual abuse incidents. During those questions, the witnesses avoided looking at the defendant in 65% of the cases, and avoided eye contact intermittently in another 9% of the cases. The witness avoided eye contact with the defendant completely in 62% of the cases while being questioned about matters other than the sexual abuse. When the defense attorney was questioning the child, the witness avoided eye contact with the defendant somewhat less. When the questions were about the abuse, she avoided eye contact completely in 50% of the cases, and intermittently in 12%

of the cases. When questioned about other matters, she also avoided looking at the defendant in 50% of the cases, and intermittently in 14% of the cases.

Although we might imagine child witnesses to be "fidgety" or frozen in their behavior while testifying, in fact their motor behavior was rated as being more or less normal. The child was relatively still, but not rigid or immobilized in 75% of the cases when questioned by the prosecutor about sexual abuse behaviors and in 87% of the cases when questioned about other matters. While being questioned by the defense attorney, 83% of the child witnesses were relatively still while they were being questioned about sex abuse, 84% when being questioned about other matters.

The child witnesses' verbal behavior was rated as normal, as well, although more so when questioned by the prosecutor rather than the defense attorney, and more so when dealing with matters other than the abuse. When the prosecutor was interviewing the child about the sexual abuse, answering behavior was rated as normal in 65% of the cases and hesitant in 35%; when the questioning was about other matters, it was normal in 84% of the cases and hesitant in 16%. When the interview was the defense attorney, 60% of the children answered normally when asked about the abuse, and 40% answered hesitantly. In response to other matters, 74% answered normally, and 25% answered hesitantly.

The child's emotional behavior tended to be rated as either normal, or flat (with little affect), although there were some children who cried during their testimony. When questioned by the prosecutor about sexual abuse, a third of the child witnesses showed an abnormal lack of affect; slightly more of them (36%) were seen as normal in their affect. Fourteen percent of the witnesses were crying during these questions. When questioned about other matters by this same prosecutor, 52% were rated as showing normal emotional behavior, and 24% as having flat affect. Ten percent of the witnesses were crying at some time during these questions. When the defense attorney was questioning the witnesses about the abuse, 44% of them seemed normal in their emotional behavior, 26% showed little affect, and 20% were crying. When the defense attorney's questions were not specifically about the abuse, 48% of the witnesses were rated as having normal emotional behavior, 28% were flat in their affect, and 12% were crying. As we will see in the next chapter, the child's demeanor and emotional behavior can have an effect on the outcome of the case under certain conditions; but there is some indication in the analysis that follows that jurors do not recognize this aspect of the case as being particularly influential in their decisions.

The prosecutor's questioning style toward the child was rated as 99% appropriate to the age of the child when questioning about the abuse and 98% appropriate when asking other questions. This is similar to the rating of appropriate that was given to the prosecutors in 95% of cases when conducting competency questioning. The defense attorney's style was rated as 88% appropriate to the age of the child when questioning about the abuse, and 89% appropriate when questioning on other matters. The defense attorney had been seen as less appropriate (78%) when conducting competency questioning than during the actual trial questions. This may be intentional, as the interest of the defense may be served by confusing the child in competency questioning as such confusion could result in the child's disqualification as a witness.

The attorneys' manner toward the child was also rated, as it had been during competency examinations. The prosecuting attorney was rated supportive in 68% of cases when questioning was about the abuse, and in 67% of cases when questions were about surrounding matters. Perceptions that the prosecutor's manner was other than supportive were the same whether he or she was questioning the child generally or about the abuse *per se*. Thirty percent of the time during abuse questioning, the prosecutor was seen by the observers as businesslike. That perception occurred 31% of the time in general questioning. Two percent of the time, regardless of the area of questioning, the prosecutor's manner was thought to be intimidating. The prosecutors were never perceived as being condescending or discrediting.

The defense attorney was rated very differently. When questioning the witness about the abuse, the defense attorney was rated as supportive only 30% of the time. Forty-four percent of the time, he or she was seen as businesslike, 18% of the time as condescending or discrediting, and 8% of the time as intimidating. When interviewing the child about matters other than the abuse, the defense attorney's manner was rated businesslike 44% of the time, supportive 39% of the time, condescending or discrediting 14% of the time, and intimidating 3% of the time. It is interesting that the defense attorney had been seen as more supportive during the competency questioning than in the trial proper.

The judge's questioning style toward the child was rated age-appropriate 91% of the cases and more appropriate for an adult witness in the other 9% of the cases rated. The judge's manner was seen as businesslike in 44% of the cases, and supportive in 56%.

As these ratings cannot be said to be objective, and they have not been proven to be reliable, they are useful only as indications of the perceptions of the volunteer data-collectors who, in this study, serve as "stand-ins" for the general public. As such, however, they show us a picture of testifying in court that is difficult for the child, at best. She is treated inconsistently by the attorneys questioning her and reacts to them differently. This difference in who is doing the questioning is more pronounced than the difference related to the subject of the questions. The witness uses the only means at her disposal to cope with her stress, while doing what is being asked of her; she avoids looking at the defendant, sometimes retreats into deadened affect, and occasionally breaks down in tears.[5]

These ratings were checked against conviction rates to see if the raters' perceptions of the child's demeanor and the court personnel's conduct were related to the outcome of the case. They were not. Only one item of all those dealt with showed significance, and this could easily have happened by chance.

JUROR DECISION MAKING

Although it was intended in this study to collect information from each juror serving on every trial observed by the volunteers, this proved impossible. In certain jurisdictions, the volunteers were not allowed by the judge to contact jurors. For those jurisdictions where the judge was supportive of collecting these data, speaking with the jurors was prohibited until after the trials. Jurors were sometimes sequestered until late at night, making contact by the volunteers impractical. On those occasions when the volunteers were able to be present when the jury was released, some jurors were too tired, or otherwise unwilling, to talk about their decisions. In the end, data was gathered from 108 jurors, representing 17 cases in five jurisdictions.

Jurors were asked questions about various aspects of the case (e.g., child witness' credibility, testimony of expert witness) that may or may not have influenced their decision to convict or acquit the defendant (see "Juror Questionnaire" in the Appendix). In general, most of the items were considered by them to be very influential in their decisions. Jurors were also asked, however, to give their perception of these same factors in the case in which they served as jurors. That way, it was hoped, we would have some notion of the relationship between their placing importance on something, and whether or not it had been available to them. The results suggest that certain factors seemed to be taken as important because they were present.

CHILD TESTIMONY

The child's description of the abuse was reported to be very influential in the juror's decisions (60.4% said their decision was influenced "a lot" by the ability of the witness to describe the event). The largest percentage of jurors (45.3%) also agreed with the statement that the child witness clearly described the event. Although there is a clear association between the child's ability to describe the event well, and jurors' being influenced by this description ($\chi^2 = 47.9$, $p < .001$), there were few trials in which the child was perceived as doing a poor job of describing what happened to her, making it difficult to determine how influential this inability would have been.

The perceived accuracy of the child's memory seems a bit more influential when the child is perceived as not accurate, but, again, the most reported category of response to the question, "How much was your decision as a juror influenced by the accuracy of the child's memory" was "a lot" (48.6% of the jurors), and the child's memory was perceived as accurate 43.9% of the time. The relationship between the perception of accuracy and the influence of this variable in decision making was strong ($x^2 = 48.7$, $\rho < .001$).

The pattern was strong for the child's ability to tell the truth. The child generally was considered to be truthful (52.8% of the jurors agreed with the statement, 25.5% strongly agreed), and this factor was considered by jurors to have been influential in their final decision in the case (59.4% were influenced "a lot" by the child's truthfulness, 18.9% "completely," $x^2 = 56.7$, $\rho .001$. Overall the child's ability to tell the truth was reported by this set of jurors to be more influential than any other factor they were asked about.

The pattern was less strong for the child's emotional behavior in court ($x^2 = 30.4$, $\rho < .05$), as a third of jurors were only "somewhat" influenced by this factor (33). Almost two-thirds (63.2%) agreed the child's emotional behavior in court was appropriate, and another 20.8% "strongly agreed." Interestingly, however, the relationship between the child's apparent level of preparation to testify, and the influence jurors thought this had on their decisions was not significant.

In general, then, data from these particular cases seem to show that when the child victim witness is perceived positively in any of several dimensions by jurors, this has considerable influence on their decisions to convict the defendant. There is less evidence to suggest (although certainly it may still be true) that the converse is correct; that is, if jurors perceive the child negatively, that they are equally influenced by this to vote for acquittal.

OTHER INFORMATION

Jurors were also asked about types of information other than the child victim's testimony that may or may not have been available in the case, and that 1) *may not have been important* to have, 2) *may have been somewhat important* to have, or 3) *may have been very important* to have in their opinion. The same pattern prevailed. For most items listed (9 out of 12); there was a significant relationship between the availability of the information and its importance. That is, the information was considered unimportant if it was unavailable, and important if available. The exceptions were testimony from the child's parents, which was considered to be equally *important* and *not important* when it was not available; results of psychological testing of the child, which varied in the importance given to it when it was not available; and the judge's answers to questions raised by jurors during deliberations, which were considered important to have both by jurors who got these answers, and by jurors who were denied these answers.

Although jurors occasionally remarked to the volunteer observers or noted on the questionnaires they filled out that they wished they had had a certain piece of testimony or evidence in making their decision, the results of detailed questioning about what was available to them, and what they considered influential or important, suggest that, in general, jurors were satisfied with the information given them and used it all to make their decisions. Whatever else may be going into making these decisions—such as any bias the jurors may bring to the situation—is not clear from these data, but may be suggested by looking at juror attitudes.

JUROR ATTITUDES

Although jurors were not polled consistently enough to determine the effect of attitudes on case outcome, and although contamination of attitudes may well have taken place during the trials (judges did not permit researchers to survey attitudes prior to jurors' serving on these cases), it is instructive to examine in the aggregate the post-trial attitudes held by jurors on these cases for points of bias that may have affected their deliberations.

Juror attitudes were investigated in this study with a survey, developed to measure attitudes and beliefs about various aspects of child sexual abuse. Response was indicated on a six-point scale ranging from "strongly agree" to "strongly disagree." Items were submitted to form this questionnaire by this author, Eugene Borgida and associates of Dr. Borgida at the University of Minnesota, and Ann Burgess, who is a national expert in child sexual abuse. As a group, and with the aid of attorneys at the Hennepin County (Minnesota) Attorney's Office who handle child sexual abuse cases and advocates in the Victim/Witness program in the Hennepin County Attorney's Office, we reached consensus on the response direction that indicated more favorable implications for the perceived credibility of a child witness in court for each item. For instance, respondents who agreed with item 26 ("Children can distinguish fantasy from reality") presumably maintain a belief about the cognitive abilities of children that has favorable implications for a child witness. For jurors who hold such a belief, the testimony of a child witness in a sexual abuse trial may be perceived as more credible, which in turn may strengthen the prosecution's case.

In general, there were few indications of bias evident in the jurors' responses to the attitude questionnaire administered to them after the trials, if bias is defined as a departure from the current understanding by child abuse researchers and treatment professionals of the issues covered by the questionnaire.[6] (In areas where the research and professional opinion is equivocal, a neutral average answer from the jurors is considered to be a condition of no bias, even the range of responses was considerable). The material covered by the survey can be roughly divided into five areas of interest: child abuse and the family, the child as witness, offender characteristics, prosecution of child sexual abuse and juror attitudes.

In the realm of child abuse and the family, respondents held views consistent with the research knowledge of the day with few exceptions. They agreed that parents are more likely to talk to their children about issues such as pregnancy, death, or abortion than about sexual abuse. They were close to neutral in their opinion of whether most wives whose husbands sexually abuse their child know about the abuse. They agreed that children who have always lived with their mothers are just as likely to be abused as children who have lived at some point without their mother, but on average their agreement with this statement was slight.

Consistent with current research knowledge, respondents

disagreed with the notion that child sexual abuse is more likely to occur in poor, rural families than rich, suburban families. They also disagreed with the idea that a child of a large versus an average-sized family is more likely to be sexually abused. They were nearly neutral in their opinion of whether daughters whose mothers discourage them from talking about sex more often experience sexual abuse than those whose mothers are more open about sex. Unaccountably, they did slightly agree with the statement that children who are physically abused are more likely to be sexually abused. They knew that if a child is sexually abused by a parent, the child will still show love for that parent, but they were unsure as to whether sexually abused children generally experience the same set of psychological reactions and symptoms.

Whether it was because of their experience as jurors or not, respondents to the attitude survey seemed to have a high level of accurate knowledge about children as witnesses in child sexual abuse cases. They knew with certainty that delays in reporting child abuse to the police or other authorities are quite common. They did not believe that children who retract their stories about sexual abuse were probably lying in the first place. They firmly disagreed with the concept that it would be wrong to convict someone of a crime if the only witness were a ten-year-old child. They seemed to understand that experts are only just beginning to study children's eyewitness memory. They disagreed with the view that children's memories for emotionally traumatic events are not as accurate as adults'. They did not think children are easily manipulated into giving false reports of sexual abuse, but they slightly agreed that when children identify strangers as having sexually abused them, the identifications are highly reliable. They agreed that children can distinguish fantasy from reality, and they thought children were only slightly more influenced by leading questions than adults.

One response in the area of children as witnesses that is puzzling, although technically in the same direction as current professional opinion (there is little research on this topic), is that the jurors only very slightly agreed that children are unlikely to fantasize about sexual activity with parents or other adults. It would seem that the influence of the psychoanalytic school (even that aspect of it that has been largely debunked, the theory of infantile sexuality) is still strong in the general public.

For the most part, juror respondents did not share some of the common misconceptions regarding sex offenders of children. They did not think these people were particularly dysfunctional in other areas of their lives, such as work, for instance. They did think that stepfathers are more frequently abusers than natural fathers, but as we have seen, there is professional disagreement about this fact, as well (see discussion of relationship of abuser to victim, Chapter 4). They apparently did not believe that child sexual abuse is primarily the result of frustrated adult sexual relations, as they slightly agreed with the statement that men who have incestuous relationships with their daughters are just as likely as other men to have normal sexual relationships with their wives. They seemed particularly clear on the fact that most child sexual abuse cases involve a relative or someone the child knows and trusts. On balance, respondents saw this form of child abuse as a sexual rather than a violent act. They thought that child molesters are overcome by sexual urges, but their agreement with this statement was only slight, and they did not think that sexual abusers are violent and aggressive in other relationships. Their confidence in the state of the knowledge base about child molesters was somewhat optimistic: they only very slightly disagreed with the statement that personality profiles of child molesters are highly accurate.

Most troublesome in this category, however, was the fact that the respondents to some extent subscribed to a common misinterpretation of the generational theory of child abuse. Knowing that people who abuse are very likely to have abuse in their own backgrounds, they assumed that the corollary was true: that is, that people who were abused are highly likely to repeat the behavior. They slightly disagreed with the statement: "Most people who were sexually abused as children do not end up sexually abusing their own children."

There were three questions regarding beliefs about prosecuting child sexual abuse specifically. Respondents knew that the majority of all reported child sexual abuse cases are not tried in court. They exhibited slight disagreement with the notion that courtroom trials are so stressful for children that we can't expect them to behave as competently as adults, presumably representing their belief in the competence of child witnesses. However, they put much stock in medical technology. They slightly disagreed with the statement that medical experts cannot usually tell if a child has been sexually abused based on a medical exam alone. But since only about a third of medical exams show definitive evidence of abuse, that statement actually would be correct.

Several of the questions were designed to get at attitudes rather than more factual beliefs or knowledge. Responses to these questions proved to be especially interesting. One question was designed to get at the "witch hunt" accusation: "Social workers and child protection agencies are more likely to see child sexual abuse where it does not exist than they did 20 years ago." Respondents slightly agreed with this characterization. On the other hand, respondents solidly agreed that steps must be taken to increase the conviction rate in child sexual abuse cases. There was firm agreement that there is much that should be done to ease a sexually abused child's trauma in court, and jurors disagreed with the belief that in the current social climate it is virtually impossible for a person accused of child sexual abuse to get an impartial trial. Of course, if they agreed with this statement, they would be indicating their own inability to complete the task which they were charged as jurors.

In general, juror's answers to the questions on the attitude survey were as we would want them to be: informed by the research and practice wisdom of the day, and relatively free of misconceptions that could pose some danger to the fair administration of their duties as triers of fact in these criminal proceedings. But the question remains: to what extent are these attitudes typical, or even reflective of the attitudes these individuals held when they began their tenure on the jury? Although imperfect as a comparison sample because of geographical differences, a random population survey conducted in Minneapolis, Minnesota, at the same time as this juror survey—but with a shortened version of the same questionnaire—shows the considerable discrepancy of beliefs between the general public and those who had already served on a child sexual abuse jury (see Table 6.3).

With the exception of two questions where the general public gave more informed answers, and two questions where the mean response was identical, the same pattern prevails throughout: the juror sample is better informed than the general sample. As shown in Table 6.3, the differences are not often dramatic. They are usually a matter of degree of agreement, rather than direction of response. In only one case did one sample substantially agree with a statement and the other sample disagree. This was the first question on both surveys, having to do with the level of functioning exhibited by sexual abusers in other areas of their lives such as work. The general public felt that these problems existed and would be noticeable; the juror sample did not. It is reasonable to assume that a good deal of educating of the jurors took place in the trials. Every one of the observed trials called upon expert witnesses (76% of these witnesses in 63% of the cases were called by the prosecution), and it is likely that much of the information came from these experts. How that information influenced the outcome of the case is unclear, however.

TABLE 6.3
Attitudes of General Public and Jurors Regarding Child Sexual Abuse

Item	General Public $\overline{X}$	Jurors $\overline{X}$
Q4. It is unlikely that most wives whose husbands sexually abuse their child know about this abuse.	2.6*	4.2

Q.10. Children who have always lived with their mothers are just as likely to be abused as children who have lived at some point without their mother.   3.0   2.8

Q12. Child sexual abuse is more likely to occur in poor, rural families, than rich, suburban families.   4.6   4.8

Q28. If a child is sexually abused by a parent, the child will still show love for that parent.   2.4   2.2

Q31. Sexually abused children generally experience the same set of psychological reactions and symptoms.   2.9   3.4

Q7. Children are no more influenced by leading questions than are adults.   4.4   4.3

Q13. Children who retract their stories about sexual abuse were probably lying in the first place.   4.9   4.9

Q29. Children's memories for emotionally traumatic events are not as accurate as adults'.   4.4   4.1

Q30. Delays in reporting child sexual abuse to the police or other authorities are quite common.   2.3   1.7

Q1. People who sexually abuse children are more likely to have noticeable problems functioning in other areas of their lives, such as work.   2.6   4.2

Q5. Children are much more likely to be abused by their stepfathers than by their natural fathers.   3.4   2.8

Q24. Most people who were sexually abused as children do not end up sexually abusing their own children.   4.5   4.3

Q27. In the current social climate, it is virtually impossible for a person accused of child sexual abuse to get an impartial trial.   3.7   5.0

Q6. The majority of all reported child sexual abuse cases are tried in court.   5.0   5.0

---

*Some conversion was necessary, as the jurors were instructed to answer on a six-point scale, whereas the general public were given only four possible responses (they were queried by telephone, and six potential responses was deemed too many to keep in mind while the question was read). The means here conform to a six-point response scale as follows: 1 = strongly agree; 2 = agree; 3 = slightly agree; 4 = slightly disagree; 5 = disagree; 6 = strongly disagree.

In summary, daily observation of child sexual abuse trials showed that the most touted reforms of the day were not extensively used. Jurors were, however, well informed individuals (perhaps because of expert testimony), who were satisfied with the information that they had been given to decide the cases they heard. The child witnesses were tense, and reacted differently to the different tactics used toward them by the opposing lawyers, but these witnesses were effective, and it was their truthfulness that the jurors identified as being the most helpful in making their decisions. Although these observations were enlightening, we are left nevertheless with a two major questions about child sexual abuse trials. First, if expert testimony did educate the jury, and if this education affected their decision making, then what were the specific elements of the experts' testimony that influenced the jurors? Second, what was it about the children's testimony that led jurors to believe them? What is it that signals to a jury that a child is telling the truth? Finally, is there any interaction between these two questions? That is, does the answer to one depend on the answer to the other? Because questions like these are so difficult to get at in the field, we engaged colleagues to design a mock jury study to further explore these questions and others under controlled conditions. The following chapter presents the results of this study.

7

Expert Testimony and Child Witness Credibility

Lessons from the Laboratory

Early in this field study, it was clear that there were real limits to the type of data that could be obtained from reviewing prosecutors' records and observing in court. While the advantage of studying *what is* over what *might be* is undeniable, real cases do not fall into desired categories in even numbers thereby facilitating investigation into the effects of different variables under different conditions. In order to augment the information that was coming forth from the criminal courts in this study, we sought the expertise of a scholar who had investigated similar questions to those we wanted to study in a laboratory setting, but had done so in the context of rape cases. The similarities between the issues in rape cases and in child sexual abuse cases are many, some of which were mentioned in Chapter 1. Juror misinformation and prejudice, special "rules" governing credibility, and the trauma of the victim witness in court are just a few. Two of these areas that were of particular interest in this study had been researched by Eugene Borgida and his colleagues. The first is rape trauma syndrome evidence in court (Frazier & Borgida, 1985; Frazier & Borgida, 1988; Frazier & Borgida, in press), and the other is the influence of different types of expert testimony, different levels of witness preparation, and different victim and defendant attributes on juror evaluation of rape victim credibility (Brekke & Borgida, 1988). We engaged the interest of Borgida and his team in working with us to apply their methodologies to the problem of child sexual abuse. Not all this work has been completed, but several of the studies have been, and these are particularly interesting for our purposes here.[1]

Perhaps the leading dispute surrounding child sexual abuse trials has been on the issue of the partisanship of the "experts." A major defense strategy has been to charge expert witnesses with leading the child to believe she was abused (if the expert was in an investigatory role vis-à-vis the child), or interpreting the facts of the case through a screen of belief that holds that "children never lie" (if the expert is providing testimony on sexually abused children in general), which these defense attorneys can easily show to be preposterous. They argue that the fear of child abuse has gotten out of hand and social workers, nursing counselors, psychologists, and other professionals are nothing more than child advocates, creating false allegations of abuse by their leading interviewing techniques. A psychologist who testifies frequently as a defense expert is quoted in a popular women's magazine as saying: "Once a professional believes a child has been abused, everything becomes evidence to support that belief. If the children deny initially, that's because they have to keep it secret. If they admit and then deny, that's because they are confused, and it means they were abused. If they deny, admit, and then retract, that's evidence that they were abused. Like Freudian and Marxist theory, nothing can count against the allegation of abuse" (Tavris, 1990).

This attitude is also evident in a scholarly article about the use of "scientific" testimony by Robert Levy, a professor of Law at the University of Minnesota: "The problem here is not that some professionals may be dishonest; the problem, rather, is that many of these experts are so committed to child protection that neither their judgment nor their statements can be trusted"

(Levy, 1989, p. 396). In other words, these professionals are not knowingly perpetrating a fraud; they are just so confused by their own feelings that they don't know what they're doing. People on the other side of the debate maintain that these professionals are not misrepresenting the truth, but rather telling what they know from experience and reasoned judgement. They contend that it is unlikely that strongly held sentiments about children would afflict only people identified as child advocates, or that this emotionalism would affect such large numbers of professionals.

Because of the centrality and the virulence of this controversy, we were very interested in learning about the partisanship of the experts who work with these cases and, in particular, those who testify in court.[2] Several questions were explored. First, to what extent are these experts, as a class, partisan toward the child in such cases? Second, to what extent is this partisanship, if it exists, a function of the type of expertise (henceforth called *expert model* in this discussion) the individual holds? Third, what are the other determinants of this partisanship: for instance, geographical location, educational background, professional specialization, gender of respondent?

This research examined the extent to which experts on child sexual abuse are "pro-victim, pro-child advocates" by examining the beliefs about child sexual abuse that are held by the members of the International Society for Traumatic Stress Studies (ISTSS). The rationale for sampling this particular organization was that the constellation of factors associated with being a victim of child sexual abuse, which is fairly well agreed upon by experts in the field and is often presented in court by these experts, resembles what has come to be called post-traumatic stress disorder, or traumatic stress reactions. Familiarity with this disorder is therefore becoming more and more important to people in the field of child abuse. Members of an organization concerning itself with this syndrome seem to qualify, then, as a logical group to survey when a sample of experts is desired. The Society is a respected and prominent national association whose membership is made up of a diversity of professionals specializing in various types of post-traumatic stress reactions.

Four hundred and ninety-three respondents were sampled from the full membership list, in conformity with a systematic randomization protocol. The Minnesota Center for Survey Research mailed questionnaires about child sexual abuse to these respondents, also asking them some questions about their expertise and area of specialization. Three hundred and forty respondents sent their surveys back, for a response rate of 69%. A demographic profile of these respondents is presented in Table 7.1. From this profile, we can see that respondents were evenly scattered throughout the regions of the United States, more were men, more had advanced academic degrees than professional degrees, most were not affiliated with an institution, and, although most reported a familiarity with the literature regarding child sexual abuse, most did not consider themselves to be experts in this type of victimization and its accompanying disorders per se and were even less likely to have been an expert witness in a child sexual abuse case.

TABLE 7.1
Demographic Profile of the International Society of Traumatic Stress Studies

Profile	% of Sample
Geographical Region*	
1. Northeast	25.9
2. South	25.1
3. Midwest	25.7
4. Mountain/Pacific	23.3
Educational Background*	
1. Bachelor's	5.4
2. Master's	35.0
3. Religious	3.9

4. Medical	14.1
5. Doctoral	33.2
6. Other	7.8

Institutional Affiliation

1. Hospitals	15.2
2. Veteran and military	8.3
3. Medical clinics	4.5
4. Private social services	7.1
5. Religious social services	1.8
6. Governmental social services	1.8
7. Educational	4.8
8. Police, prison	1.5
9. None	50.6

Gender

1. Female	42.6
2. Male	57.4

Professional Specialization

1. Veterans/Military	41.5
2. Disaster/Other	34.8
3. Child abuse/Crime victims	23.6

Percent of Caseload Involving Child Sexual Abuse

1. 0	48.1
2. 1–49	42.8
3. 50–100	9.3

Expert Witness in Child Sexual Abuse Cases

1. No	87.2
2. Yes	12.8

Self-Reported Expertise

1. Not an expert (1–3)	60.1
2. An expert (5–7)	24.4

Familiarity with Literature
1. Not at all (1–3)   36.1
2. Very (5–7)   46.9

---

*Northeast includes ME, VT, NH, MA, RI, CT, NY, PA, and NJ; South includes MD, DE, DC, WV, NC, SC, GA, FL, KY, TN, MS, AL, TX, OK, AR, and LA; Midwest includes ND, SD, NE, KS, MN, IA, MO, WI, IL, IN, MI, and OH; Mountain/Pacific includes WA, OR, CA, AK, HI, MT, ID, WY, NV, UT, CO, AZ, and NM.
†Bachelor's includes B.A. and B.S. degrees; Master's includes, M.A., M.S., M.S.W., and M.S.N. degrees; religious includes D.Div. and M.Div. degrees; medical includes M.D. and R.N. degrees; doctoral includes Ph.D. and Psy.D. degrees.

The survey, which was the same one used with jurors in the field (see Chapter 6), was developed to measure attitudes and beliefs about various aspects of child sexual abuse, later clustered into these categories on the basis of face validity: child abuse and the family, characteristics of the abuser, children's eyewitness memory, the prosecution of child sexual abuse, and general attitudes about child sexual abuse (see Table 7.2 for clustered survey questions and assigned response directions).[3]

TABLE 7.2.
Attitude Survey Questions by Category

Respondents indicated the extent of their agreement for each item on a six-point scale ranging from "strongly agree" to "strongly disagree." After each item in the cluster, the response in brackets denotes the response direction with more favorable implications for a child witness in court and for the prosecution.

Child Abuse and the Family
Q2. Parents are more likely to talk about issues such as pregnancy, death, or abortion than about sexual abuse. [AGREE]

Q4. It is unlikely that most wives whose husbands sexually abuse their child know about this abuse. [AGREE]

Q10. Children who have always lived with their mothers are just as likely to be abused as children who have lived at some point without their mother. [AGREE]

Q12. Child sexual abuse is more likely to occur in poor, rural families than rich, suburban families. [DISAGREE]

Q21. Daughters whose mothers discourage them from talking about sex more often experience sexual abuse than those whose mothers are more open about sex. [AGREE]

Q22. Children who are physically abused are more likely to be sexually abused. [DISAGREE]

Q28. If a child is sexually abused by a parent, the child will still show love for that parent. [AGREE]

Q31. Sexually abused children generally experience the same set of psychological reactions and symptoms. [DISAGREE]

Q35. A child of a large vs. average-sized family is more likely to be sexually abused. [DISAGREE]

Child as Witness
Q7. Children are not more influenced by leading questions than are adults. [AGREE]

Q9. It would be wrong to convict someone of a crime if the only eyewitness was a 10-year old. [DISAGREE]

Q13. Children who retract their stories about sexual abuse were probably lying in the first place. [DISAGREE]

Q15. Experts have only just begun to study children's eyewitness memory. [DISAGREE]

Q18. Children are easily manipulated into giving false reports of sexual abuse. [DISAGREE]

Q20. When children identify strangers as having sexually abused them, the identifications are highly reliable. [AGREE]

Q26. Children can distinguish fantasy from reality. [AGREE]

Q29. Children's memories for emotionally traumatic events are not as accurate as adults'. [DISAGREE]

Q30. Delays in reporting child sexual abuse to the police or other authorities are quite common. [AGREE]

Q32. Children are unlikely to fantasize about sexual activity with parents or other adults. [AGREE]

Offender Characteristics
Q1. People who sexually abuse children are more likely to have noticeable problems functioning in other areas of their lives, such as work. [DISAGREE]

Q5. Children are much more likely to be abused by their stepfathers than by their natural fathers. [DISAGREE]

Q8. Men who have incestuous relationships with their daughters are just as likely as other men to have normal sexual relationships with their wives. [AGREE]

Q16. The clear majority of child sexual abuse cases involve a relative or someone the child knows and trusts. [AGREE]

Q19. Child molesters are overcome by sexual urges. [DISAGREE]

Q24. Most people who were sexually abused as children do not end up sexually abusing their own children. [AGREE]

Q25. Sexual abusers are violent and aggressive in other relationships. [DISAGREE]

Q34. Personality profiles of child molesters are highly accurate. [DISAGREE]

Attitudes

Q3. Social workers and child protection agencies are more likely to see child sexual abuse where it does not exist than they did 20 years ago. [DISAGREE]

Q14. Steps must be taken to increase the conviction rate in child sexual abuse cases. [AGREE]

Q23. There is much that should be done to ease a sexually abused child's trauma in court. [AGREE]

Q27. In the current social climate, it is virtually impossible for a person accused of child sexual abuse to get an impartial trial. [DISAGREE]

Q33. After sexual abuse prevention training, children are more likely to misinterpret harmless expressions of affections by adults as sexual abuse. [DISAGREE]

Prosecuting Child Sexual Abuse

Q6. The majority of all reported child sexual abuse cases are tried in court. [DISAGREE]

Q11. Courtroom trials are so stressful for children that we can't expect them to behave a competently as adults. [AGREE]

Q17. Medical experts cannot usually tell if a child has been sexually abused. [AGREE]

Respondents were classified as experts or non-experts according to three different models. The first of these models was based on research literature familiarity. Asked whether they were familiar with the research literature on child sexual abuse, respondents assessed themselves on a seven-point scale, and those having the lowest (1–3) and highest (5–7) scores were categorized by the investigators as non-experts and experts, respectively. The second model was based on the proportion of their professional work week that they spent handling child sexual abuse cases. Fifty percent or more of their time spent on child sexual abuse was considered sufficient to qualify one as an expert on this dimension. The third model had simply to do with whether or not a respondent had ever testified in court as an expert witness on a child sexual abuse case. Those who had, were considered experts according to this model; those who hadn't, were considered non-experts. Table 7.3 presents a descriptive profile of these three groups of respondents.

As it turns out, regardless of expert model, most respondents specialized in working with victims of either child abuse or other crimes, although those considered to be experts by virtue of their caseload specialized more heavily in disorders stemming from this type of victimization than the other two expert groups. Educational background did not vary much according to expert model. Most who were experts by virtue of research familiarity and court experience were men, but more of the group categorized as experts based on caseload were women.

The responses of experts and non-experts of each type to the attitude and belief questions in each cluster were compared.

TABLE 7.3
Descriptive Profiles of Expert Models as a Function of Professional Specialization, Education, and Gender

| | Expert Model | | |
	Research	Case Load	Court Expert
Professional Specialization			
1. Veteran/Military	24.7	16.7	18.6
2. Disaster/Other	38.3	16.7	37.2
3. Child abuse/Crime victims	37.0	86.7	44.2
Educational Background			
1. Bachelor's	4.5	3.2	0.0

2. Master's	38.5	38.7	32.6
3. Religious	5.1	0.0	7.0
4. Medical	10.9	12.9	16.3
5. Doctoral	33.3	29.0	34.9
Gender			
1. Female	43.6	64.5	30.2
2. Male	56.4	35.5	69.8

Note: All numbers in the table represent the percentage of expert respondents in each model who are in the indicated category.

Results are shown in Table 7.4. Although for most expert models there are a few questions that discriminate between experts and non-experts, the number of such questions was small, and similar across models. We concluded that "taken together, these univariate analyses do not suggest that partisanship is strongly associated with a particular model of professional training" (Borgida, Gresham et al., 1989, p. 442).

TABLE 7.4
Summary of Univariate Effects for Survey Cluster as a Function of Expert Models

	Expert Model		
Survey Cluster	*Research*	*Case Load*	*Court Expert*
Child Abuse and Family (9)	4, 12	31	4, 31
Offender (8)	24	8, 16, 24	–
Child witness (10)	7, 13, 18	13	7, 15, 26
Attitudes (5)	–	–	–
Prosecuting (3)	17	–	6

Note: Entry numbers represent the survey items with statistically significant univariate effects. Numbers in parentheses indicate the number of survey items in a given category.

To investigate also the possibility that partisanship was related to both model of expertise and specific beliefs about the capability of child witnesses in some more complicated way—that is, that there is an interaction between type of expertise and a belief bias regarding child witnesses—further analyses were conducted with all expert models and the particular cluster of responses that comprises belief in the capability of children as witnesses. These "capability scores" were obtained through factor analysis, and factor scores were entered into a hierarchical regression analysis as a "belief effect," along with expert models and the interaction between expert effect and belief effect.[4] Each survey item (except those that made up the capability factor) was regressed on these three variables. Only five of twenty-nine beliefs were predicted by this interaction (see Table 7.5). The regression analysis, then, did not support the hypothesis that expert models interact with beliefs to predict partisanship. Beliefs tended to exist in consistent groupings for these experts, regardless of their training or the source of their expertise.

In order to find out more about the source of these beliefs, another analysis was conducted (Kovera, Borgida et al., in press). In this investigation, the effects on partisanship of geographical region, educational background, gender, and area of

TABLE 7.5
Summary of Hierarchical Regression Main Effects and Interactions by Survey Cluster

Survey Item No.	Expert Effects	Belief Effects	Interaction Effects
Child Abuse and the Family			
2	–	–	–
4	CE	–	–
10	–	–	B x CE
12	CE, R	-.26	–
21	–	.28	–

22	–	–	B x R, B x C
28	–	–	–
31	C	.11	B x R
35	–	–	–

Child as Witness

7	CE	–	–
15	CE	.13	–
20	–	.28	B x CE, B x C
29	–	.29	–
30	–	–	–
32	–	–	–

Offender Characteristics

1	–	–	–
5	–	.11	–
8	–	–	–
16	C	.15	–
19	–	.24	–
24	R	–	–
25	–	–	–
34	–	–	–

Attitudes

3	–	.36	–
14	–	.29	
23	–	–	–

Prosecuting

6	CE	.13	–
11	–	-.26	–
17	R	-.13	–

1. R = research model, C = case load model, CE = court expert model. All reported main effects were statistically significant at $p < .05$.

2. "Belief" is comprised of factor score items 9, 13, 18, 26, 27, and 33. Therefore, these items were not used as dependent variables. Numbers in the second column are all standardized betas.

professional specialization of the experts (determined in the same fashion as in the prior study) were examined. To do this, multivariate analyses of variance (MANOVA) were first conducted to look at the differences in respondents' beliefs (represented by their responses to the survey questions) as a function of these attributes.

The results were interesting. ISTSS respondents' partisanship did not vary as a function of educational background (Bachelor's, Master's, Religious, Medical, Doctoral, Other). That is, neither type nor level of schooling systematically accounted for experts' attitudes regarding child sexual abuse and its prosecution. There were some differences in response to particular items related to the geographical region of the experts ($F[105, 783] = 1.43$, $p < .005$). Seven of the thirty—five univariate analyses conducted subsequent to the MANOVA differed significantly by region. For five of these items, post hoc comparisons showed mean differences between the regions. Four of these agreed in their identification of the "different" region, and in the direction of that difference; that is, respondents from the South had a weaker belief in the credibility of children as witnesses in child sexual abuse cases that did respondents from other regions of the country. (The specific questions that distinguished this region were numbers 5, 15, 17, 18, 19, 29, and 33.)

Somewhat stronger and more explainable is the finding that the gender of the respondent and type of practice, specifically the type of victims the professional works with (e.g., disaster victims, veterans, sexual abuse victims) was related to partisanship ($F [35, 253] = 2.31$, $p < .001$). Women were shown to be more partisan than men, with ten survey items differing significantly according to gender. These items were representative of four of the five categories of items in the attitude survey (specifically, they were questions 3, 5, 10, 12, 13, 14, 19, 20, 28, and 29).

Perhaps the most intuitive of the findings is that professionals who work with victims of sexual assault were shown generally to have stronger beliefs in the credibility of child witnesses in sexual abuse cases than those who work with other victims of post-traumatic stress disorder ($F[70, 508] = 1.61$, $p < .002$). Eight items from three categories garnered significantly different responses according to professional specialization. (Specifically, these were questions 3, 7, 13, 18, 24, 30, 32, and 34).

The finding of regional differences, though not specifically interpretable, shows that there is a discernible impact of historical events or regional temperament on perception of children's credibility. This points out the need for public education. However, since another of these variables (gender) can be seen as a measure of experience with children in general and still another is clearly a measure of experience with sexually abused children, one way of understanding these findings is to say that a pro-child stance derives from experience, familiarity, and specific expertise, rather than from academic, historical, or professional/social influences. If this is so, then partisanship in this case, while an attitudinal proclivity in one direction, should not be seen as a bias, in the prejudicial sense. Quite the contrary. The heretofore so-labeled "neutral" stance, that of skepticism toward the child witness, particularly in sexual abuse cases, can be seen as an anti-child bias, given that it is held by those with the least direct experience with child capabilities and child sexual abuse situations.

Knowing that we can have some measure of trust in the objectivity of the experts who testify in these cases, and knowing the effect of this testimony on juror decision making are two very different things.[5] For this reason, the collaborating group of researchers sought to design a research project that would begin to bring some of these effects to light. This effort required a jury.

The Borgida team conducted a series of mock jury studies incorporating several variables of interest to us: the age of the child witness (Kovera & Borgida, 1992, unpublished manuscript), the witness' demeanor (level of preparedness), and expert psychological testimony (Borgida, Kovera et al., 1992, unpublished manuscript), videotaping the child witness (Swim, Borgida, & McCoy, unpublished manuscript), and the social class of the defendant (Gresham, 1992). The design of the studies was as follows. Jurors viewed a realistic three-and-a-half-hour videotape of a simulated child sexual abuse case that was heavily based on a transcript of an actual case that had been tried, *State v. Myers,* 1987. The defendant, the child victim, the mother, and the gynecologist were played by actors. The psychological expert, the attorneys, and the judge were played by practicing or retired professionals in those respective fields.

After viewing one version of the trial, jurors recorded their verdict, both initially and after a 45-minute deliberation process. The verdict they were asked to record consisted of guilt or innocence for each of the three possible charges: first-degree criminal sexual conduct, attempted first-degree criminal sexual conduct, and second-degree criminal sexual conduct. In addition, jurors rated the witnesses and certain aspects of the testimony in importance to their decision about each separate charge. They also rated the credibility, veracity, likability, and competence of the witnesses. Jurors were asked how strongly they felt during the child witness' testimony, and their memories for the evidence and judge's instructions were tested through a free recall process. Certain analyses planned for these data have not been finished yet, and will be published at a later date. Others can be reported her.

In one study, expert testimony and witness preparation were examined. There were three conditions of expert testimony represented in separate versions of the trial: none, standard, and use of the "hypothetical." Standard expert testimony consisted of a recitation by the expert (a clinical psychologist) of research on child sexual abuse, characteristics of victims and families, and children's emotional and behavioral reactions to this kind of abuse. The expert testimony that included a hypothetical example tied together the research and the details of the particular case confronting the jury. This device allows the attorney to describe a case that is very similar to the case at hand and to ask questions regarding the expert's opinion as to whether sexual abuse occurred in this proxy case.

The two conditions of witness demeanor were "prepared" and "unprepared." The characteristics of preparedness were based on a survey of county attorneys and victim-witness advocates who have experience preparing witnesses for child sexual abuse cases. They identified several hallmarks of preparation: calmness, control of emotions, reliability of answers, and fewer "I don't know" answers.

As there were three conditions of expert testimony and two conditions of witness demeanor, the investigators varied the nature of the witness testimony into six versions for this study, in order to test every combination of the two variables. We conjectured that the use of the hypothetical-case example in expert testimony would increase the number of guilty verdicts and raise the juror's estimation of the child witness. We further posited that preparation of the witness would increase the credibility of the witness in the juror's' eyes and also lead to more guilty verdicts.

Since a guilty verdict on the highest charge incorporates all lesser charges, discrete verdicts on the three separate charges were combined in a scale that went from 0, which stood for not guilty for all three charges, to 3, representing guilty on all charges. This scale was used as the dependent variable in an analysis of variance to test the effects of expert testimony and witness demeanor on juror verdicts.

Although analysis of the data will be further refined, preliminary results, presented in a paper to the annual meeting of the American Psychological Society in June of 1991, are provocative. There were no main effects. That is, neither independent variable alone affected juror verdicts. There was an interaction between expert testimony and child demeanor in their effect on verdicts. When jurors were exposed to the standard expert testimony and saw a prepared child witness, they judged the defendant's guilt more harshly than when they saw an unprepared child witness with the same expert testimony (see Figure 7.1). The opposite was true when they heard the expert respond to the hypothetical case when giving his or her testimony. Then the jurors who viewed the unprepared child judged the defendant more harshly.

The expert testimony–child demeanor interaction persisted in the jurors' perception of the child witness. Jurors listening to the expert respond to the hypothetical case found the unprepared child more likable, more attractive, and better on a good-bad continuum than the prepared child, while the jurors hearing standard expert testimony or no expert testimony had

FIGURE 7.1
Jurors' Combined Ratings on Three Charges

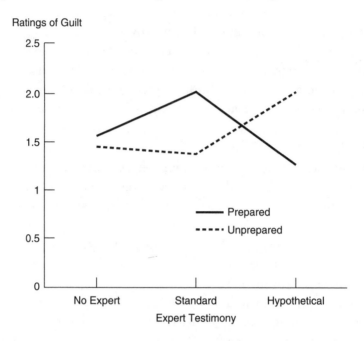

Ratings of Guilt

the opposite reaction to the child witness' likability (see Figure 7.2).

Juror ratings of the defendant were affected by the independent variables in a more complicated way. Jurors who viewed the expert testimony with the hypothetical example reacted to the defendant in line with their reaction to the victim. That is, they disliked the defendant more when the child witness was unprepared. But for jurors who heard standard expert testimony, preparation of the child witness made little difference; and those who viewed no expert at all were least favorable to the defendant when they saw a prepared child witness (see Figure 7.3).

In summary, then, this phase of the mock jury research shows that the credibility of child victim witnesses in child sexual abuse cases is affected by the presence and type of expert testimony available to the jury and the level of preparedness of the child, *in combination*. The use of the hypothetical example seems to be a better way of educating jurors than standard "scientific" testi-

FIGURE 7.2

Likability Ratings of Child Witness as a Function of Child Witness Demeanor and Expert Testimony

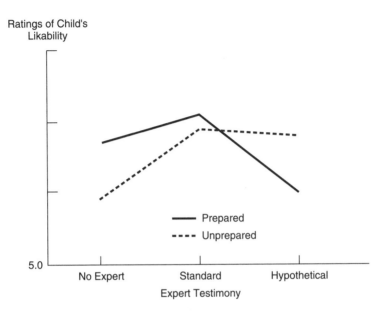

mony. In addition, the technique allows the child witness to be perceived as credible when she acts unprepared (that is, nervous and hesitant). This would seem to be better for the child and easier for the prosecutor, and to have the further advantage of circumventing charges by the defense that the child was "coached."

However, allowance of the hypothetical technique to the extent that the expert is asked to give an opinion on whether abuse occurred in this proxy case varies across jurisdictions. In some, this cannot be done, as it comes too close to the expert's giving an opinion on the truthfulness of the claim in question. In addition, preparation, if done correctly, is not the same thing as coaching and does not necessarily make the child appear unnatural. In fact, all good lawyers prepare witnesses. It is considered irresponsible not to do so (Toth, personal communication, 1992). It is of further concern that the value of the hypothetical technique in this situation may be due to the fact that certain

FIGURE 7.3

Likability Ratings of the Defendant as a Function of Child Witness Demeanor and Expert Testimony

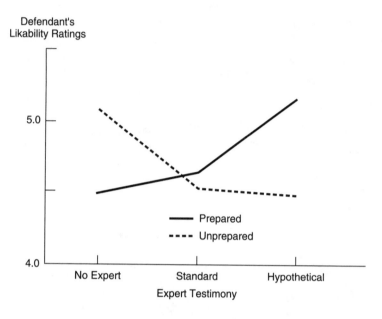

material, which may already have been presented in the standard expert testimony, is repeated by the expert witness during the course of linking it to the particular hypothetical example, rather than to the linking per se. A final question that remains has to do with the *mechanisms* by which hypothetical and standard expert testimony affect juror decisions. The next phase of investigations by this research team is attempting to answer some of these questions.

To deal with the question of repetition, the team added a *repetitive expert* condition to the research. To investigate the mechanisms by which different kinds of expert testimony—particularly the hypothetical—affect jurors' deliberations, a number of questions were added for jurors regarding how often they used various cognitive, empathic, or combination strategies during the decisions-making process. This further analysis is currently in progress, but it is already clear that the influence of hypothetical testimony is more complex than originally thought (Borgida, Kovera et al., unpublished manuscript). Work done to date suggest that hypothetical testimony only influenced juror decision making when the child witness' demeanor was consistent with the description of child abuse victims provided by the expert. This is a desirable outcome of hypothetical testimony. However, the other types of expert testimony seem to have influenced deliberations more when the child witness' demeanor was *inconsistent* with the picture of a typical child abuse victim presented in the expert's testimony. For instance, repetitive expert testimony, which was the most influential of all the types, was most effective when the witness was prepared.

While this second finding is simply puzzling, and inadequately explained by the research at this point, we might be tempted to explain the first by saying that the hypothetical example influenced jurors by increasing their empathy for the child victim witness. However, the research in progress seems to suggest that this is not true. Rather than being prejudicial to the defendant, the hypothetical testimony seems to work by affecting discussion of the child witness' behavior and her motivations for alleging that sexual abuse occurred, thereby influencing the jurors' decisions about the victim, the defendant, and the verdict. If this is so, it is a more cognitive than emotional process.

We are still, in this field, at a point where our data base regarding the actions of children who are sexually abused, and the adults who abuse them, is more made up of the practice wisdom of clinicians than the empirical findings of social scientists. Even though this practice wisdom may be well-informed and correct, those who hold the knowledge are always vulnerable to the charge of subjectivity. These studies in combination make some inroads against this charge. They show us that expert witness testimony can generally be trusted to be not unduly biased in favor of the child as a function of any particular model of expertise, although experts who are women and experts whose practice centers on child sexual abuse hold more attitudes consistent with the notion of child witness credibility than do other experts. The research further shows that the testimony of experts may affect perceptions and decisions in child sexual abuse cases, in enhancing the credibility of the child witness, and that there even are techniques that can mitigate the negative effects on witness credibility without putting excessive demands on an already traumatized child to be composed.

In the best of worlds, many ways of knowing would be seen as legitimate, and, indeed, the real experience of clinicians would be seen as superior in particular areas of inquiry into child abuse where tragic circumstances cannot ethically be reproduced in the laboratory. We are not residing in that world today, however. Knowledge gained through the scientific method is currently given more credence. Therefore, it is of utmost importance for social scientists to apply their test to the issues of child-witness credibility (as many certainly are doing, see Goodman, Aman & Hirschman, 1987; Saywitz, 1987; Penrod, Bull, & Lengnick, 1989). Whether their methods confirm or deny what the social workers, the child therapists, and the child care professionals already "know" about the veracity of these tales of abuse, we as a society have no moral choice but to listen.

8

What Do We Do Now?

We have seen that the pendulum of public opinion about proper treatment of child sexual abuse has apparently come to rest, of late, nearer the punitive end of the therapeutic/coercive continuum. As a society, we are currently in favor of sending child sexual abusers to court and to jail, and we are not sanguine about curing them of their affliction. But we have also seen, looking back through history, that the pendulum never really stops, only reaches some invisible limit in one direction, then reverse itself in reaction to the built-up momentum. It is possible and desirable to resist this knee-jerk pattern of action and reaction. If we are to take neither an unequivocal nor a reactionary position favoring therapeutic or coercive care for child sexual abuse cases, then we must decide how to process particular cases based on facts, rather than myths and misconceptions.

WHAT HAVE WE LEARNED?

In the field of child sexual abuse, research has tended to disconfirm a number of widely held views in a number of ways. Laboratory studies have shown us that children's memory is not, for the most part, inferior to adults' (Goodman & Reed, 1986;

193

List, 1986; Nigro & Gudatis, 1987; Goodman, Aman, & Hirschman, 1989), nor are children more suggestible than adults (Marin, Holmes, Guth, & Kovac, 1979; Duncan, Whitney, & Kunen, 1982; Saywitz, 1987), although there are certain studies that refute one or the other of these claims. Clinical work has deconstructed the hierarchical typology of child molesters with discrete categories of risk based mostly on the relationship of the perpetrator to the child (the closer that relationship, the less serious the threat of recidivism with this child or any other) that we had relied on, at least informally, to make many of our decisions (Abel et al., 1981; Murphy et al., 1986, Salter, 1988). And qualitative studies have begun to chip away at our conviction that going to court is a very bad experience for children (Whitcomb, Shapiro, & Stellwagen, 1985).

What does the work presented here add to this knowledge base about how we should handle these cases? It tells us first of all to be sensitive to bias. Cases with certain characteristics are more likely to end up in our criminal system. These cases disproportionately involve female victims, victims under 15 years of age, black perpetrators, perpetrators who are not family members of the victim, and an accused who is an already identified criminal. If these cases are not statistically typical of child sexual abuse in general in our society, then they must represent cases of child sexual abuse *that we think should be prosecuted*. Why is that so? Is it because this type of case is less amenable to remediation? Is it because this type of case is more likely to be referred for a complete law enforcement investigation? Is it because this type of case is more likely to result in conviction? Is it because this type of case fits what we want to believe about child sexual abuse? Or is it some combination of these attitudes?

This research also tells us that after a case is in the criminal system, the path it travels is based on some of these same attributes. Prosecutorial and judicial discretion play a major role in criminal justice in general, but this research suggests that societal bias against blacks, bias in favor of intrafamily abusers, and bias against certain-aged children and all adolescents is figuring heavily in discretionary decisions.

This research tells us that what child advocates seem to believe is useful in terms of procedural reform in the criminal court-room and what prosecutors actually use as techniques for trial do not correspond. The reforms used least often are those that supposedly relieve the stress to the child witness. Those that are used most are reforms that increase the jury's ability to hear and interpret the facts of the case in a way that they can use these facts for decision making.[1] While at first glance this may seem cold and pragmatic, and self-serving for prosecutors, it deserves a second look. The long-term effect on the child of winning a case, even at the expense of painful testimony, may be more positive than testifying under slightly more solicitous but still uncomfortable circumstances, and not being believed. Therefore, child advocates might be more effective if their efforts were directed to educating the general public regarding the extent and nature of child sexual abuse and the peculiar capabilities of child victim witnesses, than in advocating for reforms that have limited usefulness to prosecutors in the actual courtroom situation.

This research suggests that, contrary to popular belief, experts in this field are not overly partisan toward the child in these cases, nor is partisanship, to the extent that it exists, linked to any particular expert models or professional training. It also indicates, however, that the groups who are the most partisan with regard to the capability of the child as a witness and offender characteristics are those who possess the most first-hand knowledge about children in general and knowledge about children who have been sexually abused in particular. This suggests that the pro-child stance may be the more objective position and the anti-child stance the biased viewpoint. Certainly there is a need for public re-education if this is the case.

These research findings, then, as they pertain to the courtroom, point to appropriately preparing the child witness, letting the child tell the story, letting experts assist in some cases, and letting the judge and jury weigh the testimony. With regard to expert testimony, the research suggests that we should attempt to reach some professional consensus about standards for serving as an expert and the type of testimony that is given.

Extrapolating from this research, we can conclude that preparing children for court should not mean coaching them to act in accordance with public prejudice about how they would act if they were credible. Instead, it would mean helping them to be more relaxed, and therefore more able to recount the abuse they suffered. In addition, jurors should be prepared to recognize the signs of credibility when those signs are presented to them. Some children will be upset while telling their story in court, regardless of efforts to familiarize them with the process ahead of time and to offer them encouragement. The solution is to educate the jury to understand that children who act in such a manner are exhibiting reactions well within the normal range for this type of trauma. The research results show that using a hypothetical case when examining an expert witness is one effective way of so educating a jury.

An issue raised by this study, but by no means dealt with adequately, is that of utilitarian versus justice motives for criminal justice practices and inclinations toward reform. Many of the debates regarding the handling of child sexual abuse cases in the criminal justice system—through history and today—come down to this dichotomy. Several of the conventions of current criminal justice practice serve primarily utilitarian ends, either short-term or long-term. Diversion programs lighten the load on the courtroom and jails. Parole for "good behavior" makes new space in the prisons as well. Plea-bargaining frees up court time while minimally satisfying public interest in conviction. When the emphasis is shifted from what the defendant has done in committing the particular crime in question to someone's speculation of what he may do in the future, as it sometimes is in these practices, social and personal prejudices may prevail. The concept of justice is obscured in the shuffle of "managing" defendants in and out of the system.

Thus, the concept of utilitarianism is intertwined with that of discretion. All of the practices mentioned above—and others, such as separate competency hearings for child victim witnesses—entail increased exercise of discretion. A closed interview by the judge and lawyers to predetermine the competency of a child witness; a shrewd investigator's or prosecutor's ability to scare a defendant into a guilty plea to a lesser charge or obtain a guilty plea to appropriate charges by wise use of sentencing recommendations; the availability of a local treatment program to which certain kinds of offenders may be diverted from prosecution, or sent as a condition of probation; or a parole board's assessment of the relative risk of releasing an individual into society, may be—singly or in combination—the final determinates of the justice that is done vis-a-vis that person. This reduces the importance of the *triers of fact* in the case. If there is bias in society, this bias may well be exacerbated by greater discretion, as discretionary decisions are not subject to the same due process and evidentiary safeguards as the more formal aspects of the justice system. However, these are not problems unique to child sexual abuse cases but struggles in the criminal justice system, generally. What is important for child advocates outside the system to understand, is not where the system falls short of the ideal, but how they can interact with the system in order to bring about the best result for the child victims.

DIRECTIONS FOR FUTURE RESEARCH

Certainly, the findings of this study point to other research that should be done. Among such studies would be one comparing reoffense rates of intra-familial perpetrators who were dealt with only in the child welfare system with those of offenders who go through the criminal system. What are the effects on the victims, the family members, and the offenders of these very different responses to the problem?

Within the criminal justice system, there should be a study that would follow up perpetrators whose cases were diverted out of the criminal system and who received treatment and those who remained in the criminal system and received various dispositions to their cases, comparing medium- and long-range outcomes for these groups. While there is evidence that some techniques are helpful in controlling, if not in curing molesting behavior, there is at present no empirical evidence to support diversion programs on other than the obvious criminal—system management grounds of short-term reduction of trials and incarcerations. What are the relative recidivism rates connected with these different responses to child sexual abuse?

Also recommended is more sophisticated research on the effects on child sexual abuse victims of participating in the legal system. There exists in the literature, much common-sense rhetoric to the effect that the experience is harmful, as well as counter-argument and some research findings saying that the experience can be empowering. It would be very helpful to be able to identify elements of the process that contribute to one or the other of these outcomes. The exploratory phase of this research might use qualitative methods to get a deep sense of victims' feelings about their experiences. A more quantitative study could follow, using variables that were identified in the first phase.

Outside the criminal system, research that would tell us more about the causes, facilitators, and preventive agents of child sexual abuse would be helpful. Continuing research like that of Goodman et al. (1987, 1989) could illuminate the capabilities of children as witnesses, and research that could probe the source of public perceptions about children's veracity and competence as witnesses would be most valuable.

Information on false accusations would also be helpful to the field. We know little from empirical sources regarding the motives of children who falsely accuse adults of sexual abuse. Most of what has been said about this topic is opinion, conjecture, and bias. A study to identify these motives, and develop some knowledge about the signals that may be present in a case where an accusation is false, would go far to assist in evaluating the implications of fraud raised in so many court cases.

It behooves us to think clearly and without preconception about child sexual abuse, while not losing our humanity or compassion. There is no doubt that it is possible in our society to construct an intricate pattern of fear, power, manipulation, habit, and selfishness that perpetrates a fraudulent disenfranchisement of a group of victims even robs them of their status as victims, disallowing any growth as a result; history has proved that. Knowing that this possibility exists, we should be ever on the alert to its happening. There should not be "camps" when it comes to sexual abuse—whether the "witchhunt" or the "children never lie" camp. There should only be a sincere quest for truth, and the utmost protection of our youngest citizens while we find that truth.

Appendix
Data Collection Instruments

DEFENDANT CASE HISTORY

Revision 2 [2/88]

1. **ID:** Section # [____]

      Defendant identifier [_____]

      Case identifier _if_ multiple defendants [_____]

2. Prosecutor supplying this information by interview or record review:

      _____ Name

      _____ Telephone number

3. Date case brought to prosecutor's attention: Mo___Day___Yr___

4. Who (*title*) brought the case to the prosecutor's office? _____

5. Defendant characteristics:

      a. Age at time of <u>last</u> offense alleged in this case _____ # years

      b. Current age _____ # years

      c. Sex: ___1)Male ___2)Female

      d. Race/ethnicity: ___1)White ___2)Black ___3)Hispanic ___4)Asian ___5)Other

      e. Occupation prior to arrest [*unemployed/type of work/student*]: _____

      f. Education: ___1)Less than H Schl ___2)H Schl Grad ___3)Some Coll ___4)4-yr Coll Grad +

      g. Was defendant married at time of alleged offense? ___1)No ___2)Yes

      h. Was defendant married at time of trial or final disposition of case? ___1)No ___2)Yes

6. If charges were ever brought against the defendant _before this case_, fill in this section as completely as possible:

Prior Charges	Sex-Related (*circle*)		<u>Felony</u> or <u>Misdemeanor</u> (*circle*)		Convicted (*circle*)	
1._____	No	Yes	Fel	Mis	No	Yes
2._____	No	Yes	Fel	Mis	No	Yes
3._____	No	Yes	Fel	Mis	No	Yes
4._____	No	Yes	Fel	Mis	No	Yes
5._____	No	Yes	Fel	Mis	No	Yes
6._____	No	Yes	Fel	Mis	No	Yes

7. What allegedly happened in the _current case_?

      _____
      _____

8. Was *ritualistic* abuse allegedly involved? (*occult, supernatural, satanic*)

      ___1)No ___2)Yes

      a. Explain: _____

1

9. Did the alleged abuse occur in an *institutional* situation? *[day care setting, school, club, camp, Boy/Girl Scouts, Big Brother/Sister, etc.]*

    —1)No   —2)Yes

        ↓   a. Identify: _____

10. Are there other defendants charged in this case?

    —1)No   —2)Yes

               a. How many other defendants? _____

        ↓   b. List other defendants using the identifiers appearing on their case history forms:

             _____   _____   _____

             _____   _____   _____

11. Is this a <u>multiple</u>-victim case?

    —1)No   —2)Yes

               a. How many children is this defendant accused of abusing? ____

        ↓   b. List all children below using the identifiers appearing on their case history forms:

             _____   _____   _____

             _____   _____   _____

12. Was the defendant formally charged in this case?

    —2)Yes   —1)No

        ↓   13. What factors influenced the prosecutor's decision to reject the case? *[Check all that apply]*

    GO TO   Victim considered not credible because ...
    PAGE 3

                   ____a. too young
                   ____b. denies abuse happened
                   ____c. keeps changing story
                   ____d. afraid to testify
                   ____e. mentally incompetent (*mentally ill, retarded*)
                   ____f. Other (*explain*): _____

               ____g. There is evidence to the contrary

               ____h. There is no corroborating evidence

               ____i. Victim and/or victim's family does not want to prosecute

               ____j. Other (*explain*): _____

           14. What, if anything, was done about the abuse claim after the prosecutor rejected the case?

               _____

               _____

               _____

                      END HERE

                        2

202

DEFENDANT FORMALLY CHARGED IN THIS CASE

a. On what date was defendant charged? Mo___Day___Yr.____

b. All charges (sex related and other) brought against the defendant:
(*please be as specific as record allows*)

Current Charges	Sex-Related (*circle*)		Felony Misdemeanor (*circle*)	
1._____	No	Yes	Fel	Mis
2._____	No	Yes	Fel	Mis
3._____	No	Yes	Fel	Mis
4._____	No	Yes	Fel	Mis
5._____	No	Yes	Fel	Mis
6._____	No	Yes	Fel	Mis

c. Was bail set for this arrest?

___1)No ___2)Yes

a. What was the amount? _____

b. Was it paid? ___1)No ___2)Yes

d. Which of the following factors influenced the decision to file these charges?
[*Check all that apply*]

___1. Defendant acknowledged guilt

___2. Strong child witness(es)

___3. Medical evidence [*Please explain*]

_____

_____

___4. Eyewitness [*Please explain who*]

_____

_____

___5. Other [*Please specify*]

_____

_____

e. Was the the defendant <u>taken to trial on sex-related charges</u>?

___1)No **GO TO PAGE 4**   ___2)Yes **GO TO PAGE 6**

3

203

15. Date of final disposition in case: Mo____Day____Yr.____

16. Were all <u>sex-related charges dropped</u>?

___1)No \ ___2)Yes

    17. Why did the prosecutor decide not to try defendant on sex-related charges?
       [please check all that apply]

       ___a. Victim recanted story
       ___b. Victim no longer willing to testify
       ___c. Corroborating evidence weakened
       ___d. Victim's family decided not to proceed
       ___e. Victim's story contradicted by increasing evidence to the contrary
       ___f. Other (*explain*): _____

    18. Was the defendant prosecuted on any <u>non-sex-related charges</u>?

    ___1)No \ ___2)Yes

       a. Was the defendant found guilty?

    END   ___1)No ___2)Yes ___by plea ___by trial?
    HERE   b. On what charges? _____

       END c. What was the sentence?
       HERE ___Probation (#yrs ___) ___Prison (#yrs ___)

                                  END HERE ✒

19. Was the <u>defendant found incompetent</u> to stand trial?

___1)No \ ___2)Yes

    a. Was defendant institutionalized?

    ___1)No   ___2)Yes   ⟶   **END HERE**

20. Was the defendant <u>diverted to treatment</u> (*prosecution deferred*)?

___1)No \ ___2)Yes

    a. For what period of time was treatment ordered? ____mos.

    b. Is this a residential treatment program? ___2)Yes ___1)No

    c. Is it a specialized program for incest or pedophilic disorders? ___2)Yes ___1)No

    d. Did the judge stipulate what would happen if the defendant did not
       complete treatment program? ___1)No   ___2)Yes, [*specify*]_____

    _____

    e. What were the other conditions of this diversion?

       ___1. Acknowledgement of guilt

       ___2. Waiver of rights [*please specify*]_____

       ___3. Community service [*voluntary or paid, how long*]_____

       ___4. Defendant ordered to pay $_____ to victim

       ___5. Defendant ordered to pay $_____ towards own treatment

       ___6. Defendant ordered to pay $_____ towards victim's treatment

              END HERE ✒

4

21. Did the defendant plead guilty to all original sex-related charges?

___2) Yes   ___1) No

a. To what original charges *(sex-related and other)* did the defendant plead guilty?

1._____
2._____
3._____
4._____

b. To what lesser charges *(sex-related and other)* did the defendant plead guilty?

1._____
2._____
3._____
4._____

22. Was the defendant sentenced to jail after pleading guilty?

___1) No

a. Was the defendant sentenced to probation?

___1) No   ___2) Yes

b. For how long?

___# years

___2) Yes

c. How long was the sentence?

___#yrs. prison   ___#yrs. probation

d. When will defendant be eligible for parole?

___# years

END HERE

23. Was the defendant sentenced to treatment after pleading guilty?

___1) No

END HERE

___2) Yes

a. Did the judge specify a particular treatment program for incest or pedophilic disorders?

___1) No

END HERE

___2) Yes

b. Is this a residential facility?

___1) No   ___2) Yes

c. Did the judge stipulate what would happen if the defendant did not complete the treatment program?

___1) No

END HERE

___2) Yes

d. What? _____

_____
_____
_____

END

5

205

TAKEN TO TRIAL ON SEX-RELATED CHARGES

24. Date trial began: Mo ___ Day ___ Year ___   25. Date trial ended: Mo ___ Day ___ Year ___

26. Was there a jury? ___1)No ___2)Yes

27. Was the defendant represented by a court-appointed attorney?

    ___1)No   ___2)Yes

    a. Was this a public defender or a private attorney working *pro bono*?

    ___1)Public defender   ___2)Private attorney

28. Was there a conviction in this case?

    ___1)No   ___2)Yes

    a. On what <u>original charges</u>*(sex-related & other)* was the defendant convicted?

    END
    HERE

    1. _____
    2. _____
    3. _____
    4. _____

    b. On what <u>lesser charges</u> *(sex-related and other)* was the defendant convicted?

    1. _____
    2. _____
    3. _____
    4. _____

29. Was the defendant sent to jail following the trial?

    ___1)No   ___2)Yes

    a. Was the defendant sentenced to probation?   c. How long was the sentence?

    ___1)No   ___2)Yes   ____# yrs. prison

    b. For how long?   ____# yrs. probation

    ____# years   d. When will defendant be eligible for parole?

    ____# years

    END HERE

30. Was the defendant sentenced to treatment?

    ___1)No   ___2)Yes

    END
    HERE

    a. Did the judge specify a particular treatment program for incest or pedophilic disorders?

    ___1)No   ___2)Yes

    END
    HERE

    b. Is this a residential facility?   ___1)No   ___2)Yes

    c. Did the judge stipulate what would happen if the defendant did not complete the treatment program?

    ___1)No   ___2)Yes

    d. What?_____

    END
    HERE

    _____
    _____
    _____

    END

6

Revision 2 [2/88]

1. **ID:**   Section # [____]
   Defendant identifier [_____]
   Case identifier if multiple defendants [_____]
   Child identifier [_____]

2. Child's birthdate: Mo ___ Day ___ Year ___

3. Child's sex: ___1)Male   ___2)Female

4. Child's race/ethnicity: ___1)White   ___2)Black   ___3)Hispanic   ___4)Asian   ___5)Other

5. a. Child's age at onset of alleged abuse: Years ___ *AND* Months ___
   b. Date of onset of alleged abuse: Mo ___ Day ___ Year ___

6. a. Child's age at cessation of alleged abuse: Years ___ *AND* Months ___
   b. Date of cessation of alleged abuse: Mo ___ Day ___ Year ___

7. Approximate duration of alleged abuse: Days ___ *OR* Months ___ *OR* Years ___

8. How often was sexual abuse by the defendant alleged to have occurred?
   ___1)Once   ___2)Several times   ___3)Many times

9. Defendant's *relationship* to child?

   ___1)Biological mother
   ___2)Biological father
   ___3)Non-biological mother
     [*Explain:* _____]
   ___4)Non-biological father
     [*Explain:* _____]
   ___5)Bioloical brother
   ___6)Biological sister
   ___7)Step-brother

   ___8)Step-sister
   ___9)Other biological relative [*Specify:* _____]
   ___10)Other non-biol. relative (e.g., step-mother's brother) [*Specify:* _____]
   ___11)Custodial acquaintance (e.g., teacher, babysitter) [*Specify:* _____]
   ___12)Non-custodial acquaintance (e.g., neighbor, mother's boyfriend) [*Specify:* _____]
   ___13)Stranger

* [*COMPLETE ONLY IF DEFENDANT LIVES IN CHILD'S HOUSEHOLD*]

10. Was the child removed from the home prior to trial or plea?
    ___1)No   ___2)Yes
       a. Where was the child placed? _____
       _____

11. Was the defendant barred from the home prior to trial or plea?
    ___1)No   ___2)Yes, by court order   ___3)Yes, defendant in jail
       a. Were visits by/with the defendant allowed?
          ___1)No ___2)Yes, supervised

12. Did the child disclose the assault without first being questioned about it?
    ___1)No   ___2)Yes
       a. To whom initially? _____   b. Date: Mo ___ Day ___ Yr___
    c. Circumstances (*how did abuse come to light*): _____

13. Did the defendant threaten the child not to tell?
　　___1)No　　　___2)Yes
　　　　　　　　　　a. Please explain _____

14. What was the nature of the alleged sexual abuse? [Check all that apply]
　　___1)Intercourse　　　　　　　　　　　___6)Fondling by defendant
　　___2)Attempted intercourse　　　　　___7)Fondling by child
　　___3)Anal penetration　　　　　　　　___8)Exposure by defendant
　　___4)Oral-genital by defendant　　　___9)Sexual photos by defendant
　　___5)Oral-genital by child　　　　　___10)Other [Specify: _____]

15. Was the child physically abused in addition to being sexually molested?
　　___1)No　　　___2)Yes　How? _____

16. Who investigated the child's claims? [Check all that apply]
　　___1)Child Protective Service (CPS) workers　　　___3)Prosecutor's investigators
　　___2)Police investigators　　　　　　　　　　　　___4)Juvenile Court

* [COMPLETE ONLY IF MORE THAN ONE AGENCY INVESTIGATED (Q16, ABOVE)]

　　17. Did the agencies involved conduct joint or independent investigations?
　　　　___1)Independent　　　___2)Joint
　　　　　　　　　a. Which agencies? _____

18-26. Who interviewed child how many times prior to trial for reasons related to this case? What was
the purpose of each interview? Was it videotaped? Were tapes used in court? [Under each "time"
check all parties involved in interview (whether or not each asked direct questions of child), all case-
related purposes for interviews, whether it was videotaped, and whether the tape was used in court.]

	18. Time1	19. Time2	20. Time3	21. Time4	22. Time5	23. Time6	24. Time7	25. Time8	26. Time9
Parties Involved in Interview									
a. CPS staff									
b. Police staff									
c. Prosecutor's staff									
d. Therapist									
e. Medical staff									
f. Defense attorney									
Purposes									
g. Guide CPS decisions									
h. Guide DA's decisions									
i. Part of therapeutic process									
j. Prod to plea bargaining									
k. Basis for expert testimony									
l. Reduce number of interviews									
m. Replace live testimony in court									
Videotape									
n. Check if videotape made									
o. Check if video shown in court									

[Note: Record all case-related interviews with child. Use additional sheets if necessary.]

27. Did (*non-offending*) parent <u>at any point</u> give permission for the child to testify?
    —1)No   —2)Yes

        a. How difficult was it for the prosecutor to get initial parental permission?
            —1)Parent took initiative in offering child as witness
            —2)Parent agreed readily when asked
            —3)Parent agreed hesitantly when asked
            —4)Parent was difficult to persuade but finally agreed

        b. If parent was reluctant to give permission, why? _____
        _____
        _____

        c. Did parent withdraw permission before child had an opportunity to take stand?
            —1)No   —2)Yes
                b. Why? _____
                _____

28. Did the child ultimately take the witness stand?
    —2)Yes   —1)No

        a. Why not?
            —1)No opportunity -- case did not go to trial
            —2)Other reason *[explain]:* _____
        _____
        _____

29. Was there a medical examination?
    —1)No   —2)Yes

        a. Was medical evidence of sexual abuse found?

            —1)No   —2)Yes, suggestive   —3)Yes, definite
                b. Please explain the evidence: _____
                _____

        c. Was this evidence used in court?

            —1)No   —2)Yes   —3)Case did not go to trial

30. Were there eye witnesses to the sexual assault who can corroborate the child's story?
    —1)No   —2)Yes *[Describe, listing adults first.]*
        <u>Eye witness 1</u>
        a. Age: ___Adult (18 yrs or over) <u>OR</u> ___Child *[enter age at observation:* ___ years]
        b. Relation to child: _____
        c. Background: _____
        d. Did witness testify in court? ___2)Yes ___1)No -- Why not? _____
        <u>Eye witness 2</u>
        a. Age: ___Adult (18 yrs or over) <u>OR</u> ___Child *[enter age at observation:* ___ years]
        b. Relation to child: _____
        c. Background: _____
        d. Did witness testify in court? ___2)Yes ___1)No -- Why not? _____

<u>Eye witness 3</u>

a. Age: ___Adult (18 yrs or over) <u>OR</u> ___Child [*enter age at observation:* ___ years]

b. Relation to child: _____

c. Background: _____

d. Did witness testify in court? ___₂)Yes ___₁)No -- Why not? _____

<u>Eye witness 4</u>

a. Age: ___Adult (18 yrs or over) <u>OR</u> ___Child [*enter age at observation:* ___ years]

b. Relation to child: _____

c. Background: _____

d. Did witness testify in court? ___₂)Yes ___₁)No -- Why not? _____

31. Were there other (*non-eye*) witnesses who could provide <u>corroborating evidence</u>?

___₁)No\   ___₂)Yes [*Describe, listing adults first. Do not include expert witnesses who provide general information about sexual abuse not directly related to this case.*]

<u>Witness 1</u>

a. Age: ___Adult (18 yrs or over) <u>OR</u> ___Child [*enter age at observation:* ___ years]

b. Relation to child: _____

c. Background: _____

d. Did witness testify in court? ___₂)Yes ___₁)No -- Why not? _____

<u>Witness 2</u>

a. Age: ___Adult (18 yrs or over) <u>OR</u> ___Child [*enter age at observation:* ___ years]

b. Relation to child: _____

c. Background: _____

d. Did witness testify in court? ___₂)Yes ___₁)No -- Why not? _____

<u>Witness 3</u>

a. Age: ___Adult (18 yrs or over) <u>OR</u> ___Child [*enter age at observation:* ___ years]

b. Relation to child: _____

c. Background: _____

d. Did witness testify in court? ___₂)Yes ___₁)No -- Why not? _____

<u>Witness 4</u>

a. Age: ___Adult (18 yrs or over) <u>OR</u> ___Child [*enter age at observation:* ___ years]

b. Relation to child: _____

c. Background: _____

d. Did witness testify in court? ___₂)Yes ___₁)No -- Why not? _____

32. Was there other corroborating evidence?

___₁)No\   ___₂)Yes

a. What was it? _____

b. Was it used in court?

___₂)Yes ___₁)No

b. Why not? _____

Section # [   ]

Defendant [   ]

Case identifier [   ]

Child identifier [   ]

Please check one: ___ Separate competency hearing (*voir dire*)
                   ___ Competency questions after child is sworn

Child Competency Examination Checklist *

Personal Competence

Item	Asked?		Response Used to Disqualify Witness?	
	No	Yes	No	Yes
Child's first name	—	—	—	—
Child's last name	—	—	—	—
Child's age	—	—	—	—
Grade in school	—	—	—	—
Name of school	—	—	—	—
Name of present teacher	—	—	—	—
Name of past teacher	—	—	—	—
Identifies a school activity	—	—	—	—
Identifies people in home	—	—	—	—
Identifies friends	—	—	—	—
Identifies an activity with a friend	—	—	—	—
Identifies a family activity	—	—	—	—
Other:	—	—	—	—
Other:	—	—	—	—
Other:	—	—	—	—
Other:	—	—	—	—
Other:	—	—	—	—

If disqualified, please explain:

_____

_____

_____

_____

_____

_____

_____

_____

_____

_____

_____

_____

* Adapted from Grant, C.A. (1987) Child Competency Instrument, under editorial review Archives of Psychiatric Nursing

211

Intellectual Competence

Item	Asked?		Response Used to Disqualify Witness?		If disqualified, please explain:
	No	Yes	No	Yes	
Can count	—	—	—	—	_____
Knows colors	—	—	—	—	_____
Can read	—	—	—	—	_____
Can write	—	—	—	—	_____
Identifies body parts	—	—	—	—	_____
Identifies a favorite food	—	—	—	—	_____
Identifies clothing	—	—	—	—	_____
Identifies relationship	—	—	—	—	_____
Identifies a feeling	—	—	—	—	_____
Identifies a relational concept	—	—	—	—	_____
Identifies a time concept	—	—	—	—	_____
Other: _____			—	—	_____
Other: _____			—	—	_____
Other: _____			—	—	_____
Other: _____			—	—	_____
Other: _____			—	—	_____

Moral Competence

Item	Asked?		Response Used to Disqualify Witness?		If disqualified, please explain:
	No	Yes	No	Yes	
Identifies something as make believe	—	—	—	—	_____
Identifies a truth	—	—	—	—	_____
Identifies a lie	—	—	—	—	_____
Identifies the consequences of telling a lie	—	—	—	—	_____
Identifies good qualities in a person	—	—	—	—	_____
Identifies bad qualities in a person	—	—	—	—	_____
Identifies an event as right	—	—	—	—	_____
Identifies an event as wrong	—	—	—	—	_____
Other: _____			—	—	_____
Other: _____			—	—	_____
Other: _____			—	—	_____
Other: _____			—	—	_____
Other: _____			—	—	_____

Questioning Style Towards Witness

Prosecutor   —1) Appropriate for child witness   —2) More appropriate for adult witness

Defense Attorney   —1) Appropriate for child witness   —2) More appropriate for adult witness

Judge   —1) Appropriate for child witness   —2) More appropriate for adult witness

Manner Towards the Witness

Prosecutor   —1) Business-like   —2) Supportive   —3) Condescending/Discrediting   —4) Intimidating

Defense Attorney   —1) Business-like   —2) Supportive   —3) Condescending/Discrediting   —4) Intimidating

Judge   —1) Business-like   —2) Supportive   —3) Condescending/Discrediting   —4) Intimidating

Location of Witness While Testifying

—1) Sitting at a table

—2) Standing

—3) Sitting in a witness box

—4) In Judge's Chambers

—5) Other: _____

Revision 1 [9/87]

Child Witness for Prosecution

Please complete this checklist for every child witness. For each item, try to characterize the child's or attorney's behavior. That is, check the response that occurred most often, or was most apparent.

1. **Manner of child witness' dress:** ___1)casual/play ___2)school/work ___3)party/social

2. **Length of time child witness testified:**
   ___1)less than 1/2 hour ___4)1 1/2 to 2 hours ___7)3 to 3 1/2 hours Time testimony began: _____
   ___2)1/2 hour to 1 hour ___5)2 to 2 1/2 hours ___8)3 1/2 to 4 hours Time testimony ended: _____
   ___3)1 to 1 1/2 hours ___6)2 1/2 to 3 hours ___9)over 4 hours

3. **Location of child witness while testifying:**
   ___1)sitting at a table ___3)sitting in witness box ___5)other: _____
   ___2)standing ___4)in judge's chambers (*closed circuit t.v.*)

4. **Number of interruptions in child witness' testimony** (*times child left and returned to the stand, or lawyers approached the bench to clarify procedure with the judge*)
   Tally here: _____ Enter number here: _____

OBSERVATIONS WHEN CHILD WITNESS IS QUESTIONED BY PROSECUTOR:

		a. When questioned about sex abuse?	**b. When questioned about other matters?**
5.	Facial expression of the child:	___1)smiling ___2)serious ___3)anxious ___4)other _____	___1)smiling ___2)serious ___3)anxious ___4)other _____
6.	Eye contact of child to defendant:	___1)avoids completely ___2)avoids intermittently ___3)contact occasional, avoidance not obvious ___4)direct ___5)not observable	___1)avoids completely ___2)avoids intermittently ___3)contact occasional, avoidance not obvious ___4)direct ___5)not observable
7.	Child's motor behavior:	___1)excessive fidgeting ___2)relatively still (*normal*) ___3)rigid or immobilized ___4)other _____	___1)excessive fidgeting ___2)relatively still (*normal*) ___3)rigid or immobilized ___4)other _____
8.	Child's verbal behavior:	___1)answers normally ___2)answers hesitantly ___3)doesn't answer	___1)answers normally ___2)answers hesitantly ___3)doesn't answer
9.	Child's emotional behavior:	___1)flat, little affect ___2)angry ___3)frightened ___4)crying ___5)normal ___6)other _____	___1)flat, little affect ___2)angry ___3)frightened ___4)crying ___5)normal ___6)other _____
10.	Prosecutor's questioning style toward child:	___1)appropriate to age of child ___2)more appropriate for adult witness	___1)appropriate to age of child ___2)more appropriate for adult witness
11.	Prosecutor's manner toward child:	___1)business-like ___2)supportive ___3)condescending/discrediting ___4)intimidating	___1)business-like ___2)supportive ___3)condescending/discrediting ___4)intimidating

OBSERVATIONS WHEN CHILD WITNESS IS QUESTIONED BY DEFENSE ATTORNEY:

		a. When questioned about sex abuse?	**b. When questioned about other matters?**
12.	Facial expression of the child:	___1) smiling ___2) serious ___3) anxious ___4) other _____	___1) smiling ___2) serious ___3) anxious ___4) other _____
13.	Eye contact of child to defendant:	___1) avoids completely ___2) avoids intermittently ___3) contact occasional, avoidance not obvious ___4) direct ___5) not observable	___1) avoids completely ___2) avoids intermittently ___3) contact occasional, avoidance not obvious ___4) direct ___5) not observable
14.	Child's motor behavior:	___1) excessive fidgeting ___2) relatively still (*normal*) ___3) rigid or immobilized ___4) other _____	___1) excessive fidgeting ___2) relatively still (*normal*) ___3) rigid or immobilized ___4) other _____
15.	Child's verbal behavior:	___1) answers normally ___2) answers hesitantly ___3) doesn't answer	___1) answers normally ___2) answers hesitantly ___3) doesn't answer
16.	Child's emotional behavior:	___1) flat, little affect ___2) angry ___3) frightened ___4) crying ___5) normal ___6) other _____	___1) flat, little affect ___2) angry ___3) frightened ___4) crying ___5) normal ___6) other _____
17.	Defense attorney's questioning style toward child:	___1) appropriate to age of child ___2) more appropriate for adult witness	___1) appropriate to age of child ___2) more appropriate for adult witness
18.	Defense attorney's manner toward child:	___1) business-like ___2) supportive ___3) condescending/discrediting ___4) intimidating	___1) business-like ___2) supportive ___3) condescending/discrediting ___4) intimidating

OBSERVATIONS OF JUDGE'S BEHAVIOR TOWARD CHILD WITNESS

19. Judge's questioning style toward child:

    ___1) appropriate to age of child witness
    ___2) more appropriate for adult witness

20. Judge's manner toward child:

    ___1) business-like
    ___2) supportive
    ___3) condescending/discrediting
    ___4) intimidating

Revision 2 [11/87]

Daily Observation Sheet

Defendant: [_____]

[_____]-[_____]
Section#   Case identifier

Observer: _____

Date: _____

Please give your impressions of the day's proceedings by circling one number on each scale below:

Continuity:	often interrupted	1	2	3	4	5	uninterrupted
Overall style of prosecutor:	undramatic	1	2	3	4	5	dramatic
Prosecutor's mastery of details of case:	unprepared	1	2	3	4	5	prepared
Overall style of defense attorney:	undramatic	1	2	3	4	5	dramatic
Defense attorney's mastery of details of case:	unprepared	1	2	3	4	5	prepared
Technical (legal) issues addressed:	few	1	2	3	4	5	many
Judge's involvement in arguments	passive	1	2	3	4	5	active
Judge's bias apparent?	defense	1	2	3	4	5	prosecution
Presence of audience:	empty	1	2	3	4	5	packed
Appearance of defendant:	unkempt	1	2	3	4	5	immaculate
Demeanor of defendant:	uneasy	1	2	3	4	5	confident
Apparent character of defendant:	antisocial	1	2	3	4	5	upstanding
Apparent social class standing of defendant:	lower	1	2	3	4	5	upper

Witnesses

Please list all witnesses who testified on this date in order of their testimony and complete categories at right.

Witness	Age (if not adult)	Length of testimony	Relationship to victim	Relationship to defendant	Called by prosecutor (P) or defense (D)	Called as expert? 0) No 1) Yes

Jurors

Please draw vertical lines on jury box diagram to reflect the configuration of seats in the jury box of the courtroom you are observing. At exactly 10 minutes after the beginning of each person's testimony, please scan the jury and rate each juror's attentiveness using the codes at the bottom of the page, as well as an "M" or "F" to indicate gender. Enter one number for each juror in the jury box diagram. Use one diagram for each testimony.

Witness _____ Beg. time_____

Form of testimony: _____
(*live, closed circuit t.v., videotaped*)

Jury Box (front)

Witness _____ Beg. time_____

Form of testimony: _____
(*live, closed circuit t.v., videotaped*)

Jury Box (front)

Witness _____ Beg. time_____

Form of testimony: _____
(*live, closed circuit t.v., videotaped*)

Jury Box (front)

Witness _____ Beg. time_____

Form of testimony: _____
(*live, closed circuit t.v., videotaped*)

Jury Box (front)

Key: 1 = Extra attentive (*leaning forward, reacting audibly or facially, etc.*)
2 = Attentive
3 = Inattentive (*bored-looking, distracted*)

M = Male Juror
F = Female Juror

Prosecution Techniques

Please check every technique the prosecutor used/attempted to use in trying this case, including techniques invoked automatically because of statute or case law. For every technique you haven't checked by the end of the trial, ask the prosecutor: a) if the technique is automatic in your jurisdiction; b) if he/she requested the technique, and c) if it was used.

	Requested?		Used?	
	Yes	No	Yes	No
Eliminating or modifying competency criteria for child victim witness				
Presuming the competency of children by statute	____	____	____	____
Modifying the wording of the oath used to swear in child witnesses (*e.g., substituting "lie" for "falsehood"*)	____	____	____	____
Avoiding direct confrontation between child witness and defendant				
Using closed circuit television for testimony	____	____	____	____
a. child can see defendant on monitor	____	____	____	____
b. child cannot see defendant on monitor	____	____	____	____
Permitting videotaped depositions and statements	____	____	____	____
Permitting exceptions to the hearsay ruling				
Permitting hearsay that is a spontaneous exclamation	____	____	____	____
Permitting specific hearsay exception for child witnesses in sex abuse cases	____	____	____	____
Adapting the courtroom process to the child witness				
Scaling down adult language relating to sex acts and body parts	____	____	____	____
Not requiring child's appearance at the Grand Jury proceedings	____	____	____	____
Using anatomically correct dolls during examination and/or cross examination	____	____	____	____
Modifying the physical environment to reduce formality and intimidation, (*e.g., making witness chair smaller for child*) specify: _____	____	____	____	____
Keeping attorneys at a particular distance from child during questioning	____	____	____	____
Allowing leading questions on direct examination of child witness	____	____	____	____
Using child victim advocates, CASA's, or Guardians *ad litem*	____	____	____	____
Having a support person for the child present in the courtroom (*other than officially appointed advocates, above*) specify: _____	____	____	____	____
Using expert witnesses				
To testify on selected attributes of child sexual abuse	____	____	____	____
To provide developmental information to compare normal behavior patterns with those of a child who was sexually abused	____	____	____	____
To provide testimony that explains the child's behavior after the event	____	____	____	____
Protecting the child's privacy				
Limiting the access of the general public to the courtroom	____	____	____	____
a. in general	____	____	____	____
b. while child testifies	____	____	____	____
Assuring that the media not divulge the identity of the witness	____	____	____	____

PLEASE USE OTHER SIDE OF FORM FOR ANY EXPLANATIONS OR NOTES

Notes

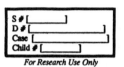
JUROR QUESTIONNAIRE

PLEASE CIRCLE YOUR RESPONSE

Revision 2 [11/87]

How much was your decision as a juror influenced by:

1. The ability of the child witness to describe the event?   not at all   a little   somewhat   a lot   completely

2. The accuracy of the child's memory?   not at all   a little   somewhat   a lot   completely

3. The ability of the child to tell the truth   not at all   a little   somewhat   a lot   completely

4. The child's apparent level of preparation for testifying   not at all   a little   somewhat   a lot   completely

5. The child's emotional behavior?   not at all   a little   somewhat   a lot   completely

Please indicate how much you agree or disagree with the following statements:

6. The child witness clearly described the event.   strongly disagree   disagree   neither agree nor disagree   agree   strongly agree

7. The child's memory was accurate.   strongly disagree   disagree   neither agree nor disagree   agree   strongly agree

8. The child told the truth.   strongly disagree   disagree   neither agree nor disagree   agree   strongly agree

9. The child was prepared to testify   strongly disagree   disagree   neither agree nor disagree   agree   strongly agree

10. The child's emotional behavior in court was appropriate.   strongly disagree   disagree   neither agree nor disagree   agree   strongly agree

Please use this space to describe any unusual behaviors of the child witness during the trial:

_____

_____

_____

Do you feel that the child witness was treated fairly and sensitively?
___ Yes   ___ No
     Please explain: _____

_____

_____

Over

INFORMATION AVAILABLE TO JURORS

PLEASE CIRCLE RESPONSES TO INDICATE WHICH TYPES OF INFORMATION WERE MADE AVAILABLE TO YOU IN THIS CASE AND HOW IMPORTANT IT WAS (OR WOULD HAVE BEEN) TO HAVE EACH TYPE OF INFORMATION LISTED WHEN MAKING YOUR DECISION AS A JUROR.

Type of Information	Was it Available?		Was it (or would it have been) important to have?		
Testimony from child witness under direct examination by prosecuting attorney	Yes	No	No	Somewhat	Very
Testimony from child witness under cross-examination by defense attorney	Yes	No	No	Somewhat	Very
Medical evidence of sexual abuse	Yes	No	No	Somewhat	Very
Testimony by an adult about what the child first said about the event	Yes	No	No	Somewhat	Very
Testimony from law enforcement personnel	Yes	No	No	Somewhat	Very
Testimony from an expert who had interviewed the child witness	Yes	No	No	Somewhat	Very
Testimony from child abuse expert having had no previous contact with the child	Yes	No	No	Somewhat	Very
Testimony from the child's parent(s) who was (were) not charged in the case	Yes	No	No	Somewhat	Very
Results of psychological testing of child	Yes	No	No	Somewhat	Very
Written transcripts or video tape of everything said during the trial	Yes	No	No	Somewhat	Very
Judge's answers to questions raised by jurors during their deliberations	Yes	No	No	Somewhat	Very
Discussion with other jurors during deliberations	Yes	No	No	Somewhat	Very

Is there any other information that was important to your decision or that you wanted but could not obtain?

_____

_____

_____

ATTITUDE SURVEY

Directions

This questionnaire deals with people's attitudes toward sexual abuse in our society. Below is a list of statements concerned with various attitudes people may have toward sexual abuse. For *each* of the statements, do the following:

A—Read each statement carefully.

B—Ask yourself: "How much do I agree *or* disagree with this statement?

C—Using the rating scale below, select the *number* which *best* represents your feeling.

D—Then, place the *number* in the blank space to the *left* of the statement.

E—Please answer *all* items. Do *not* leave any items blank.

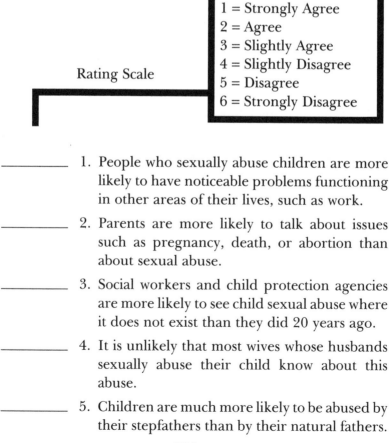

Rating Scale

```
1 = Strongly Agree
2 = Agree
3 = Slightly Agree
4 = Slightly Disagree
5 = Disagree
6 = Strongly Disagree
```

_____ 1. People who sexually abuse children are more likely to have noticeable problems functioning in other areas of their lives, such as work.

_____ 2. Parents are more likely to talk about issues such as pregnancy, death, or abortion than about sexual abuse.

_____ 3. Social workers and child protection agencies are more likely to see child sexual abuse where it does not exist than they did 20 years ago.

_____ 4. It is unlikely that most wives whose husbands sexually abuse their child know about this abuse.

_____ 5. Children are much more likely to be abused by their stepfathers than by their natural fathers.

Rating Scale

_____ 6. The majority of all reported child sexual abuse cases are tried in court

_____ 7. Children are no more influenced by leading questions than are adults.

_____ 8. Men who have incestuous relations with their daughters are just as likely as other men to have normal sexual relationships with their wives.

_____ 9. It would be wrong to convict someone of a crime if the only eyewitness was a 10-year-old.

_____ 10. Children who have always lived with their mothers are just as likely to be abused as children who have lived at some point without their mother.

_____ 11. Courtroom trials are so stressful for children that we can't expect them to behave as competently as adults.

_____ 12. Child sexual abuse is more likely to occur in poor, rural families than rich, suburban families.

_____ 13. Children who retract their stories about sexual abuse were probably lying in the first place.

_____ 14. Steps must be taken to increase the conviction rate in child sexual abuse cases.

_____ 15. Experts have only just begun to study children's eyewitness memory.

_____ 16. The clear majority of child sexual abuse cases involve a relative or someone the child knows and trusts.

_____ 17. Medical experts cannot usually tell if a child has been sexually abused.

_____ 18. Children are easily manipulated into giving false reports of sexual abuse.

_____ 19. Child molesters are overcome by sexual urges.

_____ 20. When children identify strangers as having sexually abused them, the identifications are highly reliable.

_____ 21. Daughters whose mothers discourage them from talking about sex more often experience sexual abuse than those whose mothers are more open about sex.

_____ 22. Children who are physically abused are more likely to be sexually abused.

_____ 23. There is much that should be done to ease a sexually abused child's trauma in court.

_____ 24. Most people who were sexually abused as children do not end up sexually abusing their own children.

_____ 25. Sexual abusers are violent and aggressive in other relationships.

_____ 26. Children can distinguish fantasy from reality.

_____ 27. In the current social climate, it is virtually impossible for a person accused of child sexual abuse to get an impartial trial.

_____ 28. If a child is sexually abused by a parent, the child will still show love for that parent.

_____ 29. Children's memories for emotionally traumatic events are not as accurate as adults'.

Rating Scale

1 = Strongly Agree
2 = Agree
3 = Slightly Agree
4 = Slightly Disagree
5 = Disagree
6 = Strongly Disagree

_____ 30. Delays in reporting child sexual abuse to the police or other authorities are quite common.

_____ 31. Sexually abused children generally experience the same set of psychological reactions and symptoms.

_____ 32. Children are unlikely to fantasize about sexual activity with parents or other adults.

_____ 33. After sexual abuse prevention training, children are more likely to misinterpret harmless expressions of affection by adults as sexual abuse.

_____ 34. Personality profiles of child molesters are highly accurate.

_____ 35. A child of a large vs. average-sized family is more likely to be sexually abused.

NOTES

INTRODUCTION

1. *A Dark Science: Women, Sexuality and Psychiatry in the Nineteenth Century*, by Jeffrey Masson (1986), exposes the nineteenth-century roots of the psychiatric profession's reluctance to believe women's and children's accounts of sexual abuse, and the profession's penchant for elaborate theories that blame these victims for their own victimization. The author accomplishes this disclosure by translating typical gynecological and psychiatric writings of the period that detail horrendous reabuse of these patients by their doctors complete with the rationalizations that apparently have persisted to this day.

2. *Thou Shalt Not Be Aware: Society's Betrayal of the Child* (Miller, 1986), the title of Alice Miller's third book, refers to psychoanalysis' suppression of the question of how parents consciously or unconsciously treat their children during the first years of life. By perpetrating this suppression, the profession is representing society as a whole and that society's need not to know this information for complicated reasons of psychic balance.

3. A book by journalist David Hechler, *The Battle and the Backlash: The Child Sexual Abuse War* (1988), develops the theme of the adversarial relationship between the "child savers" and the critics of the therapeutic and criminal justice systems, highlighting the current controversy that surrounds child sexual abuse.

4. My apologies to readers in the legal profession (particularly prosecutors in child abuse and sex crimes units) who may find some of these "revelations" to be obvious. I can assure them that the way the legal system operates is anything but obvious to the nonlawyer. Even for those who have a sense of judicial process in general, there is often an assumption that child abuse cases would be handled differently.

5. Although I do not know whether Billie Wright Dziech and Charles B. Schudson, authors of *On Trial: America's Courts and Their Treatment of Sexually Abused Children*, would call their book an exposé of the system, they are more qualified than I to produce such a disclosure. In any case, I commend the book highly to any reader who has not yet seen it. Due to the expertise of Schudson, a Wisconsin Court of Appeals judge, the book is very knowledgeable regarding the legal issues attendant to child sexual abuse cases in criminal court. The book differs from this one in many ways, the most important being that it deals with the trials for child sexual abuse, not with the cases that are handled with other procedures. Second, Dziech and Schudson use mostly first- and second-hand anecdotal information as data, whereas I use mostly aggregated statistics and experimental findings.

6. Patricia Toth, director of the National Center for Prosecution of Child Abuse of the American Prosecutors Research Institute, did review this manuscript thoroughly, so that it would be accurate from a legal standpoint and useful to lawyers.

CHAPTER 1. Child Abuse

1. This discussion is not intended to give the complete history of child sexual abuse through the ages, but to illustrate, through notable examples, the very different ways of officially conceptualizing the event through time, presaging our current conflicted approach to the criminalization of child sexual abuse, particularly when it occurs within families.

2. The White House Conference on Children in 1909 resulted in the creation of the U.S. Children's Bureau in 1912, which produced the Standard Juvenile Court Act in 1925. Juvenile or family courts exist in all states now, and provide an alternative to criminal court in child welfare matters, in addition to their juvenile justice role.

3. In a personal communication with Patricia Toth, director of the Center for Prosecution of Child Abuse of the American Prosecutors Research Institute, she pointed out an alternative explanation for

the coincidence of events described. Although she agreed that our system has taken a "noncriminal" approach much of the time, she stated that she believes that treatment programs grew because more people were court-ordered into treatment.

4. It is important to note that most of these references are from the early 1980s. As we learn more about how to prepare children, we realize the experience can be made less traumatic. It may, in fact, be an important affirmation for the child.

5. This is beginning to change. In a number of jurisdictions, prosecutors are taking child sexual abuse cases to trial with success.

6. There are few survey studies of child sexual abuse cases in the criminal court. Among them: Gebhard (1965) studied the convicted and incarcerated sex offenders in Indiana and California between 1941 and 1960, among whom were individuals convicted of sexually abusing a child. Charles McCaghy (1966) studied all persons who had been found guilty of a sexual offense with a child in certain counties in Wisconsin, whether they were incarcerated or on probation. Bruce MacMurray (1988) studied case processing and prosecutor discretion for sexual abuse cases in one county in Massachusetts between 1983 and 1985. Debra Whitcomb (Whitcomb et al., 1985) studied approximately 800 substantiated cases of child sexual abuse—half referred for prosecution and half not referred. These cases were from one county in each of four states: New York, Iowa, California, and Minnesota. The American Bar Association (1987) studied a random sample of 393 closed, child sexual abuse cases from the police and child welfare systems in Virginia and California to determine the extent and type of criminal prosecution carried out.

7. *Kentucky v. Stincer (96 LEd 2d 631, 647 [1987])*, in the U.S. Supreme Court, holds that a defendant does not have the right to be present at a competency hearing for the child victim witness.

CHAPTER 2. Methods and Sample Used in This Research

1. Methods for the expert survey and the mock jury experiment appear in Chapter 7, along with the results from these studies.

2. "All the requisite categories of data," in this case, means more than just the variable being looked at. It is required that this variable be measured *only* for comparable cases—that is, if gender of victims in the system is being assessed, then it would be misleading to report gender of all cases from the Jacksonville area, where cases not filed were part of the data set as well, because these cases were not also part of the data set in other jurisdictions. The basic data set for most analyses, then, was filed cases not subsequently dropped, in which the defendant was not found incompetent to stand trial.

CHAPTER 3. Eight Jurisdictions

1. After the (1980–1986) demographic statistics for each jurisdiction are presented, the narrative portion of the descriptions shifts
to the present tense for readability. Please note, however, that the
social service/judicial system and legislation pertaining to child
sexual abuse cases is changing rapidly, and these jurisdictions may
operate somewhat differently today from the process that is described.
2. Demographic statistics are accurate as of 1979, 1980, or 1985, as
indicated. More recent statistics were not compiled and published as
of this writing.
3. Every jurisdiction has some sort of speedy trial requirement. In
practice, unfortunately, cases are often continued.

CHAPTER 4. The Victims, the Defendants, the Cases

1. Outcry is the spontaneous disclosure of the abuse to a third party, and
is usually precipitated by acute stress. It is accepted in court
as evidence despite its being hearsay, because of a belief that statements made under such conditions have veracity. It is also called the
res gestae, or excited-utterance exception to the hearsay rule.
2. The terms perpetrator and defendant are used interchangeably in
this book to indicate anyone identified in the sampling procedure
who had been accused of child sexual abuse.
3. For these purposes, extra-familial relationships are custodial and
noncustodial acquaintances, mother's boyfriend, child's boyfriend,
and strangers; intra-familial relationships are all biological and step-
relatives. The inclusion of some biological and step-relatives who do
not live in the home of the victim may be a departure from other
researchers' definitions, and may therefore account in part for the
difference in proportions. Intrafamily and extrafamily should not be
read as synonymous with "appropriate for CPA" and "inappropriate
for CPA."
4. A thought-provoking discussion, pro and con, of the existence of
an incest taboo, complete with a review of sociological, anthropo-
logical, psychoanalytic, genetic, and political theories on the subject, is provided by Vander Mey and Neff in *Incest as Child Abuse:
Research and Application* (1986).
5. The numbers reported here are for only the "pure" cases, where
behaviors of only one type were reported. There are also many
cases that cross types.
6. Here, as with other findings in this study, it should be pointed out
that the statistics are not worse for child abuse cases than other

crimes. On the contrary, Patricia Toth, director of the National Center for the Prosecution of Child Abuse of the American Prosecutors Research Institute, estimates filing rates in general to be in the 50% to 60% range (personal communication, August, 1992).

7. From this point on, in this book, the victim will be referred to with the feminine pronoun and the defendant with the masculine pronoun. As we have seen, this breakdown accurately reflects the preponderance of cases.

8. A few of these cases were unaccounted for at the end of the data-collection period, as they were still pending. The figures are essentially correct, however, as even cases that were scheduled for trial but had not been tried were counted in the trial statistics.

9. Jacksonville is the exception because all categories of cases were retrieved from that site. Of all the cases that were processed by the prosecutor's office in Jacksonville, 3.8% went to trial.

10. This effect of diversion programs in general is discussed by Samuel Walker in *Sense and Nonsense About Crime* (1989).

CHAPTER 5. Which Way to Go?

1. This finding brings to mind the "conditioning continuum" of child sexual abuse posed by Alexander Zaphiris and confirmed by other researchers and clinicians, wherein an offender slowly accustoms his victim to more and more explicit and intrusive behaviors over time. We can speculate that the defendant who exposes himself to the one- or two-year-old would have progressed to fondling, and then perhaps to oral genital contact, had he not been caught at the earlier stage. (This theory does not assert, necessarily, that the molestation career of the defendant who was caught for exposure is in its earliest stages, but rather that he was in an early phase of molesting this particular victim.)

2. The grouping here is the same as in Chapter 3: extra-familial relationships include custodial and noncustodial acquaintances, mother's boyfriend, child's boyfriend, and strangers; intra-familial relationships are all biological and step-relatives.

3. The order of these case types is the order in which they explain variance in the behaviors among the cases, or the "strength" of their explanatory power—case type 1 being the strongest, and so on.

4. The categories of suggestive and definitive evidence of abuse are taken from medical documents in prosecutor's records and prosecutor's notes. As such, they represent expert opinion, but not any standardized classification.

CHAPTER 6. The Trials

1. The Federal Rules of Evidence contain 23 different hearsay exceptions, some of which can be used in child sexual abuse cases, and case law has identified still others (Dziech & Schudson, 1991). Most recently in *White v. Illinois (90 U.S. 6113 [1992])*, the Supreme Court affirmed the use of hearsay evidence explicitly in a sexual abuse case.

2. There has been some research that casts doubt on the validity of using anatomically correct dolls with alleged child sexual abuse victims (Boat & Everson, 1988; Yates & Terr, 1988). This work particularly questions the specific training and expertise of the professionals employing the dolls with these children. More recent evidence, however, presents a more sanguine picture of professional use of the dolls (Kendall-Tackett & Watson, 1992).

3. Although it was determined during the data-collection year that certain cases would be held over for trial, not all these trials took place during the time period. Those that did not were not observed. This accounts for the discrepancy between the number of cases reported in the previous chapters as having gone to trial and the number of trials observed.

4. Due to volunteer availability and scheduling difficulties, duplicate rating to assure reliability of individual children's testimony was not always possible. When it was, ratings were examined and combined. Otherwise, reliability was enhanced by the volunteer training, which included instruction and practice in observation and rating.

5. Of course, testifying about traumatic crimes is also difficult for adult victims. For example, rape victims often show all of these same behaviors on the witness stand. When it is over, however, both adults and children may feel better for having testified.

6. This contradicts the findings of another study, performed at roughly the same time by other researchers (Morison & Greene, 1992), who found considerable disparity between experts' and jurors' knowledge and attitudes. The difference, in addition to the fact that the same instrument was not used to assess this knowledge, may well be that Morison's and Greene's jurors had not necessarily served on child sexual abuse cases.

CHAPTER 7. Expert Testimony and Child Witness Credibility

1. The research presented in this chapter came about as a result of a subcontract of the federal grant supporting the NCJW project. The research was briefly outlined by this author and those individuals at the University of Minnesota referred to here as the Borgida group (some of whom have since gone to other institutions). Then, the

researchers in the Borgida group carried out the bulk of the work on these studies at their site. This author participated in the construction of the Attitude Survey used in the expert partisanship studies and provided consultation on the mock jury-trial on an ongoing basis, particularly in the preparation of the simulated trial video. For more complete information on the studies presented here, the reader is urged to see *Expert Testimony in Child Sexual Abuse Cases: An Empirical Investigation of Partisan Orientation* by E. Borgida, A. Gresham, J. Swim, M. Bull, and E. Gray; *Do Child Sexual Abuse Experts Hold Pro-Child Beliefs?: A National Survey of the Society for Traumatic Stress Studies* by M. Kovera, E. Borgida, A. Gresham, J. Swim, and E. Gray; and *Children as Witnesses in Court: The Influence of Expert Testimony* by E. Borgida, A. Gresham, M. Bull, and P. Regan, full citations of which are in the bibliography.

2. For the purposes of this research, we define partisanship as beliefs in the credibility of child witnesses that have favorable implications for the child, irrespective of the accuracy of those beliefs. By using the term partisan, therefore, we are not implying that the assessed beliefs are biased—merely that the beliefs are stronger and perhaps more polarized in terms of their favorability toward child witnesses.

3. Psychometric analysis was not performed on this instrument, and the categories are not to be taken as reliable subscales of a larger construct. The survey instrument is intended to be a means of assessing respondents' beliefs and attitudes regarding child sexual abuse and the court cases that result. Because the survey is simply assessing these beliefs and attitudes, rather than seeking to extrapolate from them to a personality trait, it is by definition valid. Categorization of groups of questions into topic areas is merely a heuristic device for greater readability, not an attempt to establish child sexual abuse attitudinal "factors."

4. These analytical techniques of factor analysis, multivariate analysis of variance, and hierarchical multiple regression are briefly explained in the discussion of method in Chapter 2.

5. People may tend to overestimate the scope of bias in such cases on the basis of a few widely publicized cases involving custody disputes or day-care center misconduct.

CHAPTER 8. What Do We Do Now?

1. It may very well be true, however, that much of the value of certain techniques is in their *potential* use, thus opening for investigators and prosecutors, many options for investigations, prosecutions, and guilty pleas that would otherwise never come about.

REFERENCES

Abel, G., Becker, J., Murphy, W. D., & Flanagan, B. 1981. Identifying dangerous child molesters. In R. B. Stuart (Ed.), *Violent behavior*. New York: Brunner/Mazel.

Abel,G., Becker. J., & Cunnningham-Rather, J. 1984. Complications, consent, and cognitions in sex between children and adults. *International Journal of Law and Psychiatry, 7,* 89–103.

American Bar Association. 1987. *Child sexual abuse: An analysis of case processing*. Washington D.C.: author.

American Humane Association. 1979. *National analysis of official child neglect and abuse reporting, Denver: Author.*

American Humane Association. 1983. *National analysis of official child neglect and abuse reporting*, Denver: Author.

American jurisprudence proof of facts, 3. 1960. San Francisco: Bancroft-Whitney Co.

American Prosecutors Research Institute (1992) *Competency of Child Witnesses*. Alexander, VA: author.

American Prosecutors Research Institute (1992a) Special Procedures: *Courtroom Closure; Reading Questions; Use of Anatomical Dolls, Length and Time of Victim/Witness Interviews' Speedy Disposition of Child Abuse Cases*. Alexander, VA: author.

Attorney General's Task Force on Family Violence. (1984, September). *Final report*. Washington, D.C.: Author.

235

Berliner, L. 1985. The child and the criminal justice system. In A. W. Burgess (Ed.), *Rape and sexual assault.* New York: Garland, pp. 199–208.

Berliner, L., & Barbieri, M. 1984. The testimony of the child victim of sexual assault. *Journal of Social Issues, 40,* (2) 125–135.

Berliner, L., & Stevens, D. 1980. Advocating for sexually abused children in the criminal justice system. *Sexual abuse of children: Selected readings.* Washington, D.C.: U.S. Department of Health and Human Services, National Center on Child Abuse and Neglect.

Boat, F., & Everson, M. 1988. Use of anatomical dolls among professionals in child abuse evaluations. *Child Abuse and Neglect, 12* (2), 171–179.

Bond, J. 1985. Children as witnesses in cases of child sexual abuse. Proposal submitted to National Center of Child Abuse and Neglect, 1986.

Borgida, E., Gresham, A., Kovera, M., & Regan, P. 1991. Children as witnesses in court: The influence of expert psychological testimony. In A. Burgess (Ed.) *Child trauma,* vol. 1: *Issues and research.* New York: Garland.

Borgida, E., Kovera, M., Gresham, A., Regan, P. & Gray, E. 1992. *Juror decision-making in child sexual abuse cases: The effects of expert testimony and witness demeanor.* Unpublished manuscript, University of Minnesota.

Borgida, E., Gresham, A., Swim, J., Bull, M., & Gray, E. 1989. Expert testimony in child sexual abuse cases: An empirical investigation of partisan orientation. *Family Law Quarterly 23,* 433–449.

Brekke, N., & Borgida, E. 1988. Expert psychological testimony in rape trials: A social-cognitive analysis. *Journal of Personality and Social Psychology 55,* 372–386.

Bremner, R. (Ed.). 1970. *Children and youth in America: A documentary history.* Cambridge: Harvard University Press.

Brownmiller, S. 1975. *Against our will: Men, women, and rape.* New York: Bantam Books.

Bruckner, D., & Johnson P. 1987. Treatment for adult male victims of childhood sexual abuse. *Social Casework, 68,* 81–87.

Bulkley, J. 1981. Evidentiary theories for admitting a child's out-of-court statement of sexual abuse at trail. In J. Bulkley (Ed.), *Child sexual abuse and the law.* Washington, DC: American Bar Association, pp. 153–165.

Bulkley. J, 1985. *Child sexual abuse and the law,* Washington, D.C.: National Legal Resource Center for Child Advocacy and Protection.

Burgess, A., & Holstrom, L. 1978. *Sexual assault of children and adolescents.* Lexington, Mass.: D.C. Health Company.

Chapman, J., Smith. B., & Brennan, N. 1987. *Child sexual abuse: An analysis of case processing.* Washington D.C.: American Bar Association.

Cole, G., Francowski, S., & Gertz, M. 1981. *Major Criminal Justice Systems.* Beverly Hills, Calif.: Sage.

Conte, J., & Berliner, L. 1981. Prosecution of the offender in cases of sexual assault against children. *Victimology, 6,* 102–109.

Conte, J. 1984. Progress in treating the sexual abuse of children. *Social Work,* May–June, 258–263.

Crewdson, J. 1988. *By silence betrayed.* Boston: Little, Brown & Company.

DeFrancis, V. 1969. *Protecting the child victim of sex crimes committed by adults.* Denver, Colo.: American Humane Association.

DeMause, L. (Ed.). 1974. *The history of childhood.* New York: Psychohistory Press.

Duncan, E., Whitney, P., & Kunen, S. 1982. Integration of visual and verbal information in children's memories. *Child Development, 53,* 1215–1223.

Dziech, B. and C. B. Schudson. 1991. *On trial America's courts and their treatment of sexually abused children, 2nd ed.* Boston: Beacon Press.

Eatman, R., & Bulkley, J. 1986. *Protecting child victim/witnesses: Sample laws and materials.* Washington D.C.: National Legal Resource Center for Child Advocacy and Protection.

Engels, F. 1968. *The condition of the working class in England.* Stanford, Calif.: Stanford University.

Faller, K. 1989. Characteristics of a clinical sample of sexually abused children: How boy and girl victims differ. *Child Abuse and Neglect, 13* (2), 281–291.

Faller, K. 1990. Sexual abuse by parental caretakers: A comparison of abusers who are biological fathers in intact families, stepfathers, and non-custodial fathers. In A. Horton (Ed.), *The incest perpetrator: The family member no one wants to treat.* Newbury Park, Calif.: Sage.

Finkelhor, D. 1979. *Sexually victimized children.* New York: The Free Press.

Finkelhor, D. 1984. *Child sexual abuse: New theory and research.* New York: The Free Press.

Finkelhor, D. 1986. *A sourcebook on child sexual abuse.* Beverly Hills, Calif.: Sage.

Finkelhor, D., Gomes-Schwartz, B., & Horowitz, J. 1987. Professionals' responses. *Child sexual abuse: New theory and research.* New York: The Free Press, pp. 200–215.

Finkelhor, D., & Russell, D. 1984. Women as perpetrators: Review of the evidence. In *Child Sexual Abuse: New theory and research,* pp. 171–187.

Ford, C. & Beach, F. 1952. *Patterns of sexual behavior* London: Eyre & Spottiswoode.

Frazer, B. 1981. Sexual Child Abuse: The legislation and the law in the United States. In P. Mrazek and C. Kempe (Eds.), *Sexually Abused Children and their Families.* Oxford: Pergamon Press.

Frazier, P. & Borgida, E. 1985. Rape trauma syndrome evidence in court. *American Psychologist, 40,* 984–993.

Frazier, P., & Borgida, E. 1988. Juror common understanding and the admissibility of rape trauma syndrome evidence in court. *Law and Human Behavior, 12,* 101–122.

Frazier, P. & Borgida, E. (in press) Rape trauma syndrome: A review of case law and psychological research. *Law and Human Behavior.*

Freund, K., McKnight, C., Langevin, R., & Cibiri, S. 1972. The female child as surrogate object, *Archives of Sexual Behavior, 2,* 119–133.

Frisbie, L. 1969. *Another look at sex offenders in California.* Sacramento, Calif.: California Department of Mental Hygiene, Research Monograph no. 12.

Fromuth, M. 1986. The relationship of childhood sexual abuse with later psychological and sexual adjustment in a sample of college women. *Child Abuse and Neglect, 10,* 5–15.

Gebhard, P., Gagnon, J. Pomeroy, W., & Christenson, C. 1965. *Sex offenders: An analysis of types.* New York: Harper & Row.

Geiser, R. 1979. *Hidden Victims: The sexual abuse of children.* Boston: Beacon Press.

Giles-Sims, J., & Finkelhor, D. 1984. Child abuse in stepfamilies. *Family Relations, 33,* 407–413.

Gomez-Schwartz, B., Horowitz, J., & Cardarelli, A. 1990. *Child sexual abuse: The initial effects.* Newbury Park, Calif.: Sage.

Goodman, G., Aman, C., & Hirschman, J. 1987. Child sexual and physical abuse: Children's testimony, In S. J. Ceci, M. P. Toglia, & D. F. Ross (Eds.), *Children's eyewitness memory.* New York: Springer, pp. 1–23.

Goodman, G., Bottoms, B. Herscovici, B. & Shaver, P. 1989. Determinants of the child victim's perceived, credibility. In S. Ceci, M. Toglia, & D. Ross (Eds.), Children's eyewitness memory. New York: Springer-Verlag.

Goodman, G. & Reed, R. 1986. Age differences in eyewitness testimony. *Law and Human Behavior, 10,* 317–322.

Gordon, L. 1988. *Heroes of their own lives.* New York: Penguin Books.

Gothard, S. 1987. The admissibility of evidence in child sexual abuse cases. *Child Welfare, 66* (1), 13–24.

Greenhouse, L. 1990, June 28. Child abuse trials can use television. *New York Times,* P. A,1.

Gresham, A., Borgida, E., Swim, J., French, S., & Bull, M. 1989. *Juror common understanding of child sexual abuse and children as witnesses.*

Paper presented at the annual meeting of the Midwestern Psychological Association, Chicago, Illinois.

Gresham, A. 1992. *Class stereotyping and the story model.* Unpublished doctoral dissertation, University of Minnesota.

Groth, N. 1983. Treatment of the sexual offender in a correctional institution. In J. Greer & I. Stuart (Eds.), *The sexual aggressor: Current perspectives on treatment.* New York: Van Nostrand Reinhold, pp. 160–176.

Groth, A. 1986. Foreword. In E. Porter (Ed.), *Treating the young male victim of sexual assault: Issues and intervention steategies.* Syracuse, N.Y.: Safer Society Press.

Harshbarger, S. 1987. Prosecution is an appropriate response in child sexual abuse cases. *Journal of Interpersonal Violence, 2,* 108–109.

Haugaard, J. 1987. *The consequences of child sexual abuse: A college survey.* Unpublished manuscript, Department of Psychology, University of Virginia, Charlottesville, 1987.

Haugaard, J., & Reppucci, N. 1988. *The sexual abuse of children: A comprehensive guide to current knowledge and intervention strategies.* San Francisco: Jossey-Bass.

Hechler, D. 1988. *The battle and the backlash: The child sexual abuse war.* Lexington, Mass.: Lexington Books.

Hugo, Victor. n.d. *les Miserables.* Paris: Hetzel.

Keckley Market Research. March 1983. *Sexual abuse in Nashville: A report on incidence and long-term effects.* Nashville, Tenn.: author.

Kempe, C. 1962. The battered child syndrome. *Journal of the American Medical Association 181,* 17–24.

Kempe, C. 1968. *The battered child.* Chicago: University of Chicago Press.

Kempe, R., & Kempe, C. 1984. *The common secret: Sexual abuse of children and adolescents.* New York: W. H. Freeman.

Kendall-Tackett, K., & Watson, M. 1992. Use of anatomical dolls by Boston-area professionals. *Child Abuse and Neglect, 16* (3), 423–428.

Kercher, G. & McShane, M. 1984. The prevalence of child sexual abuse victimization in an adult sample of Texas residents. *Child Abuse and Neglect, 8* (4), 495–502.

Kinsey, A., Pomeroy, W., & Martin, C. 1949. *Sexual behavior in the human male.* Philadelphia: Saunders.

Knopp, F. 1986. Introduction. In E. Porter (Ed.), *Treating the young male victim of sexual assault: Issues and intervention steategies.* Syracuse, N.Y.: Safer Society Press.

Kovera, M., & Borgida, E. 1992. *Children on the witness stand: The effects of witness age and expert testimony on juror decision making.* Unpublished manuscript, University of Minnesota.

Kovera, M., Borgida, E., Gresham, A., Swim, J., & Gray, E. in press. Do child sexual abuse experts hold pro-child beliefs? A survey of the International Society for Traumatic Stress Studies. *Journal of Traumatic Stress.*

Krugman, R. 1989. The more we learn, the less we know with reasonable medical certainty. *Child Abuse and Neglect, 13* (2), 165–166.

LaFree, G. 1985. Official reactions of Hispanic defendants in the Southwest. *Journal Research in Crime and Delinquency, 22,* 213–237.

Levy, R. 1989. Using "scientific" testimony to prove child sexual abuse. *Family Law Quarterly, 23,* (3), 383–409.

Liles, G., & Bulkley, J. 1985. Prior sexual acts of the defendant as evidence in prosecution for child sexual abuse. In J. Bulkley (Ed.), *Child sexual abuse and the law.* Washington D.C.: National Legal Resource Center for Child Advocacy and Protection, pp. 199–202.

List, J. 1986. Age and Schematic Differences in the Reliability of Eyewitness Testimony *Developmental Psychology, 22* (1), 50–57.

Lundberg, E. 1947. *Unto the least of these: Social services for children.* New York: Appleton-Century-Crofts, Inc.

MacFarlane, K. 1978. Sexual abuse of children, In J. Chapman & M. Gates (Eds.), *The victimization of women.* Beverly Hills, Calif.: Sage.

MacMurray, B. 1988. The nonprosecution of sexual abuse and informal justice. *Journal of Interpersonal Violence, 3* (2), 197–202.

MacNamara, D., & Sagarin, E. 1977. *Sex, crime, and the law.* New York: The Free Press.

Marin, B., Holmes, D., Guth, M., & Kovac, P. 1979. The potential of children as eyewitnesses: A comparison of children and adults on eyewitness tasks. *Law and Human Behavior, 3,* 295–305.

McCaghy, C. 1966. Child molesters: A study of their careers as deviants. Ph.D. dissertation, University of Wisconsin. Excerpted in M. Clinard and R. Quinney (Eds.), *Criminal Behavior Systems: A Typology.* New York: Holt, Rinehart & Winston, pp. 75–88.

Masson, J. 1986. *A dark science: Women, sexuality and psychiatry in the nineteenth century.* New York: The Noonday Press.

Melton, G. 1981. Children's competency to testify. *Law and Human Behavior, 5* (1), 73–85.

Miller, A. 1986). *Thou shalt not be aware: Society's betrayal of the child.* New York: Meridian.

Minnesota Center for Survey Research. 1988. Technical Report #88-17, Political Patriotism Survey, Author.

Mohr, J., Turner, R., & Jerry, M. 1965. *Pedophilia and exhibitionism.* Toronto: University of Toronto.

Morison, S., & Greene K. 1992. Juror and expert knowledge of child sexual abuse *Child Abuse and Neglect, 16,* (4), 595–613.

Muram, D. 1989. Child sexual abuse: Relationship between sexual acts and genital findings. *Child Abuse & Neglect 13* (2), 211–216.

Murphy, J. June 1985. Untitled news release (available from St. Cloud State University, St. Cloud, MN 56301). Cited in D. Finkelhor, 1986, *A sourcebook on child sexual abuse.* Beverly Hills, Calif.: Sage.

Murphy, W., Haynes, M., Stalgaitis, S., & Flanagan, B. 1986. Differential sexual responding among four groups of sexual offenders against children. *Journal of Psychopathology and Behavioral Assessment, 8,* 339-353.

National Center on Child Abuse and Neglect (NCCAN). 1988. *Study findings: National study of incidence and severity of child abuse and neglect.* Washington, D.C.: Department of Health and Human Services.

National Legal Resource Center for Child Advocacy and Protection. 1985. *Evidentiary and procedural trends in state legislation and other emerging legal issues in child sexual abuse cases.* Washington D.C.: American Bar Association.

Newberger, E. 1987. Prosecution: A problematic approach to child abuse. *Journal of Interpersonal Violence 2* (1), 112–117.

Nigro, G., Gudatis, R. April 1987. *The effects of age, context, and retention interval on memory for a single event.* Paper presented at the Biennial Meetings of the Society for Research in Child Development, Baltimore.

Norusis, M. 1990. *SPSS advanced statistics user's guide.* Chicago: SPSS, Inc.

Ohlin, L., & Tonry, M. 1989. *Family violence.* Chicago: University of Chicago Press.

Penrod, S., Bull, M., Lengnick, S. 1989. Children as observers and witnesses: The empirical data. *Family Law Quarterly, 23,* 411–431.

Peters, J., Dinsmore, J., & Toth, P. 1989. Why prosecute child abuse? *South Dakota Law Review, 34,* 649–659.

Platt, A. 1969. *The child savers. The invention of delinquency* (2nd. ed.) Chicago: University of Chicago Press.

Pleck, E. (1989. *Domestic tyranny: the making of social policy against family violence.* New York: Oxford University Press.

Porter, E. 1986. Treating the young male victim of sexual assault: Issues and intervention strategies. Syracuse, N.Y.: Safer Society Press.

President's Task Force on Victims of Crime. 1982. *Final report.* Washington D.C.: U.S. Department of Justice.

Quinsey, V., Chaplin, T., & Carrigan, W. 1979. Sexual preferences among incestuous and non-incestuous child molesters. *Behavior Therapy, 10,* 562–565.

Quinsey, V. Chaplin, T., & Carrigan W. 1980. Biofeedback and signaled punishment in the modification of inappropriate sexual age preferences. *Behavior Therapy, 11,* 567–576.

Radbill, S. 1987. Children in a world of violence. In R. Helfer & R.

Kempe (Eds.), *The Battered Child* (4th ed.). Chicago: University of Chicago Press, pp. 23–41.

Richardson, G. *Talking to abused children: Insights from the field of linguistics.* Unpublished panel presentation at Eighth National Conference on Child Abuse and Neglect, Salt Lake City, 1989.

Rogers, C., & Terry, T. 1984. Clinical intervention with boy victims of sexual abuse. In I. Steward & J. Greer (eds.). *Victims of sexual aggression.* New York: Van Nostrand Reinhold.

Runyan, D., Everson, M., Edelson, G., Hunter, W., & Coulter, M. 1988. Impact of legal intervention on sexually abused children. *The Journal of Pediatrics, 113* (4), 647–653.

Rush, F. 1980. *The best kept secret.* New York: Prentice-Hall.

Russell, D. 1983. The incidence and prevalence of intrafamilial and extrafamilial sexual abuse of female children. *Child Abuse and Neglect, 7* (2), 133–146.

Russell, D. 1984. *Sexual exploitation.* Beverly Hills, Calif.: Sage Publications.

Russell, D. 1986. *The secret trauma: Incest in the lives of girls and women.* New York: Basic Books.

Sagarin, E. 1977. Incest: Problems in definition and frequency. *The Journal of Sex Research, 13*, 126–135.

Salter, A. 1988. *Treating child sex offenders and victims.* Beverly Hills, Calif.: Sage Publications.

Sandberg, D. 1987. Child sexual abuse: To prosecute or not? *New Hampshire Bar Journal, 29* (1). 15–27.

Saywitz, K. 1987. Children's testimony: Age-related patterns of memory errors. In S. Ceci, M. Toglia, & D. Ross (Eds.), *Children's eyewitness memory.* New York: Springer-Verlag, pp. 36–52.

Sgroi, S. M. 1982. *Handbook of clinical intervention in child sexual abuse.* Lexington, Mass.: Lexington Books.

Sommerville, C. 1990. *The rise and fall of childhood.* New York: Vintage Books.

Swim, J., Borgida, E., & McCoy K. 1992. *Videotaped versus in-court witness testimony: Is protecting the child witness jeopardizing due process?* Unpublished manuscript, Pennsylvania State University.

Tavris. C. April 1990. Can Children's testimony in sexual abuse cases be trusted? *Vogue*, pp. 284–288.

Toth, P., and Whalen, M. 1987. *Investigation and prosecution of child abuse.* Washington D.C.: American Prosecutors Research Institute, National Center for the Prosecution of Child Abuse.

Tufts–New England Medical Center, Division of Child Psychiatry. 1984. *Sexually exploited children: Service and research project. Final report.* Washington, D.C.: U.S. Department of Justice, Office of Juvenile Justice & Delinquency Prevention.

U.S. Bureau of the Census. 1986. *County and city data book.* Washington D.C.: author.

U.S. Bureau of the Census. 1988. *County and city data book.* Washington D.C.: author.

U.S. Bureau of Census. 1989. *County and city data book.*Washington D.C.: author.

U.S. Department of Health & Human Services. 1979. *National analysis of official child neglect and abuse reporting* (DHHS Publication No. OHDS 81-30232). Englewood, Colo.: American Humane Association.

Vander, Mey, B., and Neff, R. 1986. *Incest as child abuse; Research and application.* New York: Praeger.

Walker, S. 1989. *Sense and nonsense about crime.* Pacific Grove, Calif.: Brooks/Cole Publishing Company.

Weisberg, D. 1984. The "discovery" of sexual abuse: Experts' role in legal policy formulation. *U.C. Davis Law Review, 18* (1), 1–57.

Weiss, E., & Berg. R. 1982. Child victims of sexual assault: Impact of court procedures. *Journal of Child Psychiatry, 21* (5), 513–518.

Whitcomb, D., Shapiro, E. R., & Stellwagen, L. D. 1985. *When the victim is a child: Issues for judges and prosecutors.* Washington, D.C.: U.S. Department of Justice, National Institute of Justice.

Wyatt, G. 1985. The sexual abuse of Afro-Americans and white American women in childhood. *Child Abuse and Neglect, 9* (4), 507–519.

Yates, A., & Terr, L. 1988. Anatomically correct dolls: Should they be used as a basis for expert testimony? *Journal of the American Academy of Child and Adolescent Psychiatry, 27,* 254–257.

Zatz, M. 1984. The timing of court processing: Towards linking theory and method. *Criminology, 23,* 313–335.

ACKNOWLEDGMENTS

I would like to thank many people for their help in producing this book and the research it represents. First, I must thank Terry Bond. Terry wrote the original grant proposal for this study, and served as director of the Center for the Child during the research planning and the data collection.

I am very grateful to Gene Borgida, who directed the jury simulation studies and the attitude surveys. It was a great pleasure to contact this eminent scholar whom I had not known before, suggest that he study child sexual abuse using his rape trial research methods, and have him say yes. He turned out to be a wonderful colleague, from whom I learned a great deal.

Patty Toth, the director of the Center for the Prosecution of Child Abuse of the American Prosecutors Research Institute, was most helpful in reading and critiquing this manuscript from a legal standpoint. Her experience and expertise make her commentary invaluable.

Other colleagues were influential in this project. Ann Burgess, who helped train the volunteer data collectors, critiqued the data-collection instruments, and introduced me to individuals and literature with whom and which I had not been familiar, also inspired me with her dedication to the victims of sexual abuse. I wish to acknowledge Jon Conte and David Finkelhor for setting a standard of academic and personal excellence in this controversial field of study. I especially thank the assistant district attorneys in the eight study sites for their candor, their lack of defensiveness in the face of so many questions, the time they spent with us describing their jurisdictions and explicating cases, and—most of all—for the time and care they spend on their cases day in and day out, despite enormous odds against them.

I would like to thank the National Council of Jewish Women for supporting this endeavor. A number of people in that organization played key roles in this project. Holly Fancher served as research assistant during the planning, data-collection, and data-entry phases of the research. Megan Lovejoy helped research and write the jurisdictional case studies, assisted in data analysis, and provided over all professional support to the project. David Kunin devoted his wealth of technical skills to this project during the latter data-analysis and report-formatting phase, producing many of the original charts and accomplishing the myriad other technical tasks associated with research and report production. Noemi Moyet, who served as project assistant throughout the term of study, was very helpful in formatting questionnaires, setting up organizational systems, and typing tables. She also assisted with grant-management tasks such as reporting requirements and proposal preparation. Jay Kantor helped to conceptualize the analysis plan for this project. Chaya Piotrkowski, the current director of the NCJW Center for the Child, suggested I write a book from the findings of the research. To all these people, my deepest thanks.

I would like, also, to acknowledge the financial sustenance received for this work. A subcontract from the American Bar Association Grant #90-CA-1402, National Center on Child Abuse and Neglect, Administration for Children, Youth and Families, office of Human Development Services was very helpful to the completion of this research, and my thanks go to Barbara Smith, Sharon Goretsky, and Howard Davidson from that organization for their support and flexibility. Thanks also to the agency providing the preponderance of the money for the research, the National Center on Child Abuse and Neglect, Grant #90-Ca-1273 for their continuing support of my work. I would like to thank my federal project officer, Jan Kirby-Gell, for her support throughout the process, and her patience in waiting for the final report of the project.

I thank Allegheny College, my current professional home, for being a place where I could finish this manuscript with support and encouragement from others who were struggling with books of their own.

Thanks to Susan Arellano, Senior Editor and Celia Knight Production Supervisor, at the Free Press for their expert help in turning this information into a book.

Most important, however, I would like to thank the NCJW volunteers who collected the data for this research. Without these women, there would be no study. Reviewing prosecutor's case records and spending long days in criminal courtrooms taking down—and taking in—stories of unspeakable acts visited on young children is physically and emotionally draining, and certainly beyond the call of duty for any volunteer. Add to that, the frustration of being one of only a handful of people doing this work in their particular location, with few opportunities to communicate with and support their colleagues on this project in other states, and their accomplishments seem even greater. I will forever be indebted to them for suffering through these difficulties and providing the material for this project.

Although there are many volunteers in the study jurisdictions who participated in collecting data, I would like to single out the site coordinators, since they provided the local training and coordination activities that could not be accomplished by the project director. To the following people, my very special thanks: Ilene Freishtat, Verna Kushel, Paula Eilbott, Marilyn Segal, Betty Barnett, Jean Pierce, Helene Coleman, Jean Edwards, Maud Fliegelman, Jeanne Frank, Sandra Heller, Frankie Wolff, Naomi Parker, Tannette Goldberg, Bernice Glickfeld, Joan Klearman, and Barbara Messing.

INDEX